The Theological Thought of Fazlur Rahman:
A Modern Mutakallim

The Theological Thought of
Fazlur Rahman

A Modern *Mutakallim*

AHAD M. AHMED

Islamic Book Trust
Kuala Lumpur

Published by
Islamic Book Trust
607 Mutiara Majestic
Jalan Othman
46000 Petaling Jaya
Selangor, Malaysia
www.ibtbooks.com

Islamic Book Trust is affiliated with The Other Press.

Perpustakaan Negara Malaysia   Cataloguing-in-Publication Data

Ahmed, Ahad M.
    The theological thought of Fazlur Rahman : A Modern Mutakallim /
    Ahad M. Ahmed.
    Includes index
    Bibliography : p.263
    ISBN 978-967-0526-34-8
    1. Theologians, Muslim. 2. Philosophers, Muslim.
    3. Knowledge, Theory of (Islam). 1. Title.
    922.97

Printed by
SS Graphic Printers (M) Sdn Bhd
Lot 7 & 8, Jalan TIB 3, Taman Industri Bolton,
68100 Batu Caves, Selangor Darul Ehsan.

Contents

Chapters

Contents vii

*To my mother and father
for their untiring support and love*

Acknowledgments

$\mathcal{I}$ would sincerely like to thank those that have helped me in completing this dissertation which has taken well over three years to complete. I would first like to thank my wife Ruba for her unmitigating support, faith and love for Allah, His Messenger and His cause. In the face of all opposition and difficult circumstances her support for me has been unwavering and tremendously valuable. Secondly, I would like to thank both my guides and mentors Dr. Nabil al-Fouly and Dr. Faruk Terzic for their loving, insightful and congenial attitude throughout my academic sojourn here at International Islamic University.

My teachers Dr. Zafar Ishaq Ansari, Dr. Muhammad al-Ghazali, Dr. Khalid Masud and Dr. Ahmad Jad guided me throughout my research with their valuable criticisms and suggestions. My friends Dr. Adeel Khan and Dr. Faruk Terzic for reading the manuscript and providing helpful suggestions and guidance.

Lastly, the publicaiton of this work could not be possible without the sincere and erstwhile interest of Mr. Haji PK Koya. In May 2016, Mr. Koya contacted me to publish my work on the late (Shaykh) Dr. Fazlur Rahman with the interest to provide a pathway on how to approach him and develop a more empathetic and deeper understanding regarding his life and work. His encouragement and belief in the value of Fazlur Rahman's work as one of the greatest thinkers of Islam whilst being gravely misunderstood by scholar and naivete alike, gave me the reassurance that work deserved to be published by such a sincere and honest publishing house. Mr. Koya's patience, sincerity and dedication deserve my heartfelt gratitude and respect.

Introduction

Since the nineteenth century, the traditional understanding of Islam has been scrutinized mainly due to the impact of Western imperialism and colonialism upon the Muslim world. Western occupation upon the Islamic world resulted in Muslims asserting their religious, socio-economic and political identities. Additionally, Orientalism and Christian missionary writings brought about an intellectual response from the Muslim intellectual elite. The effect of Western presence brought into question the viability of the traditional understanding of Islam upheld by the Ulama'. Muslim intellectuals who contended that traditional Islam was responsible for the backwardness (*takhaluf*) and political subjugation (*istibdad*) of Muslims, recommended modernism (*tajdid*), reformism (*islah*) and revivalism (*nahda*) as being necessary for the emancipation of Muslims and their progress. However, different Muslim responses were voiced towards the West and according to Masud some can be categorized under the rubric of 'Islamic modernism'.[1]

In the Indian subcontinent, Sir Sayyid Ahmad Khan is regarded as the father of 'Indian Islamic modernism'. In both the political and intellectual realms he contributed towards emancipating Indian Muslims from their decadent state. Khan contended that it was imperative that a new theology or *jadid 'ilm ul-kalām* [2] be instituted in order to respond to Western intellectualism. Other modernists like Shibli Nu'mani and Qasim Nanotawi disagreed with Khan and believed that post-formative theology (*kalām al-muta'khirin*) was sufficient in responding to Western intellectualism. Abu'l Kalam Azad resolutely believed that neither a modern nor a revival of post-formative *kalām* was the proper intellectual course to adopt. He advocated a return to the formative period of Islam (*kalām al-salaf*).[3] Muhammad Iqbal accepted Khan's recommendation for an 'Islamic theology of modernity' or *jadid 'ilm ul-kalām*.[4]

According to Masud, Iqbāl's public lectures given in the 1920's, which were later published under the title *The Reconstruction of Religious Thought in Islam* addressed the issues posed by Western modernity. In his view, this view offered a new Islamic theology of modernity in continuation of Sayyid Ahmad Khan's call for *jadid 'ilm ul-kalām*. Some urdu translations of Iqbal's work in South Asia are titled as *jadid 'ilm ul-kalām* or *jadid Illahiyat*. Iqbāl observed that traditional *kalām* was nothing more than "concepts of theological systems, draped in the terminology of a practically dead metaphysics"[5] which couldn't help the reconstruction of religious thought. He opined that "the only course open to us is to approach modern knowledge with a respectful but independent attitude and to appreciate the teachings of Islam in the light of that knowledge, even though we may be led to differ from those who have gone before us."[6]; thus, he agreed with Khan's call for a new theology.[7] In the intellectual and political realms, modern scientism, atheism and secularism were significant factors that impacted Muslim society. Muslim intellectual, social and political activists contended that Islam must be able to civilizationally and culturally respond to Western modernity.

In the twentieth century, Fazlur Rahman is considered to be amongst the most influential and significant Muslim modernists in both the Western and Muslim worlds. He took on the challenges faced by the Muslim world both in thought and in practice and contributed significantly to the discussion on *jadid 'ilm ul-kalām*. As we have discussed above *jadid 'ilm ul-kalām* does include theological topics in its gambit, however it is not limited to it as is the case with traditional *kalām*. For the purposes of this study Fazlur Rahman's contribution in the area of traditional *kalām viz.*, theology proper (*illahiyat*) and prophecy (*nubuwwat*) is scrutinized. In order to do so it is necessary to construct and evaluate Fazlur Rahman's theological thought and its implications upon the modernization and reformation of *'ilm ul-kalām* to which this thesis is committed to ascertaining.

Problem Statement

Our hypothesis is that Fazlur Rahman exemplifies a modern theologian who reformed traditional (*mutaqaddim*) and medieval (*muta'akhir*) and addressed the challenge of Western modernity by formulating an Islamic theology of modernity (*jadid 'ilm ul-kalām*). The research questions that have guided this research are as follows:

1. What are the influences that have shaped Fazlur Rahman's thought: Western and Islamic?

2. What is the nature of Fazlur Rahman modernist thought?

3. What is the methodology of Fazlur Rahman's theological thought? How does he derive his theological stance?

4. Why does Fazlur Rahman reach the conclusions that he does?

5. How does Fazlur Rahman deal with the primary sources of the Qur'an, *Sunnah*, Hadith, *Ijmā'*, Qiyas and the theological schools?

Methodology

We have attempted to use the constructivist method to analyze Fazlur Rahman's treatment of *kalām*. In this thesis, constructivism has been understood as a methodology that considers theological views as 'constructed' by particular intellectual trends and influences. Identifying these ideological and theological influences will determine, to a large extent, the characteristics of the subject's thought. Also, Fazlur Rahman's life has been reconstructed and linked to his writings to assess the role of his psychological temperament. Our analysis follows the methodology of Albert Hourani's intellectual history *Arabic Thought in the Liberal Age 1798-1939*, wherein an emphasis is placed on the importance of locating ideas within their unique intellectual context. When analyzing an intellectual, it is important to "explain as fully as possible the influences, circumstances, and the traits of personality which may have led him to think about certain matters in a certain way."[8] This way, a boundary can be demarcated between those elements of Fazlur Rahman's theology that are external to his thought and ultimately appropriated, and those aspects that he himself has introduced to the debate. Doing so allows us to determine the extent to which Fazlur Rahman is a derivative thinker, merely describing or repeating the arguments of his antecedents, and the extent that his contributions represent a dramatic break from tradition. Christian Troll, in his intellectual biography of the Indian Muslim modernist Sayyid Ahmad Khan (1817-1898), explains the necessity of viewing thought in a process of interaction and engagement between the individual thinker and his intellectual context: "It therefore seemed imperative to try to specify in which form and at what time in Sir Sayyid's life the challenges to his theological thought from outside and from within appeared and how he himself then viewed them in detail, rejecting, modifying and accommodating them."[9] Similarly, we will see how Fazlur Rahman's intellectual project is fluid and polymorphous, critically engaged with Islamic and secular sources of knowledge in a process of continuous feedback and renewal.

It is instructive that Fazlur Rahman adopted the language and conceptual framework of mid-twentieth century Orientalism in explicating his modernist theologies. By relying on the vocabulary and rhetoric of traditional Islamic exegesis, Fazlur Rahman attempted to locate himself within the *mujaddid* tradition.[10] Additionally, Fazlur Rahman positioned himself amongst the premodern and modern Islamic reformers (*muslihun*) who both defended the faith against ritual and doctrinal accretions, and asserted the proofs of Islam in the face of heresy and doubt. Further by establishing himself within the *mujaddid* lineage also boosts their claims to religious authority and legitimacy.

Literature Review

1. A Modern Muslim Intellectual: The Thought of Fazlur Rahman with Special Reference to Reason, Mary Catherine Jesse, MA Thesis, University of Regina, 1991.

This work completed in 1991 by Mary Catherine Jesse is a work that attempted to present the place of reason in Fazlur Rahman's thought. Jesse provides valuable information regarding Fazlur Rahman's close relationship with Wilfred Cantwell Smith, a Canadian Orientalist, whom he worked with at McGill University in Montreal, Canada. However, in the first section on the Young Fazlur Rahman and the pre-partition environment, does not adequately portray her knowledge of the backdrop Fazlur Rahman was born into. She stresses the political *milieu* and neglects the implications of the religious environment at the time. She does not attempt to take into consideration the cultural influence of British Colonialism and generalizes it as "westernization". Jesse fails to address the content and implications of "westernization" (*maghrabiyat*) which is impregnated with educational, cultural, economic, civilizational, religious, military and scientific elements. Further, she describes Fazlur Rahman as one of the most prominent Islamic liberal[11] thinkers in the West however she fails to explain the nature of his liberalism i.e. liberal attitude as opposed to liberalism *in re*. She generalizes the religious intellectual climate as holding a medieval worldview, whereas the religious worldview was additionally shaped by a successful Wahabi worldview that purported a pre-medieval worldview as well. She mentions rather loosely that the modern trends in reformist thoughts developed into "neo-Mutazilite tradition"[12]; we feel that she uses the word "tradition" rather casually whereas it is more appropriate to use the word "attitude or movement" towards the authority of the religious orthodoxy. Moreover, a more axiomatic doctrine in reformist thought was a rejection of *taqlid* and affirmation of *Ijtihād* and a return towards the pure bases of the Qur'an and the *sunnah*. Also, she does not make adequate mention of the political, social and ethical ramifications of British Imperial India. Further, she does not address insightfully the education he received in Pakistan at the hands of his father, Maulana Shihab ul Din Malik and at Punjab University. She does not attempt to provide information regarding his professors at Punjab University in Lahore such as Mohammed Shafi and others. [13]

In the second section she mentions the strong affection Fazlur Rahman had for H.A.R Gibb and his teaching career at Durham

University; however, she does not elucidate the long standing veneration that he had with Gibb throughout his academic career, citing him in encyclopedia articles as late as his final entry in 1988. Further, she does not properly address Fazlur Rahman's interest in Avicenna and his attempts to salvage the identity, vitality and uniqueness of Islamic philosophy. She provides valuable information regarding Fazlur Rahman's close relationship with Wilfred Cantwell Smith and time spent at McGill University as it portrays Fazlur Rahman's affinity with him as a trustworthy confidant. Further, it shows that he envisioned the Central Institute for Islamic Research in Karachi to be on the same platform as McGill University's Institute for Islamic Studies.[14]

Lastly, chapter two to five she has focused upon demonstrating Fazlur Rahman's rational approach to traditional sources of thought, law and theology and Qur'anic hermeneutics where she relies mostly on his *Islamic Methodology in History*, *Islam*, *Major Themes of the Qur'an* and *Islam and Modernity*. It seems her reason is to divide Fazlur Rahman's thought into two. The first period entails Fazlur Rahman's focus on with Islamic philosophy and in the second period solely on religious thought. This assumption is untenable because these works intrinsically portray elements from his work on Islamic philosophy in Avicenna and Mulla Sadra and the history of Islamic philosophy. We state this because Jesse failed to address the intimate passion Fazlur Rahman had in developing a system of thought which is unified and purposeful like Avicenna. She has failed to understand Fazlur Rahman's thought as a systematized unity.

2. Some Qur'anic Legal texts in the Context of Fazlur Rahman's Hermeneutical Method, Amhar Rasyid, MA Thesis, McGill University, Montreal, Canada, 1994.

Amhar Rasyid Master's thesis on Fazlur Rahman's hermeneutical method displays a thorough misunderstanding of Fazlur Rahman's thought in toto. The researcher displays a marked failure to understand his Philosophical framework and this is attributable to two factors: (1) the author's inadequate knowledge of Western and Islamic philosophy in general. (2) a partial and incomplete study of Fazlur Rahman's works. The researcher seems content to restrict himself to two works of *Islam and Modernity, Major Themes of the Qur'an* and a few articles written in Fazlur Rahman's period as Director of the Central Institute of Islamic Research.

Amhar's central thesis is that Fazlur Rahman's Qur'anic hermeneutical method is subjective and is a result of paradigms subsisting in the mind of the thinker or the scientist in his own mind. So the central point in Fazlur Rahman's 'Qur'an orientated' thought is not the Book itself but in his own mind is a fallacious statement and incorrigible. Amhar has not attempted to understand Fazlur Rahman's system of thought in its objectivity, purposiveness, totality and unity and thus methodologically his central thesis is fallacious. Further, Amhar insists that Fazlur Rahman was influenced by Jurgen Habermas is in plain contradiction with Fazlur Rahman's own rejection of Habermas's theory that "the invisible context of ideas is not just mental but environmental"[15].

3.   Fazlur Rahman's Islamic Philosophy, Fatimah Hussein, MA Thesis, McGill University, 1997.

Fatimah Hussein's work has attempted to study Fazlur Rahman's Islamic philosophy by examining his studies and critique of Muslim philosophers' works and his certitude as to the value of the Qur'anic message. The thesis is not concerned with Fazlur Rahman's opinion on the value (if any) of the *Sunnah* or tradition of the Prophet in providing answers for the needs of contemporary man. Rather, it concentrates on his opinion on the value of Islamic philosophy in the contemporary world, as mostly expressed in the Qur'an. The reason for choosing this approach lies in the importance that the Qur'an occupies Fazlur Rahman's scheme of thought. This thesis, therefore, examines the relationship between Fazlur Rahman's philosophy and his task of interpreting the Qur'anic message in the light of contemporary needs.

She argues that Fazlur Rahman does not term this specific thought as 'Islamic philosophy' but that the reason why she has chosen to refer to Fazlur Rahman's intellectual activity in this manner is because of his disagreement with the Muslim philosophers' preoccupation with metaphysical notions on the one hand, and his offer of what he regarded as a more ethics-based system of thought practically grounded in the precepts of the Qur'an. Consequently, he was not of the same opinion as those who argue – such as Hossein Nasr and Henry Corbin – that Islamic philosophy consists of pure metaphysics or that it has traditionally engaged solely in *hikmah*. On the contrary, he criticized Muslim philosophers for their focus on metaphysical issues to the neglect of the field of ethics. Indeed, Fazlur Rahman's disagreement with Muslim philosophers over their concepts of God, man, prophecy and nature emerged as a consequence of his philosophical worldview, where the notion of ethics occupied his mind – as a direct reflection of his belief – to a great extent. It is true that in his works, Fazlur Rahman employed many philosophical expressions similar to those of the Muslim philosophers. He seems however to have borrowed these expressions only in order to turn them against the philosophers as a tool of criticism.

Fazlur Rahman's philosophy is characterized by three religious terms: *īman*, *islam*, and *taqwa*. This shows the practical, rather than purely rational approach of his thought. Stated differently, Fazlur Rahman's philosophy includes his faith commitment. It should be noted, however, that Fazlur Rahman was not completely anti-metaphysics. His critique was directed towards Muslim metaphysicians due to the fact that they based their *weltanschauung* on Hellenic thought, not the Qur'an. Fazlur Rahman regarded Iqbal's *The Reconstruction of Religious Thought in Islam* as the only systematic attempt to metaphysical discourse in modern time. This work, however, cannot be categorized as a work based on Qur'anic teaching since "the structural elements of his thought are too contemporary to be an adequate basis for an ongoing Islamic metaphysical endeavor."[16]

4.   The Construction of Deobandi Ulema's Religious Authority in Pakistan: A Study of their Journal "Bayyinat", 1962-1977, Irfan Moeen, MA Thesis, McGill University, August 2004.

This work is an anthropological study on the journal "Bayyinat" published by the Deobandi Ulama' of Jami'at al-'Ulum al-Islamiya located in the largest city of Pakistan, Karachi. The Urdu, monthly journal was launched in 1962 for the express purpose of refuting the views and arguments of their opponents, and hence as a vehicle for asserting their religious identity and authority. The case of Bayyinat provides us with an opportunity to study an important and hitherto little considered phenomenon in Islamic modernity, namely, the intervention by the Ulama' to assert traditional claims to religious authority through the modem medium of print journalism in the context of the post-colonial nation state of Pakistan. The present work seeks to examine how the journal was utilized by the Ulama' in constructing their religious authority and to engage in the refutation of the two most prominent twentieth century personalities, Fazlur Rahman and Sayyid Abu'l 'Ala Mawdudi.

The author takes up Fazlur Rahman's concept of *Sunnah* and presents the debate that ensued between the aforementioned madrasah and Fazlur Rahman. The author displays a reasonable understanding of Fazlur Rahman's concept of *Sunnah* however, as is the case with Catherine Jesse and Amhar Rasyid does not attempt to understand the "system" of Fazlur Rahman's thought and as such has selected an issue in isolation of the whole. For the purposes of Irfān's thesis it may be considered suitable however for an accurate and wholistic understanding of Fazlur Rahman, the thesis is wanting. Similarly, there is a partial treatment of Fazlur Rahman's thought and seems to be a study of just bringing awareness of the refutation of the traditional Ulama'. Further, there is no attempt made by the author to address both sides critically and reach a conclusion. It seems that the author sides with the traditional scholar Muhammad Idris and leaves the reader begging the question.

Notes

[1] Khalid Masud, *Iqbal's Approach to Islamic Theology of Modernity*, Al-Hikmat, Punjab University, vol. 27, 2007, p.1-2.

Islamic theology of modernity, also known *jadid 'ilm al-kalām*, "new theology" and "Islamic modernism", is usually characterized as an apologetic approach to defend Islam against modern Western criticism. This is probably because modernity came to be known in the Muslim world in the wake of colonialism when Muslims found themselves on the defensive. To the Western colonial regimes, Islam was not compatible with modernity and hence it was to be reformed and modernized or else marginalized. Muslims, therefore, generally conceived modernity, modernism and modernization not only as Western and alien but also as hostile and threatening.

Islamic theology of modernity was not, however, entirely apologetic. It was essentially an endeavor to develop an Islamic framework to understand and respond to the questions that modernity posed to Muslim cultural outlook in general and to Islamic theology in particular. In this respect it defended Islam against particular criticism but it also developed a theological framework to explain how modernity was relevant and compatible to Islam.

Muslim responses to Western modernity range from call for reform of to call for revival of Islam, and from total rejection of either tradition or modernity to a reconstruction of Islamic religious thought.

[2] Christian W. Troll, *Sayyid Ahmad Khan: A Reinterpretation of Muslim Theology* (New Delhi: Vikas Publishing House, 1978), pp.307-332.

[3] Aziz Ahmad, *Jamal al-din al-Afghani and Muslim India*, Studia Islamica, No. 13 (1960), p.66.

[4] Khalid Masud, *Iqbal's Approach to Islamic Theology of Modernity*, Al-Hikmat, Punjab University, vol. 27, 2007, pp.1-36.

[5] Muhammad Iqbal, "The Human Ego – His Freedom and Immortality", *The Reconstruction of Religious Thought in Islam*, p.43.

[6] *Ibid.*

[7] Khalid Masud, p.12.

[8] Albert Hourani, *Arabic Thought in the Liberal Age, 1798-1939* (Cambridge: Cambridge University Press, 1983), p. v.

[9] Christian W. Troll, *Sayyid Ahmad Khan: A Reinterpretation of Muslim Theology* (New Delhi:Vikas, 1978), p. xix.

[10] In Islamic tradition, a *mujaddid* is a scholar who updates and renews the faith in times of historical change. Ahmad Sirhindī is widely recognized as a *mujaddid* of the second Islamic millennium. See also Jalal al-Din al-Suyuti's *Tuhfat ul-Mujtahidin fi asma' ul-Mujadidin*, unpublished manuscript.

[11] *The Development of a Muslim Intellectual*, chapter 1, p.1.

[12] *Ibid*, p.9.

[13] Calendar of Punjab University, 1936-1948.

[14] *Ibid*, p.13-23.

[15] Fazlur Rahman's criticism of Habermas' Hermeneutic in *Islam and Modernity,* pp. 8-11.

[16] Fazlur Rahman, *Islam and Modernity*, p.132.

Chapter I
Fazlur Rahman's Life:
A Biographical Overview

Fazlur Rahman: Youth, Curiosity and the Making of an Intellectual; In the Footsteps of an Icon, Iqbal (1919-1946)

Fazlur Rahman was a notable scholar of Islamic philosophy and an important liberal Muslim thinker of the twentieth century. He was characterized in his lifetime as "one of the most learned and acute of modern Islamic thinkers,"[1] as "an outstanding intellect, an immensely erudite scholar straddling traditional and modern learning,"[2] and "one of the clearest and wisest Islamic thinkers in the world today."[3] He was born on the 21st of September, 1919 AC/1332 AH, in the Malik family, but it is not certain where he was born: Catherine Jesse[4] records the village of Buchhal Kalam in north-west India; Rasyid[5] records Seraislhe, in the Hazara District of North West Frontier Province of Pakistan; whereas, Fazlur Rahman states that "in 1933, we moved from our ancestral home in what is northwest Pakistan to Lahore."[6] Born into a scholarly family, his father Shihab al-Din was a graduate from Dar ul-Uloom, Deoband, under the tutelage of Rashid Ahmad Gangohi (d.1905) and the

"Sheikh al-Hind" Mahmud ul-Hasan (d.1920). His uncle was a Naqshbandi Sheikh and taught him *Fiqh* and the Mathnawi of Maulana Rūm. Fazlur Rahman began his traditional studies in Dars-i-Nizami with his father at a very early age. By the age of ten, Fazlur Rahman had memorized the Qur'an. Both left a lasting impact on Fazlur Rahman but more so his father, whom he admitted had a deep impact on him intellectually. Fazlur Rahman states reverently about his father, "Unlike most traditional Islamic scholars of the time, who regarded modern education as poison both for faith and morality, my father was convinced that Islam had to face modernity both as a challenge and an opportunity.[7]

In 1933, at the age of fourteen, Fazlur Rahman moved to Lahore and continued his Dars-i-Nizami degree. In the 1940's the cultural and intellectual milieu was shaped by Muhammad Iqbal's philosophical, poetic and political ideas of Lahore. Charles Adams posits that Fazlur Rahman 'was powerfully influenced by the thought of Iqbal, whose intellectual activity, I think it no exaggeration to suggest, was a kind of model for him'[8]. He goes on to argue that he was 'no doubt stimulated by the political agitation in which Indian Muslims were swept up during the 1930's and 40's and had some personal contact with certain of the leading figures'[9] and intellectuals such as M. Saeed Sheikh, Khalifa Abdul Hakim, B.A. Dar, A.Z. Bazmee, A.K. Brohi. Religious figures such as Abu'l 'Alā Maudūdī, Ghulam Ahmad Parvez, Inayatullah al-Mashriqī, Abu'l Kalām Āzād were all contemporaries of Fazlur Rahman.

In 1938, at the age of nineteen, he enrolled in Punjab University in the B.A. (Hons) in Arabic. The university was under British Imperial administration and the Department of 'Arabic, amongst other departments, was affiliated with Oxford

University. Fazlur Rahman completed his Bachelors in 1940 and Masters in 1942 standing as class first. It seems probable that he studied 'Arabic language and Literature, Philosophy and English at the Bachelor level and Master level. It is important to note here that philosophy was taught with a balance between American Pragmatism, British Platonism and Logical Positivism and we shall endeavor to illustrate the influence of these schools of philosophy on Fazlur Rahman's thought based upon his critical study of Modern Western philosophy and his unique position regarding it.[10]

In 1942, he completed his Master's degree and was accepted as a research student at the Oriental College at Punjab University, a position which he held till 1946. His supervisor was the great scholar of Arabic at the Oriental College, Mohammad Shafi under who research students in the department of Arabic were responsible for editing of Persian and 'Arabic manuscripts. Whilst in Pakistan, Fazlur Rahman also learned German and translated Ignaz Goldziher's fundamental study of classical Qur'an commentary, *Die Richtungen der islamischen Koranauslegung* (Lieden, E.J. Brill, 1920) into English but lost the manuscript in the confusion of India's partition in 1947.[11]

Fazlur Rahman and Gibb: Post World War II, Reformed Orientalism, Independent Pakistan and the Making of a Scholar (1946-1958)

In 1946, Fazlur Rahman was nominated for a scholarship to Oxford University for doctoral research at Oxford University. Charles Adams considers that the most decisive and formative influence was Fazlur Rahman's time spent in England.[12] The director of his studies was the renowned reformist Orientalist H.A.R Gibb[13] and the thesis supervisor was Simon van der

Bergh, a scholar in Ancient and Medieval philosophy. Both supervisors insisted that a preparation for the serious study of Islamic philosophy and thought required a thorough grounding in Greek philosophy, including the languages of the original texts. He was, therefore, subjected to a rigorous course of instruction in the history of ancient philosophy. As a result, he achieved a 'magisterial command' of both Ancient Greek texts and the main themes of Greek and Islamic philosophy. He completed his doctorate in 1949 on Avicenna's Psychology.

In 1950, Fazlur Rahman accepted the position of Lecturer in Persian Studies and Islamic philosophy at Durham University; a position he held till 1958. It seems that during his time at Oxford and Durham University his personal commitment to change the Western belief that Islamic philosophy ceased after al-Ghazālī in the Islamic World led him to undertake a concerted effort to introduce the two sub-continent religious thinkers, Ahmad Sirhindī[14] and Shah Walī Ullah al Dehlawi.[15]

Smith & Fazlur Rahman: Visionaries, Islamism Within and Outside the Faith (1958-1961)

In 1958, he was visited by the renowned Canadian Islamicist, Wilfred Cantwell Smith at the recommendation of H.A.R Gibb and was so impressed with Fazlur Rahman that he offered him the post of Associate Professor at the Institute for Islamic Studies at McGill University, in Montreal, Canada. Fazlur Rahman accepted the post, and Smith's vision "to establish an institute comprised of equal numbers of Muslim and Western professors and students, where the study of religion could occur in an authentic and honest setting."[16] Fazlur Rahman remained at McGill University till 1961 and in the opinion of Jesse was to "leave an indelible mark on him."[17] The Islamic Institute was a pioneering endeavor. It was the first major academic enterprise to examine contemporary Islamic themes, and that focus coupled with the balanced participation of Muslims and Westerners resulted in an immensely stimulating environment. The institution's objective was to concentrate on current developments in Modern Islam and in so doing increase Muslim critical self-understanding, Westerners' knowledge of Islam, and encourage communication between the two.[18]

Fazlur Rahman's experience at McGill University ushered in a new area of study for him and resulted in a departure from Classical Islam which was the area of focus at Oxford and Durham to Contemporary Islam. Fazlur Rahman's strong background in Classical Islam and his grasp of modern issues made him stand out as the leading participant among the Institute. Also, Fazlur Rahman influenced many scholars and students alike at McGill University and consequently McGill University influenced Fazlur Rahman. Wilfred Cantwell Smith commented on him:

> "He was a person of integrity; a religious man with a brilliant mind using it as part of his religion. He was a moral person; a serious Muslim motivated by deep concern for his culture and his people."[19]

Ayub Khan, Fazlur Rahman – Director of Central Institute for Islamic Research (1962-1968): Philosophico-Religious Reformer

In 1961, Field Marshall Ayub Khan as President of Pakistan invited Fazlur Rahman to take up the position of Director at the Central Institute of Islamic Research. Ayub Khan envisioned a modern Islamic state and established the Institute with the following goals:

1. To define Islam in terms of its fundamentals in a rational and liberal manner. To emphasize among others, the basic Islamic ideals of universal brotherhood, tolerance, and social justice;

2. To interpret the teachings of Islam in such a way as to bring out its dynamic character in terms of the more intellectual and scientific progress of the modern world;

3. To carry out research in the contribution of Islam to thought, science and culture with a view to enabling Muslims to capture an eminent position in these fields;

4. To take appropriate measures for organizing and encouraging research in Islamic history, philosophy, law and jurisprudence, etc.[20]

Initially, Fazlur Rahman hesitantly accepted the position and moved to Karachi. He was appointed the Director in August 1962 till he resigned in September, 1968. Fazlur Rahman's position as Director of the Institute represents the practical imperative of his thought in general combining both the intellectual and practical. Fazlur Rahman believed that the real objective of both Islam and faith was to establish a socio-moral order[21]; furthermore, that the function of Prophethood was of socio-moral reform.[22] Hence, his decision to accept the Directorship of the Institute was to achieve this religious goal. However, the methodology for achieving this two-fold objective *viz.*, as a Muslim and a citizen of the twentieth century attained perennial importance for both Fazlur Rahman and Ayub Khan. Thus, Fazlur Rahman's tenure as Director brings to light his practical or activist side and this represents Fazlur Rahman's concerns with both intellectual and practical Islam.

One of the goals of the Institute as we have mentioned above required that young Muslims be educated and trained in modern scientific educational methods in order that they be more intellectually capable to address contemporary issues. In consonance with his modernist-reformist predecessors – Sir Syed Ahmad Khan, Shibli Nu'mani and Muhammad Iqbal – Fazlur Rahman also contended that Islam must be studied with modern methods and that the traditional system of education taught in the madaris in Muslim countries was Medieval and outmoded and required reform. It is important to stress here that the *élan* since the nineteenth till Fazlur Rahman's time was 'anti classical or anti orthodox' not only in Pakistan but in the Muslim World in general.[23] Thus the religious sciences of *falsafa, tasawuf, kalām, fiqh, usul ul-fiqh, ḥadith* methodology, *tārīkh* and *tafsīr* were considered inadequate to meet the needs of modern times and necessitated reform. Conversely, Fazlur Rahman expressed concern about the western model of education established in Pakistan that it did not offer an adequate study of Islam although it did provide an elements of objective approach to learning and a modern scientific world view, it offered no social and ideological values.[24]

Fazlur Rahman proposed that North American scholars were to visit the Research Institute to provide expertise in research methodology, and that Muslim scholars from other regions of the world provide input on Islamic matters. It would seem that this model for the Institute was influenced by the co-operative scholarship between Muslims and non-Muslims at McGill University and Azhar University. To achieve this end he instituted three journals: *Islamic Studies* in English, *Darasāt al-Islāmīyya* in 'Arabic and *Fikr-o-Nazar* in Urdu.

The second objective of the Research Institute was related to the nation state towards social reform and national development to establish a Modern Islamic state. Fazlur Rahman wrote extensively on educational, legal, theological and historical matters.

The collaboration between the State and the Institute, Ayub Khan and Fazlur Rahman, resulted in a politico-religious environment that was strongly volatile. The politico-religious parties such as the Jama'at-i-Islami headed by Maulana Maududi and the Jamī'at-i-Ulama'-i-Islam headed by Maulana Mufti Mahmood staunchly opposed Ayub Khan's modernization programs. Maulana Yusuf Binori, a Deobandi scholar and founder of Jamia Binorīya, a Madrasa in Karachi, 'waged a six year battle' (1963-1968) against Fazlur Rahman and the Institute. Binori instituted the monthly journal *al-Bayyinnat* to counter the 'sedition of Fazlur Rahman' (*fitna-i-Fazlur Rahmani*). Binori and other leading scholars of Deobandi, Barelvi, Ahl-i-Hadith, Shi'a, fundamentalist and neo-fundamentalist dispositions scrutinized Fazlur Rahman's work considering them to be a composite of Qadiyani-Mashriqi-Parvezism concocted by Jewish and Christian Western Orientalists against Islam for the purposes of Colonialism and anti-Islamism. The Ulama' considered him to be an ignorant, heretic, atheist, enemy of Islam and a Western Orientalist agent. They suspected his "Modern Islam" and "Reformed Islam" to be a mere lip-service to Islam moreover, a much greater conspiracy against Islam in the form of seditious Orientalism *'fitna-i-istishraqiyat'* through the agency of Fazlur Rahman to distort Islamic teachings.[25]

Fazlur Rahman published his *magnum opus, Islamic Methodology in History*[26] in 1964 (Karachi) and *Islam* in 1966.

Also, he wrote extensively in English and published them in the Institute's journal, *Islamic Studies*. The journal published articles by notable Western Orientalists and Muslim researchers from the Institute, from both Arab and Pakistani background.[27] Mazhurudin Siddiqqui translated two chapters of Fazlur Rahman's *Islam* (1967) into Urdu and published it in the Institute's journal *Fikr-o-Nazr*. Additionally, Fazlur Rahman wrote numerous articles in Urdu, on themes related to Islam's early developmental and post-developmental stages, legal matters, social change, culture, Iqbal, Ibn Sīna, the Qur'an and Muhammad (ṣ). His writings in Urdu portray an attempt to communicate his historical, modernist and reformist ideas to the larger religious segment of Pakistani society which resembled Orientalist interpretations of Islam. Moreover, Fazlur Rahman's characterization of Early and Medieval Islamic thought to be 'outmoded', 'backward', 'unsuitable' and 'stagnant' echoed similar opinions held by non-Muslim Western Orientalists such as Ignaz Goldziher and Joseph Schacht.

The publication of Orientalist interpretations of Islam in the Institute's *Islamic Studies* coupled with the similitude of Fazlur Rahman's conceptualization of Islam's cardinal (*musalamāt*) sources, figures, history and intellectual contribution aroused the ire of the religious scholars in Pakistan fueling the sentiment of a Jewish and Christian conspiracy with Fazlur Rahman being perceived as the 'strategically appointed agent' against Islam. In addition, Ayub Khan's dictatorial military rule and secular disposition voiced resentment and protest against Fazlur Rahman. Furthermore, Ghulam Ahmad Pervez, a twentieth century Islamic modernist's recommendation to Ayub Khan to assume the title of "Khalifa" to eliminate the "mullas Islam" coupled with followers of Pervez's *Tolu-i-Islam* changing of allegiances to Fazlur Rahman, capitulated anger and vociferous outrage against Ayub Khan and Fazlur Rahman.[28]

Two examples can display the clash between the Ulama' and religious parties, and Ayub Khan and Fazlur Rahman which eventually led to the resignation of the former from Head of State and the latter from Director of the Institute. In 1963, the press reported that it had received a copy of a document from the Director of the Central Institute for Islamic Research to an advisory body of the Pakistan government on the subject of *ribā* (usury), with Fazlur Rahman's assessment that simple interest was *halal* (permitted) while compound interest was *haram* (forbidden). A few days later, Maulana Ehtishamul Haq Thanvi, a member of the Board of Governors of the Institute,[29] organized a press conference challenging Fazlur Rahman's views and charging him with "distorting the canons of Islam" and "exploiting the Central Institute of Islamic research in collaboration with foreign Christian missionaries". Thanvi criticized his Institute's plan to invite Western Islamicists to assist in training Muslim researchers and quoted extensively from private correspondence between Fazlur Rahman and Wilfred Cantwell Smith, and from one of Smith's books in which he is critical of various policies and personalities in South Asian Islam. Fazlur Rahman, while expressing distress that private letters and confidential government documents had been unethically obtained, welcomed scholarly critique of his work regarding *ribā*, and clarified his educational goals for the Institute. While acknowledging that only Muslims can conduct "constructive Islamic research", Fazlur Rahman stated that such research requires both understanding of traditional Islamic texts and concepts and the modern analytical tools of the West, the latter of which Muslim religious scholarship lacked. He concluded his response to the Thanvi:

> "I think that constructive Islamic research cannot be developed except by Muslims themselves. But the Muslims, in order to do this, have to combine the analytical and critical modern approach with the knowledge of the traditional materials of Islam. When they have done so, they will become entirely independent of the western Orientalists and will be able to displace them. Unfortunately, our religious scholars have been unable to develop this scientific technique of research...We must remember however, that Western Orientalist techniques of research are one thing and the interpretations and the conclusions they may have reached quite another. If a Muslim is intellectually an adult he can be expected to distinguish between the two and to necessarily accept the one and equally necessarily reject the other. It is we, however, who have to decide whether we want adulthood."[30]

Based upon this example, it becomes apparent that Thanvi was outraged by the nascent Institute's liberalism and secularism to allow non-muslim Western Orientalists to be published in the official government Institute for Islamic Research. In subsequent years, speculation and suspicion about the Institute's ulterior motives increased sharply and whence the Institute published a translation of Fazlur Rahman's *Islam* (1967) in *Fikr-o-Nazr* the Ulama' became convinced that he was playing homage to his Orientalist masters. On the other hand, Fazlur Rahman and his modernist-reformist predecessors, such as Sir Sayyid, Amīr 'Alī and Muhammad Iqbal, believed that the understanding of Islam in the twentieth century was replete with Medieval overtones. Also, similar to Shibli Nu'mani, Fazlur Rahman believed that the study of Islam should be conducted according to modern and scientific methodologies. Furthermore, Fazlur Rahman was cognizant of the prejudice that nineteenth century Orientalists had against Islam and was critical of Goldziher, Schacht, Margoliouth, Snouck Hurgronje and Lammens evaluations and judgments and highlighted them in both his works. However, he was acquiescent of the methodological and scientific approach to the study of Islam that Orientalists employed such as the History and Sociology of Religion. Further, he believed that the standards of Islamic research needed to become more scholarly, profound and meaningful for society at large. Finally, he was theologically convinced that the role and function of a Prophet was of a moral reformer and the community (*millat*) was to establish a socio-moral order. Thus the confrontation between Haq and Fazlur Rahman, two members of the same Institute, in a public press conference instead of an intellectual debate in the closed intellectual quarters of the Institute, 'sensationalized' the issue and presented the issue to the public at large as a perpetration between pure and true Islam vs. maligned and corrupted Islam.

On September 6, 1968, Fazlur Rahman resigned from the Directorship of the Central Institute for Islamic Research. The confrontation between Haq and Fazlur Rahman depicts the concerns that the Ulama' had *vis-a-vis* changing established conceptions about Islam. If the consequence of Modern Islam meant westernization in all of the public and private areas of life; furthermore, had Qadiyani-Mashriqi-Pervezian objectives of denuding Islam of its 'glorious past' *viz.*, its domination over the Muslim world, debasing its intellectual heritage, corrupting its teachings and subverting its cardinal beliefs; finally, to be motivated by Christian Missionary and Western imperialistic intentions, then this "Modern Islam", may seem acceptable to an Ayub Khan but was unacceptable and more so an outright abomination, a conspiracy, a sedition – the sedition of Orientalism (*fitna-i-istishraqiyat*). On the other hand, Fazlur Rahman's decision to accept the Institute's directorship was influenced by his conviction for Muslims to reform a narrow, self-righteous and authoritarian conception of Islam to a more universal, creative, dynamic, progressive and authentic conception of Islam. Fazlur Rahman believed that this could only be through new thinking and approach to Islam (*Ijtihād*) and that this door must be opened in order for the dynamic, progressive, positive and creative potentialities of Muslims can become actual. Fazlur Rahman thought of himself to be a twentieth century Ibn Sīna that had to deal with crass religious thought that was in dire need of Philosophical reawakening. He also felt his circumstances were similar to that of an 8th century Ibn Taymīya who had to deal with a languid society, self-righteous, stagnant and repressive Ash'arism, and political instability due to internal corruption and external war with India and power struggle with the Americans. He considered himself to be in the same circumstances of a sixteenth century Ahmad Sirhindī who faced a political elite that was metaphysically secular and positivistic. However, he found the greatest resemblance between himself and Shah Walī Ullah Dehlawi in his systematic (*tatbiq*) approach and intellectually he believed he had to develop a system of thought (*tatbiq*) for the Modern era of Islam.[31] He shaped his attitude similar to a 18th Century Abdul Wahab al Nadji, towards Medieval Islamic thought that it had to be purified from foreign elements and only the Qur'an and the *Sunnah* of the Prophet (ṣ) must be emphasized.[32] Lastly, he felt his insistence upon the Qur'an as the *sola scriptura* brought him closer to be a Muslim Luther and Calvin.

Fazlur Rahman and America: Scholar, Activist (*Dā'ī*), Religious Savant & Legacy – Shaping an Islamic Discourse (1968-1988)

In 1968, Fazlur Rahman with his wife Bilqis and five children left Pakistan never to return and lived in self-exile for the next twenty years till his death in 1988. Fazlur Rahman spent a year at the University of California in Los Angeles as a visiting professor. In 1969, he moved to Chicago where he joined the University of Chicago's Department of Near Eastern Languages and Civilizations. Jesse provides a list of courses that Fazlur Rahman taught at Chicago that are illustrative of his scope and wide learning: (1) Islamic Theology (2) Islamic Modernism (3) Business Aspects of Islamic Law (4) Islamic Political Thought (5) Islamic philosophy (6) Comparative Study of Muslim Family Law (7) Islamic Mysticism (8) Readings in Ibn al-'Arabi (9) Islamic Law (10) Readings in Muhammad Iqbal (11) Readings in the Qur'an (12) Islam and Social Change; and (13) Comparative Christian/Islamic Theology. [33] Fazlur Rahman taught both undergraduate and graduate students and they would be drawn from as far distant as Bosnia, Turkey, Indonesia and Malaysia; he had more graduate students than anyone else in the department. Professors and students alike appreciated the stature of Fazlur Rahman's scholarship and deeply respected in the academic community.

In 1975, Fazlur Rahman published *The Philosophy of Mulla Sadra*. The work addresses two critical issues in the Western treatment of Islamic philosophy *viz.*, addressing the perception that philosophy had died after Imam Ghazālī and secondly, to persuade the study of intellectual Islamic philosophy not to be restricted to Mystical philosophy.[34]

In 1980, Fazlur Rahman published his second *magnum opus*,[35] *Major Themes of the Qur'an* and represented his life's work of understanding and contemplating the Qur'an. Fazlur Rahman believed that for Islamic research in the West to be meaningful, it required a thorough grounding in the Qur'an. Furthermore, his criticism of the "atomistic approach to the study of the Qur'an" [36] prevalent in the Muslim world encouraged him to present his methodology for a sound study of the Qur'an that comprised of a philological-historical-thematic-logical and systematic expression.

In 1982, Fazlur Rahman published his last work *Islam and Modernity: The Transformation of an Intellectual Tradition* which historically and thematically analyses the Islamic tradition from its medieval era till its modern period. The work represents his commitment to reform of the Islamic tradition and education in both its Western and Eastern institutions. Moreover, it stresses the revival of the Qur'an and the *Sunnah* of the Prophet (ṣ) and the need to make Islamic scholarship more meaningful than mere historical studies of Islam.

In 1983, he received the notable distinction of being the ninth and only Muslim to be awarded the Giorgio Levi Della Vida Medal which is awarded biennially "to give recognition to an outstanding scholar whose work has significantly and lastingly advanced the study of Islamic civilization."[37] The list of eminent Islamicists awarded this distinction in its history include the likes of Joseph Schacht, G. E. von Grunebaum, Franz Rosenthal and W. Montgomery Watt. In 1986, he was honored by appointment as the Harold H. Swift Distinguished Service Professor.[38] He was also a founding member of the Editorial Advisory Board of the American Journal of Islamic Social Sciences since its inception, as originally titled, the American

Journal of Islamic Studies.[39] Additionally, he was consultant to the United States' State Department and the White House.[40]

Fazlur Rahman's Writings

Historically, Fazlur Rahman's writings can be categorized into four time periods: (1) Initial Pakistan period (2) UK and Canada period (3) Final Pakistan period and (4) American period. The initial Pakistan period which spans from his birth in 1919 to the time he left for his doctorate at Oxford University in 1946, we do not find any extant writings that he wrote during this period. At Oxford University, Fazlur Rahman completed his doctorate on *Avicenna's Psychology*.

Avicenna's Psychology

During his stay at Oxford Fazlur Rahman's supervisors were Simon van den Bergh, Professor H. A. R. Gibb and Dr. Richard Rudolf Walzer. Gibb left a very deep and pronounced mark on Fazlur Rahman and this can be seen in his manner of expression. Also, the second edition of Gibb's *Mohammedanism* as compared to its first edition displays a marked contribution in the chapter on Islam in the Subcontinent – this can be most likely attributable to Fazlur Rahman's influence on Gibb. Further Fazlur Rahman can be compared with Charles Adams and Wilfred Cantwell Smith. Both writers primarily wrote in the History of religions and adopted this methodology as the most appropriate means by which to convey an understanding of Islam.

In order to understand the second period in Fazlur Rahman's life which comprised of an eleven year hiatus in the UK and Canada he wrote three books that focused on the psychological aspect of Ibn Sīna's philosophy. His doctoral thesis focused upon Ibn Sīna's psychology, in which he elaborates the medieval conception for the philosophy of the soul. It seems probable that he was interested in resuscitating the Islamic philosophical tradition in response to the accepted opinion that Islamic philosophy died after al-Ghazālī. Secondly, Sir Syed Ahmad Khan and Shibli Nu'mani who advocated a modernist interpretation attempted to revive the works of Ibn Sīna. Finally, Fazlur Rahman regarded the early Muslim philosophers at seriously attempting a synthesis between Islam and Hellenism – philosophy and *Din* and Law and Shari'ah. Thus, it seems probable that Fazlur Rahman found himself a thousand years later in the same position of attempting to synthesize Western knowledge with Islam. Finally, his specific interest in Ibn Sīna's psychology is because of his original attempt at presenting a theory of prophecy and revelation.

Avicenna's De Anima

In 1959, Fazlur Rahman published *Avicenna's De Anima* being the psychological part of his *Kitab al-Shifa*. It is important to note that Avicenna did not write a separate tract by the name of *De Anima* but Fazlur Rahman specifically selected the psychological part of his book. This work comes after Fazlur Rahman's doctoral thesis on Avicenna's *Kitab al-Najat* and *Prophecy in Islam*. This work resonates with Aristotle's *De Anima* and it is extremely necessary to point out the significance and nature of this work. It is consciously purported by Fazlur Rahman in *Prophecy in Islam* that the orthodoxy had chiefly relied and been influenced by Avicenna's ideas. Subsequently, the impact of Avicenna on the medieval Islamic intellectualism was that the "environment" became acclimatized by Avicenna's philosophical thought.[41]

This text serves to show Fazlur Rahman's pre-occupation during his second time period, with establishing prophecy as the starting point of his religious philosophy. In doing so, Fazlur Rahman had found evidence to critique Avicenna and Islamic philosophy for establishing a metaphysical *viz.*, God-world relationship that was untenable with Islam's religious epistemology and secondly, that Ibn Sīna's religious epistemology is based on a purely intellectual intuitionism which does not provide any religious mode of knowledge – the moral imperative or conscience.

The fourth essay is of paramount significance and is deemed the primary objective behind Fazlur Rahman's undertaking of presenting Avicenna's *De Anima viz.*, the prophetic mood and its relationship with the animal motive faculty, that is discussed in the fourth chapter of this essay: (1) The universal (*kullī*) argument for the internal senses of animals (2) Of the internal senses, the cogitative and representative faculties (3) Actions of the faculties of memory and estimation (4) the conditions (*aḥwāl*) of the motive faculty and its relationship with prophetic mood (*nabuwwa*). In the fifth essay levels of intellectual actions are discursively argued and the highest of its levels is the Holy Intellect (*al-'Aql al-Qudusī*) to which the prophetic intellect is elevated to. It appears that Fazlur Rahman feels that complete denial of authority of religion is not correct and thus that prophetic authority is the only authority that is valid to be maintained.

Prophecy in Islam: Philosophy and Orthodoxy

In Fazlur Rahman's second work *Prophecy in Islam* we see that he focused upon in depth on the philosophy and psychology of prophecy i.e. the unique nature of a prophet in comparison to a normal human being. In the former work Fazlur Rahman enunciated the archetypal position that Avicenna held in the history of Islamic thought. Fazlur Rahman considered that Avicenna was the first and most systematic thinker in the history of Islamic thought. Thirdly, Fazlur Rahman realized that any thought of modernization or reformation of Islam could not be executed without the *Sunnah* of the Prophet (ṣ). Thus to unravel the concept of prophethood was of primary importance because the Muslim community was never going to disown the prophet in search for progress, industrialization and social development. So, the first step which Fazlur Rahman undertook was to understand the difference between the medieval Islamic man and the modern Muslim man. According to Russell if modernity implied that all medieval metaphysical knowledge was to be rejected as being sheer fanciful definiteness then the metaphysical doctrines ascribed to the concept of prophethood had to be removed. Thus the search to understand the Prophet Muhammad (ṣ) became of quintessential importance in the first leg of Fazlur Rahman's thought. Hence, questions related to the soul in the modern world had shifted to it being regarded as the center of consciousness and in Islam it was moral consciousness.

Selected Letters of Aḥmad Sirhindī

Selected Letters of Aḥmad Sirhindī deal with the philosophical, mystical and theological doctrines of Ahmad Sirhindī. Fazlur Rahman's objective in this book is to present Sirhindī's criticism of Ibn 'Arabī's Sufi system of thought. Sirhindī presented the concept of prophethood that was adopted by the great mystics and mystical philosophers of Islam estimating the status of prophethood to be less than that of a *wali*. He attempts to reestablish the religious notion that a prophet's role is both worldly and saintly, not as the Sufis – primarily under the influence of Ibn 'Arabi, had held to be saintly. Fazlur Rahman concludes that the Aristotelian and Platonean conception is not entirely logical and contains a metaphysical duality – God and matter – and a purely ethical dualism – good and evil (expressed in terms of being and non-being) that renders the ontological argument untenable.[42] He further concludes that the Muslim *falāsifa* developed an ontological-cum-cosmological argument for the existence of God.[43]

Fazlur Rahman indicates a pronounced error on the part of medieval philosophers and by modern historians of medieval philosophy that they attempted to reduce the *fact* of existence to a concept or an abstract quality would inevitably commit the error of making existence a co-ordinate of essence, a kind of extra-essence, a quality. He rectifies this error by stating "it is a *fact* that the existence of the contingent is not given in its essence but is bestowed by God."[44] Further, he discusses Ibn 'Arabi's doctrine of Unity of Being, followed by al-Suhrawardi's critique of it, followed by Ahmad Sirhindī's criticism of Ibn 'Arabi's position. Subsequently, Fazlur Rahman discusses the *ontic* concept of the Qur'an with the terms of *'Amr-Khalq*. It should be noted that Shah Walī Ullah of Dehli also held the same ontology. Thereafter, once the metaphysical and ontological arguments have been presented Fazlur Rahman presents the Sirhindī's criticism of the status of sainthood (*willayat*) with that of prophethood and supports Sirhindī's world-affirming, confirmed with changing history and reforming mankind. Lastly, he presents Sirhindī's criticism on the theological doctrines of al-Ash'arī, al-Bāqillani and al-Isfarā'ini that pertain to pre-determinism and the freedom of human will.[45] Fazlur Rahman again accepts and adopts

Sirhindī's position regarding this theological doctrine that human free will is absolutely free otherwise it could not be held accountable for the acts committed if the willing, creating and producing agent is not the human being himself.

In this text, Fazlur Rahman labors at presenting the effect of metaphysical and ontological arguments resulting in a conception of prophethood that purported the role of the Prophet (ṣ) as *wall* – mystical connection with God and hence world-negating and was in open contradiction to the Qur'anic concept of prophethood *viz.*, its primary role was social-reform and world affirming. Also, Fazlur Rahman discusses Sirhindī's position with respect to the concept of a tri-world of reality namely, *ʿālam al-Amr, ʿālam al-Mithāl* and *ālam al-Khalq*. Fazlur Rahman restates Sirhindī's position regarding *ʿālam al-Mithāl* (the world of similitude) that it does not bear any effect on *ʿālam al-Amr* or on *ʿālam al-Khalq* and reduces Ibn ʿArabi's position to his uncontrolled imagination. [46] Lastly, Fazlur Rahman's criticizes the miracles (*karamat*) performed by saints are an 'auxiliary concomitant of saintship and not an essential part of it.'[47] Again, we find Fazlur Rahman's pre-occupation with the concept of prophethood and the prophetic experience all intimately related to his primary concern of reforming the concept of the Prophetic *Sunnah*.

Islamic Methodology in History

Islamic Methodology in History is a complex work and has been described by Fazlur Rahman[48] along with his *Major Themes of the Qur'an* as his *magnum opus*. This is a work on the historical development of *Usul ul-Fiqh* or the principles of Islamic Jurisprudence. This book comprises of five chapters: (1) Concepts *Sunnah, Ijtihād* and *Ijmāʿ* in the Early Period (2)

Sunnah and Ḥadīth (3) Post Formative Developments in Islam (4) *Ijtihād* in the Later Centuries (5) Social Change and Early *Sunnah.* This work was a compilation of several articles that Fazlur Rahman wrote whilst director of the Central Institute of Islamic Research in Karachi. The articles were translated in Urdu and Arabic and probably done so because of the relationship between Pakistan and Iraq as can be determined from the newspapers, *Dawn* and *Pakistan Times* 1960-1968.

As we have stated earlier, Fazlur Rahman pre-occupation with unearthing and properly depicting the Prophetic *Sunnah* in its most broadest terms, continued throughout his Early studies in Pakistan, his doctoral and professorship in the United Kingdom and Canada and his time in Pakistan. *Islamic Methodology in History* represented a shift in focus from Islamic philosophy, theology and mysticism towards the study of *usul al-fiqh.* Fazlur Rahman did not consider the phenomena of Hadith to be a body of knowledge that was innocent from the influences of history. Therefore, he applied the same rigors of his unique Qur'an centric ethical historicism to Ḥadith as he did to *fiqh, kalām, falsafa* and *tasawwūf* in attempt to salvage 'true' Prophetic *Sunnah* as depicted by the Qur'an of a social reformer intent on establishing a socio-moral order.

Fazlur Rahman's objective in studying the phenomena (*dhāhira*) of Ḥadith was to ascertain the noumena (*haqīqa*) of the Ḥadith which he deemed should be equivalent to the *Sunnah* of the Prophet (ṣ) as depicted in the Qur'an. The main categories that he took into consideration were the following: (1) Qur'an (2) *Sunnah* (3) *Ijmā'* (4) *Ijtihād* (5) *Qiyās* (6) *R'ay* (7) Ḥadith (8) *Fiqh* (9) Socio-political factors, both internal and external (10) *Kalām*-cultural, both internal and external.

Islam

The book *Islam* was completed whilst Fazlur Rahman was the Director of the Central Institute for Islamic Research in Karachi, Pakistan. The book provides a panoramic view of Islam and is presented using the methodology employed in the history of religions. Thus this book can be categorized amongst the works written by Margoliouth, Goldziher, Gibb, Adams and Smith. The book comprises of fourteen chapters, each chapter discussing succinctly a significant category in the history of Islamic thought and its corresponding effect on the trajectory of Islam. However, what distinguishes Fazlur Rahman's work as opposed to the aforementioned Orientalists "criteria" by which Fazlur Rahman weighs Islamic thought and action on. The inherent nature of this "criteria" is the key to unlocking the mind of Fazlur Rahman. It is truly a unique work that is unlike any other text in the history of Islam up to date. The argumentation is extremely powerful both in tone and in style. His writing style if compared to his earlier work *Selected Letters of Ahmad Sirhindī* is different. In his work on Sirhindī there is a significant alteration in the boldness of his writing as compared to *Islam*. It is believed that the audience to whom Fazlur Rahman was addressing in his work on Sirhindī is the Philosophical and English speaking elite of Pakistan. If the writing style is compared with his contemporaries in Pakistan one can see how resemblance of Fazlur Rahman change in tone as if to suit the temper of his audience *viz.,* if compared with the English writings of Bashir Ahmad Dar, M.M. Sheikh and the like of this era we see a considerable change in *boldness* of his writing.

This work is divided into fourteen chapters: (1) Muhammad (2) The Qur'an (3) Origins and Development of the Tradition

(4) The Structure of the Law (5) Dialectical Theology and the Development of Dogma (6) The Shari'ah (7) Philosophical Movement (8) Sufi Doctrine and Practice (9) Sufi Organizations (10) Sectarian Developments (11) Education (12) Pre-Modernist Reform Movements (13) Modern Developments (14) Legacy and Prospects. It is a comprehensive treatment of Islamic history taking into consideration the history of ideas that have influenced its growth, the political events that steered the destiny of the community towards or away from the Qur'anic ethos and prophetic rubric, the principle figures that have altered its course, the cultural and religious influences external to the community, criticism of modern Orientalist studies of Islam. The original thought (*Ijtihād*) displayed by Fazlur Rahman, in comparison to other works in the same genre, is the Qur'ano-Sunnatic or ethical historicism employed as a criterion on evaluating Islam.

The objective of these studies was to understand the *Sunnah* of the Prophet (ṣ) and we find that the product of this labor is to be found in his book *Islam* published in 1966 in London and New York. This work seems to be the product of his lectures and discussion during his early career at Durham University and McGill University where he had to address the Orientalist conceptions of Islam. It is worthy to note that Goldziher, Margoliouth, Gibb and Adams had written similar tracts on the history of Islam but had titled these works as *Mohammadanism* whereas Fazlur Rahman titled his work on the same subject as *Islam*. Again we see that Fazlur Rahman's preoccupation with the Prophet (ṣ) concepts and and doctrines related to him. It seems that during his early teaching period at Durham and McGill University he was contemplating the positions he has arrived at from his study of the Qur'an. This activity was a demonstratively daunting because the great Orientalists had preoccupied themselves with the Qur'an and the *Sirah*. Thus, the intellectual culture of the age had influenced Fazlur Rahman's study of the *Sirah* in the light of the Qur'an and *vice versa*. In this era of Orientalist studies on Islam, there are copious writings on the *Sirah* and the Qur'an which all together attempted to establish the following:

1. Psychology of the Prophet (ṣ): the psychological state of the Prophet (ṣ) was one who experienced epileptic fits and the product of these fits was the Qur'an.

2. Jewish-Christian influences on the Prophet (ṣ): the Jewish and Christian societies that influenced the Prophet (ṣ) through the cultural milieu surrounding Makkah.

3. The non-divine nature of the Qur'an: Due to the two aforementioned factors, the nature of the Qur'an was considered to be not Divine and consequently, the concept of Revelation was considered to be untenable within the precarious Western philosophical and cultural milieu during the early twentieth century was one of extreme skepticism, pessimism and nihilism due to the influence of Logical Positivism, Scientific Realism and Nietzschian pessimism. Further, the political milieu of the early twentieth century was a combination of the degeneration of the Western Imperial Empire in the Muslim World coupled with the collapse of the Ottoman Empire and the Ideological polarization of Europe ravaged by two World wars. Lastly, the success of Biblical historicism and hermeneutics of the nineteenth

century resulted in a strong skepticism towards all revealed religions *en masse.*

Additionally, Fazlur Rahman made a concerted effort to ascertain the root cause for the attitude of the Muslim world which he repeatedly described as world-denying, [49] antinomianism, monism, occasionalism and obscurantism which he concluded to be anti-Islamic and representing doctrines that were contradictory to the Qur'an and the *Sunnah.*[50]

The Philosophy of Mulla Sadra

The Philosophy of Mulla Sadra published in 1975 was his first publication after a hiatus of seven years. Fazlur Rahman's interest in Mulla Sadra can be traced to early references in his *Avicenna's Psychology, Avicenna's De Anima,* and *Selected Letters of Shaikh Ahmad Sirhindī.*[51] Secondly, from the 1950's onwards the works of Henry Corbin on Islamic philosophy principally shifted the focus towards Islamic Mysticism, as Fazlur Rahman himself states in the preface to his work:

> "Indeed, considerable valuable work has been done during the past two and a half decades in the field of post-Ghazālīan Islamic thought, notably on al-Suhrawardī (d.1191), the founder of the Illuminationist School. But most leading scholars [Henry Corbin] in this activity, have, through their own spiritual proclivities, been led to emphasize the Sufi and esoteric side of this literature at the cost, as I believe, of its purely intellectual and philosophical hard core, which is of immense value and interest to the modern student of philosophy...It is hoped, therefore, that the present work will further stimulate sorely needed *philosophic* research into this hitherto little explored but rich field of Islamic thought."[52]

This work comprises of three parts: (1) Ontology (2) Theology (3) Psychology: Man and his Destiny. It is a work that attempts to synthesize four separate journeys: The first journey is from the world of creation to the Truth and/or Creator (*min al-khalq ila'l-haqq*) where Sadra addresses the questions of metaphysics and ontology known also under the rubric of 'general principles' (*al-Umur al-'Āmmah*) or 'divine science in its general sense' (*al-'Ilm al-Ilahi bi'l-Ma'na al-A'lām*). It is in this part of the *Asfār* that Sadra deals with the ontological foundations of his system including such issues as the meaning of philosophy, being (*wujud*) and its primacy (*asalah*) over quiddity (*mahiyyah*), gradation of being (*tashkik al-wujud*), mental existence (*al-wujud al-dhihni*), platonic forms (*al-muthul al-aflatuniyyah*), causality, substantial movement, time, temporal origination of the world, the intellect, and the unification of the intellect with the intelligible. The second journey is from the Truth to the Truth by the Truth (*min al-haqq ila'l-haqq bi'l-haqq*).

In the second journey, we find a full account of Sadra's natural philosophy and his critique of the ten Aristotelian categories. Among the issues discussed extensively are the categories, substance and accidents, how physical entities come to exist, *hylé* and its philosophical significance, matter and form (hylomorphism), natural forms, and the roots of the hierarchy of the physical order.

The third journey is from the Truth to the world of creation with the Truth (*min al-haqq ila'l-khalq bi'l-haqq*) where Sadra goes into his reconstruction of theology, which is discussed under the name of 'metaphysics' or 'divine science in its particular sense' (*al-'ilm al-ilahi bi'l-ma'na'l-akhass*). It is in this section of the *Asfar* that the theological dimension of Sadra's thought and his relentless attacks on the theologians (*mutakallimun*) come to the fore. Among the issues Sadra addresses are the unity and existence of God and the previous *kalām* proofs given of it, the ontological simplicity of the Necessary Being, the names and qualities of God, God's knowledge of the world, His power, divine providence, speech (*kalām*) as a divine quality, good and evil (theodicy), procession of the world of multiplicity from the One, and the unity of philosophy ('wisdom', *hikmah*) and the divine law (*shari'ah*).

The fourth and final journey is from the world of creation to the world of creation with the Truth (*min al-khalq ila'l-khalq bi'l-haqq*) where the great chain of being is completed with psychology, resurrection, and eschatology.

Major Themes of the Qur'an

Major Themes of the Qur'an published in 1980 is to be considered Fazlur Rahman's second *magnum opus* after his self-declared first *Islamic Methodology in History*. This work seems to be a culmination in one volume of Fazlur Rahman's understanding of the Qur'an. It is a work that represents the final presentation of a well nigh forty year career spent in the study of the Qur'an. In an attempt to deconstruct this work we have labored extensively to decipher the meaning and implications of a thematic approach to the study of the Qur'an and shall present our finding in the chapter on the Qur'an in this thesis.

Islam and Modernity

This book commemorates Fazlur Rahman's scholarly contribution to the study of Islam and Modernity. The book was compiled as a result of a research project undertaken at the

University of Chicago and was originally part of a much larger project on "Islam and Social Change".[53] He wrote the book in light of writing a general work on the:

> "medieval Islamic educational system, with its major features and deficiencies, and on the modernization efforts undertaken during the past century or so. In the last chapter I have tried to delineate certain general lines along which I believe these efforts should proceed in order to be really fruitful."[54]

Fazlur Rahman focused upon the Islamic intellectualism created as a result of the medieval learning attained from higher Islamic education. He further stresses that the "growth of a genuine, original and adequate Islamic thought that must provide the real criterion for judging the success or failure of an Islamic educational system."[55] Thenceforth, he states the need for a correct method of interpreting the Qur'an and its central position in Islamic intellectualism and in the faith of Muslims.

Health and Medicine in the Islamic Tradition

Health and Medicine in the Islamic Tradition: Change and Identity, was the last book published by Fazlur Rahman. His goal is twofold: he first articulates the overall Qur'anic approach to the subject matter, distinguishing between that and various later interpretations from extra-Qur'anic sources, and stressing the contiguity of the physical and moral realms in Islam. Just as physical health cannot be separated from moral health, he claims in a clear bid for a holistic approach to the practice of medicine, neither can the physical sciences be separated totally from moral sciences (ethics). He then outlines the historical development of Islamic thought about health and medicine, including its fruition in the great ethical issues in Islamic medicine. His purpose here is to critique certain developments he considers to be deviations from Qur'anic norms and to indicate issues he believes Islamic medicine focuses on today, particularly in the area of contraception.

Revival and Reform in Islam: A Study of Islamic Fundamentalism

Revival and Reform in Islam: A Study of Islamic Fundamentalism is a posthumous publication edited by Ebrahim Moosa. Fazlur Rahman in his critique of the orthodox view which was developed by the Ḥadīth scholars (*muhadithūn*) was incorrigible from two aspects. One from the point of view of the Qur'an itself emphasizing that the Qur'an was revealed upon the Prophet's heart and secondly that from the Medieval conception of the soul and mind that orthodoxy had formulated a dogma that was not correct with the process of revelation.

The Influence of Orientalism on Fazlur Rahman and Its Significance in the Acceptance of his Works

In order to properly understand the ground realities and the context in which Fazlur Rahman's work and personality were examined it is vital that we have a clear understanding of how orientalism is viewed in Pakistan and the Muslim world. In addition, we need to evaluate how the West has approached the study of the Orient. Edward Said in his *Orientalism* (1978) cites Jacques Waardenburg's *L'Islam dans le miroir de l'Occident* and contends that it offers a valuable and intelligent study of Orientalism. Waardenburg examines five important experts as makers of an image of Islam whom Fazlur Rahman was coeval to: (1) Ignaz Goldziher, (2) Duncan Black Macdonald, (3) C. Snouck Hurgronje, (4) Carl Becker, (5) Louis Massignon.

Waardenburg's mirror-image metaphor for late nineteenth and early twentieth century Orientalism is apt. In the work of

each of his eminent Orientalists there is a highly tendentious –
in four cases out of the five, even hostile – vision of Islam, as if
each man saw Islam as a reflection of his own chosen weakness.
Each scholar was profoundly learned, and the style of his
contribution was unique. The five Orientalists among them
exemplify what was best and strongest in the tradition during
the period roughly from the 1880's to the interwar years. Yet
Ignaz Goldziher appreciation of Islam's tolerance towards other
religions was undercut by his dislike of Muhammad's
anthropomorphism and Islam's too exterior theology and
jurisprudence.[56] Duncan Black Macdonald's interest in Islamic
piety and orthodoxy was vitiated by his perception of what
he considered Islam's heretical Christianity; Carl Becker's
understanding of Islamic civilization made him see it as a sadly
undeveloped one; C. Snouck Hurgronje's highly refined studies
of Islamic mysticism (when he considered it the essential part of
Islam) led him to a harsh judgment of its critical limitations; and
Louis Massignon's extraordinary identification with Muslim
theology, mystical passion and poetic art kept him curiously
unforgiving to Islam for what he regarded as its regenerate revolt
against the idea of incarnation. The manifest differences in their
methods emerge as less important than their Orientalist
consensus on Islam: latent inferiority.

Waardenburg's study has the additional virtue of showing
how these five scholars shared a common intellectual and
methodological tradition whose unity was truly international.
Ever since the first Orientalist congress in 1873, scholars in the
field have known each other's work and felt each other's
presence very directly. Edward Said in his *Orientalism* (1978)
points out that Waardenburg did not stress enough that most of
the late-nineteenth century Orientalists were bound to each

other politically as well. Snouck Hurgronje went directly from his studies of Islam to being an adviser to the Dutch government on handling its Muslim Indonesian colonies; Macdonald and Massignon were widely sought after as experts on Islamic matters by colonial administrators from North Africa to Pakistan. All five scholars shaped a coherent vision of Islam that had a wide influence on government circles throughout the Western world. What we must add to Waardenburg's observation is that these scholars were completing, bringing to an ultimate concrete refinement, the tendency since the sixteenth and seventeenth centuries to treat the Orient not only as a vague literary problem but to penetrate into the secrets of the Orients history.

The Orientatlists – Renan, Goldziher, Macdonald, von Grunebaum, Gibb and Bernard Lewis – saw Islam, as a "cultural synthesis" that could not be studied apart from the economics, sociology, and politics of the Islamic peoples. For Orientalism, Islam had a meaning which, if one were to look for its most succinct formulation, could be found in Renan's first treatise: in order best to understand Islam, it had to be reduced to "tent and tribe". The impact of colonialism, of worldly circumstances, of historical development all these were to Orientalists never taken seriously enough to complicate the essential Islam.

The career of H.A.R. Gibb illustrates within itself the two alternative approaches by which Orientalism has responded to the modern Orient. In 1945 Gibb delivered the Haskell Lectures at the University of Chicago and opined that Orientalism should be approached with a new methodological approach known as Area Studies – where an Arabist and sociologist would be combined into one. [57] In his *Modern Trends in Islam* (1951) Gibb contended that it is a fact that Arab literature displays both remarkable signs of imaginative power on the one hand and literalism on the other. The Arab mind has an intense feeling for the separateness and the individuality of the concrete events; thus, despite there being great Muslim philosophers they were few and exerted minimal influence. The cumulative effect is the "lack of a sense of law" and "the aversion of the Muslims from the thought-processes of rationalism". The rejection of rationalist modes of thought and of the utilitarian ethic which is inseparable from them has its roots, therefore, not in the so-called "obscurantism" of the Muslim theologians but in the atomism and discreteness of the Arab imagination.

Edward Said categorized Gibb's contentions as "pure Orientalism … If Islam is flawed from the start by virtue of its permanent disabilities, the Orientalist will find according to his views, 'reform' is a betrayal of Islam: this is exactly Gibb's argument."[58] Fazlur Rahman countered this racial categorization and attributed this *Gibbsian* portrayal of the Arab mentality as being attributable to the Islamic educational system being in need of serious reform. Second, Fazlur Rahman focused his efforts in his second period in Pakistan towards legal and theological reform above all despite his deep attachment to Islamic philosophy. This provides us with a valuable insight into Fazlur Rahman's overall appraisal and attitude towards Orientalist thought; firstly, not to resort to reactionarism and apologetics, secondly, to treat Orientalist criticism as constructive criticism and thirdly, that Orientalism and Islamic modernism *should* work in a collaborative manner to achieve a common goal "the good of humanity". Hence, a consistent feature that is noticeable in Fazlur Rahman's treatment of Orientalism is to be tolerant, fair and just. For example, Orientalist criticisms of the Arab or Muslim world under the rubric of any ethnic generalization, racial inferiority or religious intolerance are completely rejected. Whereas, Islamic thought requiring a thorough scientific and systematic reformation is accepted. Further, if the Muslim world and the West faced a common enemy in communism then they would form an alliance to confront it. But a wholesale acceptance of Westernism is neither acceptable. Fazlur Rahman believed that the underlying deficiencies prevalent generally in Muslim thought not restricting it to Islamic thought, in the directives put forth by Muslim modernists that both scientific approaches and Western methodologies need to be cultivated with the original sources of Islam to usher in a modern Islamic thought free from the shackles of Medievalism.

On the other hand, the Muslim reception of Orientalism has been mostly viewed with suspicion, rejection, racism, religious hatred, Western supremacy and polemicism. Muhammad Karam Shah (1998) states that:

> "this is an astonishing reality that those intellectual sources that Orientalists rely upon for their results, they are either entirely mute about this movement or if there is any mention of Orientalism or Orientalist then they are extremely insufficient and self-contradicting. The reason for this is typically in the way that Orientalists conceal their objectives and the policies which they adopt to fulfill them; and, in this same manner they do not want to popularize this name Orientalism." [59]

Abu'l Hasan Ali Nadwi:

> "By Orientalists it is meant those people that are Western and have specialized in Islamic studies and spent their entire lives in it. These people have attained repute amongst Muslim circles due to their interest in Eastern sciences on the basis.

> Their attempts are to distance Muslims from their religion and by creating doubts about their history and repugnance towards Islam's present and future; they create confusion and doubts about Islam and the Prophet of Islam; they stress and actively engage in reform and modernization of Islamic law."[60]

Khaliq Ahmad Nazami identifies five stages through which the Orientalist movement had passed through based upon its behavior and focus. He argues the objectives and methods have evolved in each period and are intrinsically distinct. In the first and second stages, from the birth of the Prophet (ṣ) to the end of Europe's middle age, Orientalism confined itself to Christian polemicism about prophet Muhammad (ṣ), Qur'an and Islam's teachings as an impostor and false religion. During these stages Islam was militarily, territorially, civilizationally and culturally superior to Christendom. In the third stage the Muslim world became subjugated to Western colonial and imperialism.[61] Orientalism experienced a paradigm shift and studied Muslims from a more wholistic approach: social, historical, geographical, economic, religious, ethical and political. Oriental scholarship became more refined and erudite with scholars possessing greater profundity with Arabic and Islamic history with the aim of maintaining an imperial stronghold upon the Muslims. They engaged in carefully cataloging manuscripts and preserved them in museums and libraries across the major cities of Europe. Orientalists also paid great attention to the teaching of the Arabic language and Oriental religions. They also established societies that allowed students to receive financial aid and scholarships in Islamic civilization, history and many other Islamic sciences. They established Asiatic societies or Asia specific societies that would focus upon area-specific studies. Annual international conferences were held and Orientalists from all over the world would present papers upon various issues related to Islam.

In the fourth period, Western colonial and imperialistic powers began loosing their grip upon the Muslim world as it demanded independence and freedom from them. Orientalism had largely continued along the same lines as it did in the previous stage. After the Second World War, H.A.R. Gibb in his *Modern Trends in Islam* writes about the future course of Orientalism. Regarding this Muhammad Karam Shah responds:

> "Reality is so that after the imperialistic powers departed, Muslims actively became the West's slaves. Colonialist and Imperialist countries began giving weaker countries loans and bound them in the strait jacket of debt and upon these grounds both internal and external policies were shaped and drawn. If one were to scrutinize and carefully study this course in Orientalism one finds that this period is not dissimilar than any other period in the history of Orientalism."[62]

In the fifth period new preferences and policies were drawn up in the light of the new prevailing post Second World War geopolitical situations:

1. The global economic reliance of East upon West and West upon East.

2. Recognition of imperialistic intentions of the West.

3. Freedom and Independence from Western occupation and subjugation.

4. The defeat of colonialist ventures.

5. Discoveries and developments in science and technology.

6. Capitalistic and Communist ideologies and their promulgation.

They realized that Christian literature compiled against the Prophet of Islam and Islam itself had to be modified and the portrayal of the Prophet (ṣ) and Islam had to be changed.[63] During this period Orientalists modified their approach and in general their appreciation of Islam and the Prophet (ṣ) changed based upon certain factors:

1. Access to original manuscripts and documents.

2. In depth knowledge of the Arabic language.

3. New research upon important and central issues allowed to acknowledge a definite manipulation and modification of the texts and an unreasoned bias against Islam.

4. Internal factors: Europe facing their own problems with relation to modernism, scientific developments and racial discrimination. These factors led to a more sympathetic, truthful and reasonableness where baseless inaccurate and falsified accounts were less likely to be made, accusations became occurred less. It seems that the talismanic power of the Church upon the Orientalist reduced and in this new age some bold and courageous writers challenged the pedantic ideas that had been held and an intellectual honesty and just representation of Islam began to surface, however unfortunately despite the truthful and just image portrayed of Islam they were incapable of accepting it and Islam as the truth. Moreover, this outward appreciation of Islam was in

contradiction to the inner prejudice that lay in the minds of the Orientalists.

5. The changing civilization and resource allocation amongst the East and West.

6. Part time scholars were replaced by full time faculty at universities in Britain, France and America.

The result is that Orientalist studies became more focused and less prejudice began to surface in their writings. Examples of moderation are like the writings of Goethe and Carlyle. On the one side the Orientalists were able to find a clientele for their writings and on the other criticism of Islamic sources increased in an exponential manner and this was only to increase the hesitation, skepticism and confusion amongst the people of the East. Thus, during the fifth period unlike the previous four, the Qur'an and Ḥadīth became the target of the Orientalists. During this period a shift in focus was made from classical studies upon Islam to the contemporary situation of Muslim societies – politically, socially and economically. Here focus was not made upon Oriental societies but only those that were financially affluent or politically significant.

Ahmad Samayalofitsh argues that since Islam lost its political supremacy and unity due to the Crusades it also lost its societal, moral, civilizational and cultural supremacy. He states that the motives and objectives of Orientalism have been the following:[64]

1. Imperialism: After the defeat of the Crusaders, the Europeans reflected deeply upon how the defeat could be vanquished. They resorted to effacing the beliefs of Islam that were in opposition to Christianity. Further, they created a mental and intellectual status quo that

Western imperialism could not be even dreamt of. Upon this dismissal from power the importance and significance of the Orientalist became more apparent. These Orientalists provide in-depth studies and expert articles are compiled and published.

2. Ideological: Ideologically Orientalism is primarily a Jewish and Christian enterprise to study the religion of Islam and Muslim people. The differences between Islam, Judaism and Christianity theologically and historically have impregnated deep-seated ideological differences, both in the civilizational and cultural realms.

3. Political Motive: In the Muslim world, the Europeans have established embassies in which secretaries are present, that are Muslim and are fully literate of Arabic to gain awareness of thinkers, journalists and political leaders and have an approach of them. This person is the pioneer of the Western governments. Intellectual support is given by Western governments.[65] These first hand conspirators provide knowledge of the Eastern nations manners, behaviors, natures, conduct, way of living, language, literature, emotions and psychologies they have in depth knowledge and in doing so spread their ideas, concerns and cause the civil and Muslim conflicts between them.

4. Economic: Religious and political affiliations result in economic interests as well. From the early periods the East and West exchanged economic ties. Many of the publishers and publications receiving government endorsements and books of such would attain much financial gain.

5. Intellectual: The Westerners lost militarily to the Muslims as a reaction they took to the intellectual revenge. Muhammad Tufayl cites two Orientalists in his *Naqush Rasūl*:

   "Now on the military front the crusader wars ended however Westerners did not cease to make Islam the eye of their prejudice and they continued to do so in their writings. In another place, a French Orientalist cites that after the Christian losing the Turks took up the battle in the field of literature."[66]

6. Historical: The colossal width and length of the Islamic empire stretching from the Far East to the West, over mainly Christian lands, led many to hate Islam.

7. Crusades: The Crusades are also one factor that has strongly influenced the Orientalist movement. In Western history the Crusade bear a heavy importance and significance. Palestine before Islam's conquest over it belonged to the Christians and was extremely holy and blessed land. Mustafa Sibai has provided a summary of Orientalism as follows:

   a. Prophethood, revelation, Qur'an, *Sunnah* and law to place in doubt and scepticism.

   b. For Muslims to doubt and think that their present cannot be improved and to be pessimistic about their futures.

   c. To remove Islam's intellectual heritage from Muslims.

d. To remove the sense of brotherhood amongst Muslims and replace it with the era of ignorance (*jāhilīya*).

Religious: The religious factor is the promulgation and spreading of the Christian religion. By doing so, Christianity would seem better, preferable and supremacy to be self evidently apparent – according to them they lay claim that Islam was incapable of dealing with modern challenges *viz.*, that the time of the Prophet (ṣ) has passed and that time has passed when these laws and rules cannot be and are not applicable because the realities of the modern world and those of previous generations are infinitely different. Science and technology have given way to new discoveries thus it is not rationally acceptable to accept the way of life of gone and lost times and instead adopt a modern way of life. Thus, much of Orientalism and Evangelism go hand and hand a great deal of Orientalists are actually religious clergy men and a great number of them are Jewish.

Sources of Fazlur Rahman's Islamic Thought

Fazlur Rahman considers that Islamic doctrine, law and thinking in general are based upon four sources, or fundamental principles (usul): (1) Qur'an, (2) *Sunnah* ("Traditions"), (3) *Ijmā'* ("consensus"), and (4) *Ijtihād* ("individual thought"). He opines that the Qur'an (literally, reading or recitation) is regarded as the Word, or Speech, of God delivered to Muhammad (ṣ) by the angel Gabriel. The surahs' revealed at Makkah during the earliest part of Muhammad's (ṣ) career are concerned with ethical and spiritual teachings and the Day of Judgment. The surahs' revealed at Madinah at a later period in the career of the Prophet (ṣ) are concerned with social legislation and the political-moral principles for constituting and ordering the community. *Sunnah* ("a well-trodden path") was used by pre-Islamic Arabs to denote their tribal or common law or 'the bulwark of Arab practice'; in Islam it came to mean the example of the Prophet (ṣ); *i.e.*, his words and deeds as recorded in compilations known as Hadith.[67]

It seems that much of Fazlur Rahman's inspiration for his critique on the traditionalist account of Hadith is based upon Ibn Sīna's concept of Prophethood. Ibn Sīna in his *Al-Najat fi-l Illahiyat wa-l Mantiq* dedicates a chapter to the *Fasl fi Ithbat al-Nabuwwwah wa kaifiyat da'watul Nabi Ila Allah wa'l Mi'ad* – that it is necessary that human beings are dependent upon one another and are unable to function without one another, thus, there exists a civil and social contract (*'aqd al-mudn wa-l Ijtima'at*) between members of a society. Further, every human being is responsible in fulfilling a particular function in the fabric of society; similarly, a prophet is responsible for fulfilling a particular function in society. It is necessary, therefore, that for the survival of the society and mankind in general that cooperation (*musharaka*) and interaction (*mu'amala*) exists between members of society. In this interaction there must be two essential elements (1) *Sunnah* (2) *'Adl*. The prophet must 'establish his path' (*Sunnah*) and a legislator (*mu'addl*). The prophet should be able to communicate and commit to his *Sunnah*. He should not allow people to leave his *Sunnah* or to disagree with his authority – his subjects should be aware of what is acceptable and unacceptable before him. It is of paramount importance to point out that his role permits the survival and existence of a good (*salih*) human being. Fazlur Rahman modernized Ibn Sīna's concept of good and reformulates it with the good of Plato, the *amor intellectualis des* of Spinoza, the good will of Kant and connects with prophetic insight *viz.*, creative of knowledge and values."[68] This requires that the prophet establish a good order (*nizam ul-khayr*). Hence, the need and function of a prophet is fundamental (*wajib*). Hadith (a report, or collection of sayings attributed to the Prophet) provide the written documentation of the prophet's word and deeds. Six of these collections, compiled in the 3rd century AH/9th century AD came to be regarded as especially authoritative by the largest group in Islam, the *Ahl ul-Sunnah*. Another large group, the Shi'a, has its own Hadith.

Ijmā' and Ijtihād: The Influence of Kalām

The doctrine of *Ijmā'*, or consensus, was introduced in the 2nd century AH/8th century AD in order to standardize legal theory and practice, and to overcome individual and regional differences of opinion. Thought conceived as a "consensus of scholars," (*Ijmā'*) in actual practice was a more fundamental operative factor. From the 3rd century AH *Ijmā'* connotates accepted interpretations of the Qur'an and the actual content of the *sunnah* (i.e., Hadith and theology). Thus, *Ijmā'* amounted to a principle of rigidity in thinking where consensus had reached in practice interpretations that were considered closed questioning and further substantial questioning on them prohibited.[69] Fazlur Rahman contends that it is this principle of *Ijmā'* that resulted in the doors *Ijtihād* closing.[70] In contrast, the Shi'a developed the doctrine of Imamology, emphasizing a subjective form of idealism and transcendentalism in conscious contrast with Sunni pragmatism. Thus, whereas the Sunni believe in the *Ijmā'* of the community as the source of decision making and workable knowledge, the Shi'a believed that knowledge derived from fallible sources is useless and that sure and true knowledge can come only through a contact with the infallible *Imām*.[71]

Fazlur Rahman opined that *Ijtihād*, literally meant "to endeavor" or "to exert effort," was required to find the legal and doctrinal solution to a new problem. In the early period of Islam, because *Ijtihād* took the form of individual opinion (*ra'y*) a wealth of conflicting and chaotic opinions surfaced. In the 2nd century AH *Ijtihād* was replaced by *qiyās* (reasoning by strict analogy), a formal procedure of deduction based on the texts of the Qur'an and the Hadith. The transformation of *Ijmā'* into a conservative mechanism and the acceptance of a definitive body of Hadith virtually closed the "gate of *Ijtihād*". Nevertheless, certain outstanding Muslim thinkers (e.g. al-Ghazālī, died 1111 AD) continued to claim the right of new *Ijtihād* for themselves, and reformers of the 18th and 19th centuries, because of modern influences, have caused this principle to once more receive wider acceptance. Fazlur Rahman reformed and modernized the concept of *Ijtihād*, under the influence of Shah Walī Ullah Dehlawi double movement theory, that is in an intellectual endeavor or jihad, including the intellectual elements of both the moments – past [prophetic] and present – is technically called *Ijtihād* which means "the effort to understand the meaning of a relevant text or precedent in the past, containing a rule, and to alter that rule by extending or restricting or otherwise modifying it in such a manner that a new situation can be subsumed under by a new solution. This definition itself implies that a text or precedent can be generalized as a principle can then be the principle can be formulated as a new rule. This implies that the meaning of a past text or precedent, the present situation, and the intervening tradition can be sufficiently objectively known and that the tradition can be fairly objectively brought under the judgement of the (normative) meaning of the past under whose impact the tradition arose. It follows from this that tradition can be studied with adequate historical objectivity and separated not only from the present but also from the normative factors that are supposed to have generated it."[72]

Fazlur Rahman's position on the "closing of the gates" of *Ijtihād* in the 4th century is that the there was a general state of affairs that led to the gradual constriction of the *Ijtihād* or "fresh thought."[73] Fazlur Rahman attributes specific factors that caused this general state of affairs. He points out six main factors:

1. Formalism: He attributes formalism to the framework of the Islamic methodology which he considers to be – (1) Qur'an (2) *Sunnah* (3) *Ijmā'* (4) *Ijtihād*. Post-formative developments led to both *Sunnah* and *Ijmā'* being cut off from the process of *Ijtihād*. Further the content of this formalism became enshrined in the prophetic authority and this content prevented the nature of methodology to play any further part in its development. The influence of the *Ahl ul Sunnah wa'l Jama'ah* at the hands of the Ash'arī and Maturidī formulations that there was a direct interdependence between theology and law in Islam and hence the formalism of juristic thinking is in no small measure due to the formalism of the *kalām*. The result of this formalism is the existence of blatant contradictions in the juristic doctrine due to *kalām*. Further these theological dogmas, as they were formulated and subsequently held with tenacity, were in themselves one-sided reactions rather than genuine syntheses. Fazlur Rahman recommendation is that to integrate jurisprudence into the larger field of Islamic

thought should be done to develop a synthetic whole inconsonance with the general Islamic worldview.

2. Inconsistencies between *kalām* and *fiqh*: After enunciating the relationship between *kalām* and law, Fazlur Rahman focuses his attention towards to the inconsistencies between the two. These contradictions become accentuated when *kalām* theology enters into jurisprudence. He states that Ibn Taymīya criticized the traditional *kalām* on human free will, stating "the natural assumptions of law which presumes man to be free and responsible and those of Sunni *kalām* which considers man to be a divine automaton."[74] The second inconsistency is that in matters of belief the foundation is reason where as the foundation of law is *taqlīd* (unquestioning acceptance of authority).

3. The imperfection of human knowledge: The imperfection of human knowledge is that human knowledge based on reason and experience cannot be trusted at all and, therefore, cannot lead to action. Further, that man is incapable of knowing anything true or doing anything good without being commanded on authority. This depreciation of human faculties, which is in conflict of the Qur'an to man to think, understand, reflect and ponder is the standard dogma of Sunni theology. Its net result is cynicism. Furthermore, the implications of this theological dogma becoming the prolegomena of legal philosophy, its consequences for the Sunni view of human action and its value are moral relativism. Lastly, if there is nothing good or evil in itself, then neither human reason nor yet Divine Revelation

can declare anything to be either good or evil in itself. Fazlur Rahman argues that the difficulty, however, remains unsolved for many reasons not the least being that if things become good or bad by a Divine declaration – although they are not so in themselves – why can they not become good or bad by a declaration of the human reason?

4. The denial of *Ijtihād* in practice has been the result not of externally over-strenuous qualifications but because of a deep desire to give permanence to the legal structure, once it was formulated and elaborated, in order to bring about and ensure unity and cohesiveness of the Muslim ummah.

Sunnah and Hadith

Fazlur Rahman considers that the *Sunnah* of the Holy Prophet (ṣ) was an ideal which the early generations of Muslims sought to approximate by interpreting his example in terms of the new materials at their disposal and the new needs "that arose in their society; he connoted that this continuous and progressive interpretation was called the "living *Sunnah*", even if it varied according to different regions. He considers that this point is so fundamentally important for grasping the true nature of the early development of Islam and appears – after the full development of the science of Hadith."[75] The first point to be noticed in the above account is that it obviously implies (i) that *Sunnah* is an authoritative precedent that can be set by any competent person, and (ii) that the 'Sunnah of the Prophet' over-arches all other precedents and has priority over them. (iii) in light of the 'situation' an exception to the rule must be applied as a rule.[76] He comments that this freedom of interpretation of the Prophetic *Sunnah* – in order to formulate the concrete *Sunnah* i.e. the actual practice of that community – presents to the rigid and inflexible doctrine of *Sunnah* inculcated by later legists. Fazlur Rahman contends that his concept of *Sunnah* provides a freely flowing situational treatment of the Prophetic activity, there a once and for all, positing of immobile rules; here a ceaseless search for what the Prophet (ṣ) intended to achieve there a rigid system, definite and defined, cast like a hard shell. (iv) the *Sunnah* concept as used by early lawyers including al-Awza'i, although it ideally goes back undoubtedly to the Prophetic Model (*uswa hasana*),[77] is nevertheless, in its actual materieux, inclusive of the practice of the community. Indeed, al-Awza'i constantly speaks of the 'practice of the Muslims,' 'of the political (and military) leaders of the Muslims (*a'immat al Muslimin*)' and 'of the consonance of the learned' as synonmous terms as Malik talks of the practice of Madinah. It is absolutely clear that we are here face to face with the living practice of the early generations of the Muslims. It is also quite obvious that this *Sunnah* – which we called "*Sunnah*" may be called the "living *Sunnah*" – is identical with the *Ijmā'* of the community and includes the *Ijtihād* of the Ulama' and of the political authorities in their day to day administration.

The second important point that emerges is that although the "living *Sunnah*" is still an on-going process – thanks to *Ijtihād and Ijmā'* – there is at the same time noticeable, by the middle of the second century, a development in the theoretical framework of the *fiqh*, which contends that not any and every decision by a judge or a political leader may be regarded as part of the *Sunnah* and that only those well versed in law and possessed of a high degree of intelligence may be allowed to extend the living *Sunnah*. The idea of the living *Sunnah* is certainly not denied but a firm and sure methodology is sought to base this living *Sunnah* upon it.[78]

Fazlur Rahman's rejection of the popular Orientalist contention at the time that Hadith must have existed from the very beginning of Islam and must be deemed a fact which may not reasonably be doubted. He argues that rejection of this natural phenomenon is tantamount to a grave irrationality, a sin against history. Their new *Sunnah* – the living *Sunnah* of the Prophet (ṣ) – was much too important (an importance so emphatically enshrined in the Qur'an itself) to be either ignored or neglected: the *Sunnah* of the Community is based upon, and has its source in, the *Sunnah* of the Prophet (ṣ).

Fazlur Rahman goes on to argue that the recording of Hadīth was largely an informal affair, for the only need for which it would be used was the guidance in the actual practice of the Muslims and this need was fulfilled by the Prophet (ṣ) himself. After his death, the Hadith seems to have attained a semi-formal status for it was natural for the emerging generation to enquire about the Prophet (ṣ). There is no evidence that the Hadith was compiled in any form even at this stage because the purposes of recording Hadith was to generate and elaborate a practice for the Community. For this reason, it was interpreted by the rules and judged freely according to the situation at hand and something was produced in course of time which we have described as the "living *Sunnah*".[79]

In the third and fourth quarters of the first century, the living *Sunnah* expanded vastly in different regions of the Muslim empire through this process of interpretation and in the interests of actual practice, and difference in law and legal practice widened, the Hadith began to develop into a formal discipline.

The exact relationship between the lawyers and the transmitters of the Hadith in the earliest period is obscure for lack of sufficient materials, this much seems certain that these two represented in general the two terms of a tension between legal growth and legal permanence: the one interested in creating legal materials, the other seeking a neat methodology or a framework that would endow the legal materials with stability and consistency.

Fazlur Rahaman agrees with Joseph Schacht's contention that the majority of the Hadith did not go back to the Prophet (ṣ), due to the natural paucity of the Prophetic Hadith, but to later generations.[80] Schacht, however, bitterly opposed Fazlur Rahman's attempt at challenging the classical Orientalist conceptualization established by Margoliouth, Brunschvig and Schacht himself.[81] The extant works in the second century, most of the legal and even moral traditions are not from the Prophet (ṣ) but are traced back to the Companions, the "Successors" and to the third generation. But as time went on, the Hadith movement, as though through an inner necessity imposed by its very purpose, tended to project the Hadith backwards to its most natural anchoring point, the person of the Prophet (ṣ). The early legal schools, whose basis was the living and expanding *Sunnah* rather than a body of fixed opinion attributed to the Prophet (ṣ), naturally resisted this development.[82] By the middle of the second century, the Hadith movement had become more advanced and although most Hadith was still being attributed to persons other than the Prophet (ṣ) – the Companions and especially the generations after the Companions – nevertheless a part of the legal opinion and dogmatic views of the early Muslims had begun to be projected back to the Prophet (ṣ). But still, the Hadith was interpreted and treated with great freedom.

Thus, Fazlur Rahman rejects Schacht's contention that *all* Hadith are fabrications and falsely attributed to the Prophet (ṣ). He argues that there are two *Sunnahs*: (1) Prophetic *Sunnah* – which the Qur'an declares as the Prophetic Model (*uswa hasana*) (2) Living *Sunnah* – this is the Community's attempt at theorizing (*ra'y*) the correct Prophetic *Sunnah* and upon reaching concensus (*Ijmā'*) upon it. Hence, he attempts to do justice to both the orthodox and Orientalist contentions *viz,*. that the recording of Hadith must have been practiced during the time of the Prophet (ṣ) informally – thereby satisfying the orthodox claim about the recording of Hadith to be a practice of the Sahabah. On the other hand, he accepts the Orientalist contention, those of Goldziher and Schacht that the majority of Hadiths are redactions that were formulated several centuries after the Prophet (ṣ) and attributed to the Prophet (ṣ) himself in order to be deemed authoritative. This process Fazlur Rahman terms as the 'living *Sunnah*'.

Fazlur Rahman accepts Abu Yusuf's method of interpreting Hadith on a situational basis and agrees with him that the expert lawyers are those that elaborate the Prophetic *Sunnah* and are the creators of the living *Sunnah*. Further he rejects lonely (Ahad) Hadith by which he does not mean, as was done later, a Hadith which has only one chain of narrators but a Hadith which stands alone as a kind of exception to the general *Sunnah*. Fazlur Rahman similar to Abu Yusuf issues a general warning against the uncritical acceptance of Hadith and advocates keeping close to the 'collective spirit (*al-jamā'ah*) of Hadith' which he considers to be the well-known *Sunnah*. This collective spirit of Hadith is intimately connected with the term *Sunnah* and is then used to designate the majority or the collectivity of Muslims (*Ahl ul Sunnah wa'l Jama'ah*). Shafi'i's efforts for expanding the influence of Hadith over the living *Sunnah* gained currency during the Hadith movement thus represented the new change in the religious structure of Islam as a discipline and continued to encompass social, moral and religious problems.

Fazlur Rahman considers that a significant feature of Hadith formation is that the "moral maxims and edifying statements and aphorisms may be attributed to the Prophet (ṣ) irrespective of whether this attribution is strictly historical or not". He emphasizes that, "it was legal and dogmatic Hadith, i.e. that concerning belief and practice which must, strictly speaking belong to the Prophet (ṣ)."[83] He goes on to criticize that if the principle of non-historicity is introduced at some level then the Hadith corpus would gainsay be rejected. However, his conclusion is that the majority of the contents of the Hadith corpus is, in fact, nothing but the *Sunnah-Ijtihād* of the first generations of Muslims, an *Ijtihād* which had its source in individual opinion but which in course of time and after tremendous struggles and conflicts against heresies and extreme sectarian opinion received the sanction of *Ijmā'*, i.e. the adherence of the majority of the Community. In other words, the earlier living *Sunnah* was reflected in the mirror of the Hadith with the necessary addition of chain of narrators. There is, however, one major difference: whereas *Sunnah* was largely and primarily a practical phenomenon, geared as it was to behavioral norms, Hadith became the vehicle not only of legal norms but of religious beliefs and principles as well.

One of Fazlur Rahman's general principles of interpreting Hadith is that a Hadith which involves a prediction, directly or indirectly, cannot, on strict historical grounds, be accepted as genuinely emanating from the Prophet (ṣ) and must be referred to the relevant period of later history.[84] He rejects all specific predictions but not those that are general. This principle has been accepted by most classical traditionalists themselves but has never been applied by them with the full rigor of strict historicity. While they reject absolutely specific predictions, *viz.*, those which claim to indicate a specific day or date or place, they swallow without qualms predictions about the rise of Muslim theological and political groups and parties. Fazlur Rahman posits that a massive campaign carried out from the second century onwards to preserve the unitary fabric of the community and to crystallize a middle of the road orthodox majority, i.e. a majority which by being both a majority and middle-of-the road would be deserving of the designation "orthodoxy". Additionally, the companions, their Successors and the Successors of the Successors – are to be regarded as the Fathers of the Islamic doctrine and practice and their teachings as the permanent basis for the religious structure of the community. It is a point of great importance and interest to not that it is after approximately these three generations that the "living *Sunnah*" of these very generations starts getting canonized in the form of the Hadith. The relationship between Hadith and the orthodox (*Ahl ul Sunnah wa'l Jama'ah*) is that the *Ahl ul Hadith* were responsible for the structure of the orthodox. Their attempts were to develop doctrine that could provide some kind of synthesis and *via media viz., Sunnah,* was done so to reduce the effects of the political, theological and legal differences that threatened the integrity of the community – the idea to preserve its unity asserted itself.[85]

The political wars, and, in their wake, theological and dogmatic controversies, gave rise to a specifically prominent type of predictive Hadith known as the Hadith about civil wars (*Hadith al Fitan*). Its clear purpose was to steer a middle course especially between the Khariji and Shi'a political and theological extremes. To justify Hadith about civil wars, certain over-arching Hadiths were circulated. Fazlur Rahman believes that the Qadariyah, Khawarij and Shi'i were groups that developed after the death of the Prophet (ṣ). He argues that the very doctrine of *Ijmā'* itself rooted is in 'dire political necessity.'[86] Further he sees that this phenomenon, *viz.*, that the *Ahl wa'l Sunnah wal Jama'ah* have included in their doctrine certain elements from the right and certain others from the left wing, is an evidence of a policy of synthesis and mediation and is indeed, the essence of the *Ahl ul-Sunnah*.[87]

But the idea of the "middle-path-majority", although certainly in its earliest phase born of political necessity, was bound to be applied in a theological-legal sense also as the political factions tended to create for themselves a theological-moral-legal basis. Fazlur Rahman contends Abu Hanifa to be of Murj'ii tendency and considers that his self-description of "*Ahl al-adl wa'l-Sunnah*" (people of balance and middle path in the context of a theological controversy). In this connection one should also recall such terms as "*al-jama'ah min al-Hadith*" (i.e. the Hadith recognized by the majority or the collective nature of Hadith) and "*al Sunnah al-ma'rufah*" used frequently by Abu Yusuf to distinguish these from the "peripheral" and "obscure" opinion. This controversy indeed, was the most acute, not only because it was the first general moral-theological controversy in Islam but also because to its very nature, it threatened the fabric of the Muslim community most seriously. This controversy was precisely this: What is the definition of a *mumin* or a Muslim and can a man continue to be regarded as a Muslim even if the commits a grave moral error? Fazlur Rahman argues based upon a Hadith in Bukhari and Muslim that due to the 'uncompromising fanaticism' of the Kharijis that the more tolerant and religiously pluralistic opinion of the Murj'iis be substituted for political expediency – probably favored by the Umayyad state. Thus the Murjii solution took into consideration the majority and thus began to tread a more middle-of-the-road or catholic definiton; and this modified Murjiism through making some sort of a distinction between Islam and Iman – came, in course of time, to constitute an essential factor of orthodoxy, i.e., the beliefs of the majority of the Community. As a result of this painstaking and heart-searching Hadith activity amidst an atmosphere of interminable conflict, the Muslim orthodoxy – the *Ahl ul Sunnah* (i.e. the majority of the Community) finally formulated – at the hands of al-Ash'arī and al-Maturidi and their successors – a catholic definition of Islam which silenced Kharijism and Mutazilism and saved the Community from suicide.

Fazlur Rahman states that "it is absolutely imperative to be exactly clear about the real issues at stake particularly because there are strong trends in our which in the name of what they call "progressivism" wish to brush aside the Hadith and the Prophetic *Sunnah*. Fazlur Rahman goes on to inquire what is the real relationship between *Sunnah* and Hadith? He answers that in his time the lengthy disquistions on Hadith yield no real answer. He comments that not even the Khawarij or the Mu'tazilah ever denied the validity of the *Sunnah* and that what they objected to was the formulation of the *Sunnah* in Hadith terms. He regards the rejection of Hadith based upon the anti-Hadith argument would yield a yawning chasm of fourteen centuries between us and the Prophet (ṣ)? And in the vacuity of this chasm not only must the Qur'an slip from our fingers under our subjective whims – for the only thing that anchors it is the prophetic activity itself – but even the very existence and integrity of the Qur'an and, indeed, the existence of the Prophet (ṣ) himself become an unwarranted myth.

Fazlur Rahman argues that technical Hadith are by in large not historical and normative in a basic sense. These two factors distinguish technical Hadith from historical and biographical Hadith. The issue of the non-historicity of Hadith is addressed as follows: the first that Fazlur Rahman considers that the fundamental Hadith are those that are concerned with the Islamic methodology itself. These Hadith deal with the fundamental principles of *Ijmā'* and Hadith and he declares that they prove its non-historicity: "the prima facie case for the historicity of most other Hadith is demolished." [88] Fazlur Rahman addresses his all-encompassing statement by pointing out that his choice of words are that he is not referring to *all* Hadith but *most.* Secondly, Fazlur Rahman under scores the *isnad* and it seems to be on the basis of Caetani and Schacht's thesis that the Isnad itself is a relatively late development originating around the turn of the first century. [89] The second objection that Fazlur Rahman posits for the non-historicity of Hadith is not scientific but religious which he goes on to conclude would render Hadith to be a gigantic conspiracy. The second issue about the normativity of Hadith is that if it proven that Hadith is mostly non-historical then that does not logically lead to it being divorced from the Prophetic *Sunnah.*

He considers that the Prophetic Model (*Sunnah*) was correctly interpreted by the early community in the interests of the needs of the Muslims and the resultant product in each generation was the living *Sunnah.* Thus, for Fazlur Rahman the Hadith is nothing but a reflection in a verbal mode of this living *Sunnah.* The Prophet's (ṣ) *Sunnah* is, therefore, in the Hadith just as it existed in the living *Sunnah*. But the living *Sunnah* contained not only the general Prophetic Model but also regionally standardized interpretations of that model – thanks to the ceaseless activity of *Ijtihād* and *Ijmā'*. Fazlur Rahman believes that this would explain the innumerable differences that existed in the living *Sunnah*. But this is exactly true of Hadith also. This is because Hadith reflects the living *Sunnah*. He observes a striking feature of Hadith is its diversity and the fact that almost on all points it reflects different points of view. This point, while it shows the lack of strict historicity of Hadith, just like the earlier living *Sunnah*, has been the most potent fact of catholicity in the hands of the *Ahl ul Sunnah*, i.e. the majority of the Muslims. For the *Ahl ul Sunnah*, through Hadith, tried – largely successfully – to steer a middle course and produce a middle of the road synthesis. Here Fazlur Rahman highlights that critical development and point in Islamic thought which seems to him to be what caused stagnation and formalism. He attributes stagnation to the efforts of the orthodoxy in their attempts to formalize the content of the living *Sunnah* of the Prophet (ṣ), which the early community maintained as a creative and dynamic process. Hadith, in fact, is the sum total of aphorisms formulated and put out by Muslims themselves, ostensibly about the Prophet (ṣ) although not without an ultimate historical touch with the Prophet (ṣ). It's very aphoristic character shows that it is not historical. It is rather a gigantic and monumental commentary on the Prophet (ṣ) by the early community. Therefore, though based on the Prophet (ṣ), it also constitutes an epitome of wisdom of classical Muslims.[90]

Henceforth, Fazlur Rahman is brought to explain how the *Ijmā'* of the early community can be rendered dynamic. He states that the character of Hadith is essentially synthetic:

"... *Ijmā'* may be changed by a subsequent *Ijmā'* and further that *Ijmā'* is a matter of practice and not that of pure theory involving truth values. An *Ijmā'* can be right or wrong, or partly right and partly wrong, rather than true or false. The Community, indeed, cannot take itself for granted claiming theoretical infallibility. It must always aspire both to understand and to do the right."[91]

Fazlur Rahman posits that the Prophet (ṣ) and the community were commanded to do based upon the emphasis of the Qur'an on "*shūrā*" and he asserts that this catholic and synthetic character of Hadith is not confined to this one point – it runs through almost the entire gamut of moral, social, legal and political doctrines.

Fazlur Rahman throughout his writings consciously attempts to reevaluate each Hadith independently according to the following principles: (1) Situational Interpretation – Revaluation of different elements in Hadith and their thorough reinterpretation under the changed moral and social conditions of today must be carried. This can be done only by a historical study of the Hadith – by reducing it to the "living *Sunnah*" and by clearly distinguishing from the situational background the real value embodied in it. (2) Progressive moral re-interpretation – After completion of situational interpretation to resurrect the moral value, the problem of legal Hadith must be reformed according to the true nature of the Qur'an and *Sunnah* which is a 'progressive moral re-interpretation' and not 'rigid formalism'.[92] Through the previous steps we can reduce Hadith to *Sunnah* and by situational interpretation can resurrect the norms which we can then apply to our situation today. Here Fazlur Rahman addresses the concerns of Orientalists *viz.*, Schacht and Margoliouth and to the traditionalists. The former considered Hadith to be a forgery or a concoction to which Fazlur Rahman responded to it was more appropriate to consider it as "formulation":

> "We cannot call Hadith a forgery because it reflects the living *Sunnah* and the living *Sunnah* was not a forgery but a progressive interpretation and formulation of the Prophetic *Sunnah*".[93]

In response to the latter Fazlur Rahman "Hadith, verbally speaking, does not go back to the Prophet (ṣ) , its Spirit certainly does, and Hadith is largely the situational interpretation and formulation of this Prophetic Model or spirit."[94] (3) Biography of the Prophet (ṣ) – Fazlur Rahman considers that historical Hadith can be interpreted soundly in light of the biography of the Prophet (ṣ) because it serves as the "chief anchoring point of the technical Hadith itself when the latter is interpreted." (4) Background of the early community – In light of the biography of the Prophet (ṣ) and the background of the early community, which are 'indubitably fixed' and in its essential features Hadith can be interpreted.

Throughout Fazlur Rahman strikes at the rigid formalism and attributes it to be the cause of Muslim stagnation and this holds testament to his overall project of modernizing and reforming Islamic thought. Thus his methodology is to reduce the Hadith to *Sunnah* – what it was in the beginning – and by situational interpretation resurrect the norms which we can apply to our situation today. Fazlur Rahman responded to the views of most Orientalists and some contemporary Muslim modernists of his time who had rejected Hadith entirely as well criticizing the uncritical acceptance by traditionalist Muslims of Hadith by finding the middle term and this is a characteristic pattern in all of his analyses in any field. In response to the Orientalist reference to Hadith as a "forgery" or "concoction" he uses the term "formulation":

> In response to the traditional picture he states that his approach does involve a reversal of the traditional picture on one salient picture in that we are putting more reliance on pure history than Hadith and are seeking to judge the latter partly in light of the former (partly because there is also the Qur'an) whereas the traditional picture is the other way round.

In conclusion, Fatma Kizil considers that the conceptualization of Fazlur Rahman of *Sunnah* and Hadith is similar to Joseph Schacht's in reaching the same conclusions in practice. However, he departs from Schacht's ideas in theory by accepting that the Prophetic *Sunnah* and the traditions regarding the Prophet (ṣ) and his deeds had existed since the beginning. His primary concern is to deremine the historical traditions because traditions, according to him, are verbal form of the living *Sunnah,* so they represent an on-going process. Accordingly, authenticity of a tradition does not mean its ascription to the Prophet (ṣ) unlike the concept in the classical theory. In Fazlur Rahman system the traditions lost their direct connection with the Prophet (ṣ). However, he realizes, or rather 'feels' what this loss is supposed to mean. Hence, he often tries to emphasize the 'continuity'[95]:

> "The Prophet (ṣ) founded not merely a religion but a developing large-scale Community ... This public continuity between the Prophet (ṣ) and his Community is the real guarantee of the Prophetic *Sunnah* ... It is this double connection, of spirit and of his historical continuity, that rendered the Hadith, despite a lack of strict historicity on the

part of much of its contents, impregnable to all attacks in Classical Islam." [96]

Notes

[1] Charles J. Adams, *Fazl al-Rahman as a Philosopher*, Journal of Islamic Research, Vol 4, no. 4, October 1990, p.265.

[2] *Ibid*, p.265.

[3] Bermann, Phillip L., *The Courage of Conviction*, New York: Dodd, Mead & Co., USA, 1985, p.193.

[4] Mary Catherine Jesse, *A Modern Muslim Intellectual: The thought of Fazlur Rahman with special reference to Reason*, MA Thesis, University of Regina, Canada, 1991, p.2.

[5] Amhar Rasyid, *Some Qur'anic Legal Texts in the Context of Fazlur Rahman's Hermeneutical Method*, MA Thesis, McGill University, Montreal, Canada, 1994, p.4.

[6] Bermann, Phillip L., *The Courage of Conviction*, p. 154.

[7] *Ibid*, p.154.

[8] Charles J. Adams, *Fazl al-Rahman as a Philosopher*, Journal of Islamic Research, Vol 4, no. 4, October 1990, p.265.

[9] *Ibid*, p.265.

[10] See Punjab University, University Calendar 1938-1945.

[11] Frederick M. Denny, *The Legacy of Fazlur Rahman, Muslims in America*, edited by Yvonne Yazbeck Haddad, Oxford University Press, New York, 1991, pp. 96-108.

[12] *Ibid.*

[13] H.A.R Gibb – Abdul Rehman Badawi records that Gibb was born in Alexandria, Egypt on the 2nd of January, 1895 and died on the 22nd of October, 1971. His father was an agriculturalist and was employed at a

company called Abu Qayr for the irrigation of lands. He completed his secondary school at Edinburgh in Scotland and then took admission at Edinburgh University in 1912. He specialized in Semitic languages and from 1914-1918 he was a soldier in the Royal British Army. After the war he became a research student at the school of Oriental Languages in London. In 1922 he attained his Master degree from the University of London. In 1926 till 1927, he traveled to the East and studied Contemporary Arab literature whilst on his sojourn. In 1929, he was appointed as a reader in Arabic History and Language. Whence in 1930, Thomas Arnold passed away, Gibb was appointed as Chair of Arabic language at Oxford University, after which he remained at Oxford till 1955 and thence was appointed as a Professor at Harvard University as the James Richard Jewett Professor of Arabic and in 1957 was made incharge for Middle Eastern Studies. In 1971, Gibb passed away due to brain hemorrhage. According to Badawī, Gibb's intellectual work can be divided into three areas. He considered Gibb's work to be scholarly very poor and insignificant contributions. Also, Badawī felt that Gibb's prestigiousness is more attributable to his non-scholarly activities. See entry H.A.R. Gibb, 'Abdul Raḥmān Badawī, *Maūsū'āt al-Mustashriqiyīn*, Dār al-'Ilm al-Milāyīn, (Beirut, 1992). (1895-1971), pp. 174-175.

Qamar al-Huda records that "Orientalism immediately following World War II, academic interest in Orientalism underwent a transformation, ultimately splitting out into specialized area studies across a variety of disciplines, including philology, literature, economics, political science, sociology, anthropology, gender studies, history, and religious studies. The field of Orientalism was no longer based in any one department or discipline, and this is credited to such illustrious scholars as Phillip Hitti, Gustave von Grunebaum, and Hamilton Gibb, who developed Orientalism curricula and divisions in major universities in the United States." Refer to pp.515-516, See *Orientalism, Encyclopedia of Islam and Modern World*.

[14] Shaykh Ahmad Sirhindī (1564-1624) was born in Sirhind, near

Delhi, India. The head of a Sufi lodge as well as a competent religious scholar; he was initiated into three Sufi lineages: the Chishtiyya, the Qadiriyya, and the Suhrawardiyya. The turning point of his life came with a meeting with Muhammad Baqi billah (d. 1603), a Central Asian Naqshbandi Sheikh. In three months Sirhindī returned to Sirhind with unconditional permission to transmit the teachings of the Naqshbandi lineage. Three years later Baqi billah died and Sirhindī was recognized by most of Baqi billah's disciples as the principal successor. From this point Sirhindī elaborated a new set of Sufi doctrines and disciplines grounded in following the prophetic example (*Sunnah*) and Islamic law (shari'ah). More than any other Naqshbandi since Baha'ud Din, Sirhindī became the pivotal figure in India who redefined Sufism's role in society and who integrated Sufi practice into strict juristic notions of shari'ah observance. Indeed, after Sirhindī's death, the Naqshbandiyya became renowned as the Naqshbandiyya-Mujaddidiyya, named after Sirhindī's title of "the renewer of the second millennium" (*mujaddid-i-alf-e-thani*). In the twentieth century selective interpretations of Sirhindī's thoughts have been utilized by Pakistani nationalists to legitimize the creation of Pakistan. p. 632, *Encyclopedia of Islam and Modern World.*

[15] Shah Walī Ullah of Delhi (1703-1762) Shah Wali Ullah was the most prominent Muslim intellectual of eighteenth century India and a prolific writer on a wide range of Islamic topics in Arabic and Persian. The fact that his writings are often characterized by a historical, systematic approach coupled with an attempt to explain and mediate divisive tendencies leads him to be considered a precursor to modernist/liberal Islamic thought. His most important and influential work, *Hujjat Allah al-Baligha,* in which he aimed to restore the Islamic sciences through the study of the hadith, was composed in Arabic sometime during the decade after his return to India. After Shah Wali Ullah's death in 1762, his teachings were carried on by his descendants, in particular his sons, Shah 'Abd al-'Azīz (d. 1823) and Shah Rafi' al-Din (d. 1818), and his grandson Shah Isma'īl Shahīd (d.

1831). Shah 'Abd al-'Azīz was a noted scholar and teacher with a wide circle of pupils some of whom are linked directly with the establishment of the Deoband madrasa. South Asian Muslims with an anti-Sufi, puritan outlook such as the *Ahl ul Hadith*, and even the followers of Maulana Maududi, find in Shah Wali Ullah's return to the fundamentals of Shari'ah and political rejection of alien influences a precursor to their own reformist beliefs. Another group of his successors, best exemplified by his closest disciple and cousin, Muhammad 'Ashiq (1773), seems to have pursued Wali Ullah's mystical inclinations. See entry on Shah Wali Ullah, *Encyclopedia of Islam and Modern World*, p. 730.

[16] *Op. cit*, Mary Catherine Jesse, p.14.

[17] *Ibid.*

[18] *Ibid.*

[19] *Op. cit.* Mary Catherine Jesse, p.15.

[20] Abdur Rauf, *"Central Institute of Islamic Research"*, Pakistan Times (Lahore) 4th March, 1966, p.10.

[21] Āl 'Imrān:104.

[22] *Selected Letters of Shaykh Ahmad Sirhindī*, p.32.

[23] Qureshi, I.H., *A Short History of Pakistan,* (University of Karachi Press, 1st ed., 1967), p.111.

[24] *Op. cit.* Mary Catherine Jesse p.17, and Fazlur Rahman, "The Qur'anic Solution of Pakistan's Educational Problem," *Islamic Studies* 6, no. 4, December 1967, p.321.

[25] Yusuf Ludhyanavi, *Daur-i-hazir kay tajaddud pasandon kay Afkār*, Maktaba Ludhyanavi, Karachi, 2000. Ludhyanavi records in his preface that Binori had applied all of his exterior and interior forces to combat the 'sedition of Fazlur Rahman' (*fitna-i-Fazlur Rahmani*).

[26] Dr. Saleem Akhtar interview 12th August, 2011: stated that Fazlur

Rahman considered *Islamic Methodology in History* to be his *magnum opus.*

[27] A thorough reading of print archives published during Ayub Khan's rule exacts a Pan-Islamic spirit. Delegations of scholars from Egypt, Syria and Iraq visited and attended conferences at the invitation of the Institute. The Institute was not limited to operating as a Research facility but more wholistically it was established for a dialogue between Pakistan and the Muslim world and the West. It was an entity that was envisioned to have both global and local influence. During Fazlur Rahman's directorship the Institute employed foreign scholars from the Arab world. However, this is not with in the scope of this thesis to discuss the nature of the Institute in depth.

[28] Yusuf Ludhyanavi, *Daur-i-hazir kay tajaddud pasandon kay Afkār,* Maktaba Ludhyanavi, Karachi, 2000, p.22.

[29] *Islamic Studies,* 1963, p.286.

[30] *Op. cit.,* Mary Catherine Jesse, p.20.

[31] Fazlur Rahman, 'The Thinker of Crisis, Shah Waliyullah', *Pakistan Quarterly,* VI, 2, Karachi, 1956, pp.1-5.

[32] Fazlur Rahman, *Islam,* p.155.

[33] *Op.cit,* Mary Catherine Jesse, "Fazlur Rahman Course Listing", *Department of Near Eastern Civilizations and Languages,* (University of Chicago), n.d., p.24.

[34] Fazlur Rahman, *The Philosophy of Mulla Sadra,* p.vii.

[35] Dr. Saleem Akhtar interview 12th August, 2011: stated that Fazlur Rahman considered *Major Themes of the Qur'an* to be his second *magnum opus.*

[36] *Islam and Modernity,* p.2.

[37] *Ethics in Islam: Proceedings of the Ninth Giorgio Levi Della Vida Conference,* May 6-8, 1983, (University of California, Los Angeles,

1983).

38 Muhammad Khalid Masud, Obituary Notes, *Islamic Studies*, vol. 27, no. 4, 1988, p.397.

39 Amhar Rasyid, *Some Qur'anic Legal Texts in the Context of Fazlur Rahman's Hermeneutical Method (MA. Thesis)*, (McGill University, Montreal, Canada, 1994), p.7.

40 Donald L. Berry, *'Dr. Fazlur Rahman (1919-1988): A Life in Review'*; in Earle H. Waugh and Frederick Mathewson Denny, *The Shaping of an Islamic Discourse: A Memorial to Fazlur Rahman*, (Atlanta, Georgia, Scholars Press, 1998), p. 39.

41 Fazlur Rahman, *Islamic Philosophy*, Encyclopedia of Philosophy, Paul Edwards, vol. 4, 1967, pp.219-224.

42 *Ibid*, p.3.

43 *Ibid*, p.7.

44 *Ibid*, p.8.

45 *Ibid*, pp.65-71.

46 *Islam*, Encyclopedia Britannica, 15th ed., p.17.

47 *Ibid*, pp. 62-64.

48 In an interview with Dr. Saleem Akhtar, a colleague of Fazlur Rahman, he mentioned Fazlur Rahman was asked about which of published works he considered to be his *magnum opus*. Fazlur Rahman replied it was his book *Islamic Methodology in History*. Thereafter, in 1980 when his *Major Themes of the Qur'an* was published, Dr. Saleem inquired from Fazlur Rahman if this work was also his *magnum opus* and he replied in the affirmative.

49 *Selected Letters of Shaikh Aḥmad Sirhindī*, p. v.

50 *Islam and Modernity: Transformation of an Intellectual Tradition*, "that does mean that Ash'arite theology represented Islam more

faithfully than Iqbal, on the contrary that theology (Ash'arī) represents, in my view, an almost total distortion of Islam and was, in fact, a one-sided and extreme reaction to the Mutazilite rationalist ideology." p.133.

[51] See *'ālam al-Mithal in Selected Letters of Ahmad Sirhindī*, p.68.

[52] *The Philosophy of Mulla Sadra*, p.vii.

[53] *Islam and Modernity*, p.1.

[54] *Ibid*, p.1.

[55] *Ibid*, p.1.

[56] Fazlur Rahman considered Goldziher to be "the first great perceptive student of the evolution of the Muslim Tradition, all though occasionally uncritical of assumption" and was strongly influenced throughout the extent of his life by the latter's cultural and socio-historical method. *Islamic Methodology in History*, p.4.

[57] It is pointed out that Gibb was Fazlur Rahman's mentor at Oxford University during his doctoral studies. Also, throughout Fazlur Rahman's publications he considered and maintained Gibb as an authority on Islam and only in two instances does he disagree with Gibb. One, on Islam being both an individual and social religion; second, on Iqbal's *The Reconstruction of Religious Thought* not to be understood as a new creedal formula. It is also believed that Fazlur Rahman's permanent position at the University of Chicago from 1968-1988 was highly influenced by Gibb's recommendation.

[58] *Ibid*, p.215.

[59] Karam Shah, Ḍiyā' al-Nabī, vol. 2, p.120.

[60] Abu'l Hasan Ali Nadwi, *al-Islam wa-'l Gharb*, Mu'assat al-Risalat, (Beirut), 2nd ed., 1987, p.16.

[61] Faruq 'Umar Fawzi, *Al-Istishraq wa al-Tarikh al-Islami: Al-Qurun al-Islamiya al-Ula Darasat Maqaranat bayn wijhat ul-Nazr al-

Islamayat wa wijhat al-Nazr al-Urubiya, (Beirut), 1st ed., 1998, pp. 25-49.

[62] Karam Shah, *Ḍiyā' al-Nabī*, vol. 2, p.155.

[63] Salim Yafut, *Hafriyat al-Istishraq fi naqd al-'Aql Istishraqi*, al-Markaz al-Thaqafi al-'Arabi, 1st ed., 1989, (Beirut), pp.69-82.

[64] Ahmad Samayalofitsh, *Falsafat ul-Istishraq wa athruha fi al-Adab al-'Arabi al-Mu'asir*, Dar al-Fikr al-'Arabi pp.40-51; See also Muhammad Ali Kandahlawi, *Ma'alim al-Tanzil*, Dar ul Uloom Shahabiya, vol. 4, Sialkot, 1977, pp.420-444; Muhammad al-Bihiyyi, *Al-Fikr al-Islami al-Hadīth wa silatuhu bi al'Isti'mar al-Gharbi*, Maktaba Wahba, 4th ed., (Cairo, 1964), pp. 15-57.

[65] Abdullah Muhammad, *Mu'assat ul-Istishraq wa al-Siyasa al-Gharbiya tijah al-'Arb wa l'-Muslimin*, Markaz al-I'marat li-darasat wa-l' buhuth al-Istratijiya, No. 57, 1st ed., (Beirut, 2001), pp.39-67.

[66] Muhammad Tufayl, *Naqush Rasul*, pp. 32-34.

[67] See *Functional Interdependence of Law and Theology*, p.94.

[68] *Fundamental Ideas in the Philosophy of Value*, p.13; Ibn Sīna, *A History of Muslim Philosophy*, p.499.

"This [Prophetic] insight, creative of knowledge and values, is termed by Ibn Sīna the active intellect and identified with the angel of revelation".

[69] *Islam, Encyclopedia Britannica*, 15th ed., p.5.

[70] *Islamic Methodology in History*, p.149.

[71] *Islam, Encyclopedia Britannica*, 15th ed., p.17.

[72] *Islam and Modernity*, pp.7-8.

[73] *Islamic Methodology in History*, p.149.

[74] *Islamic Methodology in History*, p.152.

75 *Islamic Methodology in History*, p. 27.

76 *Ibid*, p. 28.

77 See *uswa hasana* in the Qur'an: *Surah al-Aḥzāb*: 21, and *al-Mumtaḥanah*: 4, 6.

78 *Islamic Methodology in History*, pp. 27-31.

79 *Islamic Methodology in History*, p.188.

80 Joseph Schacht, *Origins of Muhammadan Jurisprudence*, pp. 58-80, See also, Ignaz Goldziher, *Introduction to Islamic Theology and Law*, pp. 37-43.

81 "Dr. Fazlur Rahman has realized this but in order to make his program acceptable to his traditionalist-minded readers, he presents them, instead of the real alternative, with an imaginary, watered-down one which he tries, by verbal gymnastics, to bring into agreement if not with traditional doctrine, at least with traditionalist feeling." See Joseph Schacht, *Fazlur Rahman: Islamic Methodology in History*, Bulletin of the School of Oriental and African Studies, XXIX/2 (1966), p.395; Also, Fatma Kizil, *Fazlur Rahman's Understanding of the Sunnah/Hadith – A Comparison with Joseph Schacht's Views on the Subject*, Hadis Tetkikleri Dergisi (HTD), VI/II, 2008, pp.31-45.

82 Fazlur Rahman intellectual inclination is always to find the 'middle term' binding two concepts otherwise he is inclined to attempt a synthesis between two disparaging views. In this case, he attempted to forge a synthesis between the Orientalist and modern Islam.

83 *Islamic Methodology in History*, p.44.

84 *Islamic Methodology in History*, p.46.

85 *Ibid*, p.53.

86 *Ibid*, p.56.

87 *Ibid*, p.58.

[88] *Islamic Methodology in History*, p.72.

[89] L. Caetani's *Annali Dell' Islam* and J. Schacht's, *Origins,* Shibli Nu'mani, *Al Faruq,* Dar ul-Isha'at pp.30-36.

[90] *Islamic Methodology in History*, p.76.

[91] *Ibid*, p.77.

[92] *Ibid*, p.80.

[93] *Islam*, p.65.

[94] *Islamic Methodology in History*, p.80.

[95] Fatma Kizil, *Fazlur Rahman's Understanding of the Sunnah/Hadith – A Comparison with Joseph Schacht's Views on the Subject*, Hadis Tetkikleri Dergisi (HTD), VI/II, 2008, pp.44-45.

[96] *Islam*, p.66.

Chapter II
Emergence and Development
of Islamic Theology

Stages and Evolution

The historical studies of Fazlur Rahman on Islamic theology (*kalām*) have attempted to analyze and evaluate the entire history of *kalām*. His analytical method is synthetic – in that he has attempted a synthesis between Modern Orientalist methodology and the history of *kalām* literature. Based upon a thorough study of Fazlur Rahman's argument it becomes apparent that the methodology which he implemented in his studies is strongly influenced from Shah Walī Ullah Dehlawi *double movement* theory and synthesis (*tatbiq*) serve as two instruments which Fazlur Rahman applied throughout his writings. Muhammad al-Ghazālī a contemporary specialist on Shah Wali Ullah's thought posits that Dehlawi's understanding of the history of Islam is based upon the writings of Ibn Taymīya. Fazlur Rahman's opinion of the history of *kalām* up till Ibn Taymīya is based upon the latter's work. On the other hand, Fazlur Rahman is indebted in particular to Ignaz Goldziher's *socio-historical* method to reinterpret Islamic thought and practice according to modern research methods.

In our evaluation of Fazlur Rahman's study and opinions on *kalām* we have found that his early writings were based upon his 'response' to 'Western Orientalist' study of *kalām viz.*, either agreeing or disagreeing with their views. Fazlur Rahman's attitude towards new research on *kalām* was accepting of contemporary modern Western Orientalism. For Fazlur Rahman, a purely rationalistic, objective and historical analysis of Islam, and for our purposes – *kalām*, did not serve the purposes of reforming *kalām viz.*, it being systematic, meaningful and purposeful:

> "involves an analysis of that teaching in both historical and systematic terms; that is, it views the unfolding of the Qur'an and the *Sunnah* historically, so as to understand their meaning then systematically arranges values in order of priority and posteriority, subordinating the more particular to the more general and ultimate, and thus obtains an answer from this system for a given problem or a given solution."[1]

Secondly, Fazlur Rahman formulated his 'doctrine of Islamicity':

> "that a doctrine of an institution is genuinely Islamic to the extent that it flows from the total teaching of the Qur'an and the *Sunnah* and hence successfully applies to an appropriate situation or satisfies a requirement, then it will not be Islamic to the extent that it does not flow from the teaching of the Qur'an and the *Sunnah* as a whole and hence will not solve a given problem or apply to a given situation Islamically."[2]

Fazlur Rahman's categorization of *kalām* is into four major stages: (1) Classical (2) Medieval (3) Classical Modernism (4) Contemporary Modernism. The classical period refers to the emergence and subsequent initial development of *kalām*. Fazlur Rahman outlines three major issues that lead to solidifications of theological views: (1) Islam and *Iman* (2) Qadar (human freedom) and *Jabr* (predeterminism) (3) *Irjā'*. The uniformity of theological opinion was during the time of the Prophet (ṣ) till the Caliphate of 'Umar. The schisms that developed within the Community began in the Caliphates of 'Uthman and 'Ali: (1) Khawarij (2) Shi'a and (3) Murjia.

Fazlur Rahman in his *Islam and Modernity* argues that the companions of the Prophet (ṣ) had witnessed the historical unfolding of the Qur'anic message in the performance of the Prophet (ṣ) whereas the subsequent generations – the Successors and the Successors of the Successors – did not. In the historical unfolding of *kalām*, there were several developments that led to the formulation of its specific content. As the Muslim community expanded its borders an important result of the interaction of Islam with foreign cultural currents, particularly Hellenism and Hellenized Christianity, was the sudden eruption of conflicts of opinion on matters of theology and theological ethics and the emergence of a large number of heresies and early sects in Islam.[3] The events and agents responsible for these developments brought about a 'distancing from' and a 'metamorphosis' *vis-á-vis* its "original" state and the teaching of the Qur'an. Fazlur Rahman considers that the point at which Sunnism gained self-reflection and formed its conscious being it had already passed through this "radical change".[4] This fact and the smoldering opposition to the Umayyad rule on the part of the non-Arabs, notably the Persians subsequently resulted in the overthrowing of the Umayyad Caliphate and the installation of the Abbasids in Baghdad with the aid of the Persians in 750 AD. The Umayyad regime had seen the growth of the early Arab religious sciences of Islam and the eruption of the heresies but it had not lasted long enough to see the full-fledged development of the lay intellectualism of Islam.

Fazlur Rahman argues that the Abbasid Caliphate witnessed two mutually somewhat inconsistent developments both of which were results of deliberate policy. On the one hand, the Abbasids sought to meet the claims of the dissatisfied religious leadership under the Umayyads and implemented the results of the religious achievements through the state machinery, thus removing the gulf which had largely separated religion from the Umayyad state; on the other hand, they hastened the process of the intellectual awakening of Islam by officially patronizing wholesale translations of Greek philosophy, medicine and science into Arabic. Fazlur Rahman contends that the "pure intellectualism that resulted from this activity reacted on the religion of Islam and produced the rationalist religious movement of the Mu'tazila."[5]

The entire development could not fail to react on religious intellectualism as well, and during the 2nd/8th and 3rd/9th centuries the Mu'tazila movement developed rapidly and was in full swing. Mu'tazilism developed under the influence of Hellenic rationalism, thereby creating the first major tension in the religious history of Islam. The leaders of Muslim orthodoxy, representing the old tradition, at first suffered at the hands of this rationalist movement which was raised to the position of a state creed during the time of the Caliph al-Ma'mun but subsequently, by mustering political strength and by borrowing the very weapons of Greek dialectic, effectively gained the upper hand. Gradually, the orthodox Ulama' brought almost all education under their control, and worked out and implemented curriculum to realize their own intellectual and spiritual ideals.[6]

The practical attitude that developed within in the community was the practice of adduction – citing verses from the Qur'an. Fazlur Rahman in his work *Islamic Methodology in History* argues that the development of Hadith was a process of where *Ijtihād* and *Ijmā'* of the community attempting to establish the 'living *Sunnah*'. The Hadiths were then projected back to the Prophet (ṣ) in order to achieve 'stability, cohesion and unity' within the nascent community. In his *Revival and Reform in Islam*, he argues that the schisms that developed within the community were due to political factors and the subsequent reaction of the community initiated the practical attitude of *Irjā'* which later developed into the doctrine of *Irjā'*. Lastly, Fazlur Rahman contends that the community had developed and maintained a functional interdependence between theology and law.

Fazlur Rahman's criticism of the role of *kalām* in the history of Islam overall is negative. He considers that the early *kalām* had developed Qur'anically one-sided solutions to *kalām* problems. The early *kalām* between the Khawarij and the Shi'a illustrated this behavior. The subsequent development of the Murjia brought about a temperament of pacificism and tolerance at the expense of doctrinal correctness. Thus, he finds that there is an *action-reaction* relationship between the theological positions upheld.

The action and reaction between the theological groups led to development of reason (*'aql*) expressly belonging to the Mu'tazila, whereas its antithesis, tradition (*hadīth*) belonging to the *Ahl ul Hadith*. The synthesis attempted between the two opposing groups gave birth to the Ash'arīs, whom Fazlur Rahman viciously and vehemently argues developed doctrines that were contradictory to each other and conflicting with the

Qur'an and the *Sunnah* of the Prophet (ṣ). The Maturidites, he declares to be closer to the Qur'an and the *Sunnah* which he probably does to buttress the theological systems upheld by Ahmad Sirhindī and Shah Wali Ullah.

It seems that Fazlur Rahman considered Ibn Taymīya's evaluation valid *viz.*, the downfall of the Muslims during the medieval period to be due to the introduction of philosophical ideals, tools, methods and argumentation into theological discourse. He deems the role of al-Ghazālī instrumental in shaping the first half of the medieval period in developing a '*kalām*-internalized Sufism, belittling of law and deviation from the Qur'an and *Sunnah*'. Subsequently, Razī and Ijī extending and expanding the Ash'arī influence in more philosophical issues and by employing more philosophical tools to develop stronger arguments. Ibn 'Arabī's Sufi mystification of Ash'arī *kalām* doctrines further developed more deviant theological doctrines in developing a 'monistic pantheistic worldview' that was against the *élan* of the Qur'an and the *Sunnah*. Fazlur Rahman agrees with Ibn Taymīya attempt to reestablish the supremacy of the law over *kalām* and Sufism and eradicating Ash'arīsm as the interpreters of the Community.

Fazlur Rahman drew strong inspiration from the eighteenth century Wahhabi movement which was effectively a puritan enterprise influenced heavily by Ibn Taymīya. Fazlur Rahman found that Abdul Wahhab's efforts to purify, remove and purge Islam of innovations and incorrect beliefs needed to be extended to its logical end *viz.*, removal of Ash'arīsm as the doctrinal interpretation of the Qur'an, *Sunnah* and early Community. To achieve this end Fazlur Rahman relied expressly upon Ibn Taymīya. However, Fazlur Rahman criticized Ibn Taymīya's acceptance of *Irjā'* Hadith which had a bearing both on his political and theological thought.

In the premodernist period Fazlur Rahman considered three figures of paramount significance: (1) Ahmad Sirhindī (2) Muhammad b. Abdul Wahhab and (3) Shah Walī Ullah Dehlawi. Fazlur Rahman considered Sirhindī's concept of prophethood as reinstating a 'positive world-affirming' attitude as opposed to the 'sainthood world-negating' attitude. Fazlur Rahman opines that the positive influence in history of this doctrinal change led to the creation of Pakistan.[7] However, we find that although Fazlur Rahman in his *Revival and Reform in Islam* presents very elaborately Sirhindī's concept of God he does not adopt it as his personal conceptualization most probably for being the product of contemplative thought. On the other hand, Fazlur Rahman's acceptance of Dehlawī's theological thought in fulfilling the criteria which he had established of "soundly flowing from the Qur'an and *Sunnah* of the Prophet (ṣ)" and "accurate pre-modern" rational expression of the Orthodox belief. Dehlawī's *tatbīq* of Islamic theology inclusive of social change (*irtifaqat*) fulfills service to God (*'ibāda*) and nearness to God (*i'qtirab*).[8]

The subsequent period which Fazlur Rahman identifies as Classical Modernism was in the wake of Western Imperialism and Colonialism. The representative of theological thought during this period are: (1) Sir Syed Ahmad Khan (2) Shibli Nu'mani (3) Jamal al-Dīn al-Afghanī (4) Muhammad Iqbal; the cumulative result of their thought bringing about the political independence of the Muslim world from the West.

Finally, contemporary modernism is demarcated by the political independence of the Muslim world from the West. This period is identified with the Muslim world's response to the West both Communist and Capitalist.

Classical period of *Kalām*

Fazlur Rahman's studies on the history of *kalām* attempted to ascertain the underlying theological and moral doctrines that influenced the temper and trajectory of the community.[9] Fazlur Rahman analysis yielded that the doctrines of: (1) Islam and *Iman* (2) *Qadar* (3) Human Freedom and Accountability; were the most significant in shaping the 'historical trajectory of the community'. These doctrines had implications in the realms of: (1) Politics (2) Law and (3) Sufism (4) Hadith. Politically, the doctrine of *Irjā'* was borne forth from the practical attitude towards belief (*iman*) and non-belief (*kufr*). Legally, the doctrine of *qadar* influenced the doctrine of reason (*'aql*) and revelation (*naql*). In the realm of Sufism, the doctrine of human freedom and accountability influenced the Qur'anic worldview. Finally, the community's attempts at achieving the value of social cohesion forced them to formulate *kalām* content through the principle of *Ijtihād* and *Ijmā'* or 'living *Sunnah*'. He accepted Ibn Taymīya's evaluation of *kalām* that the *kalām al-muḥdath* – neo-*kalām* or innovated *kalām*, was a departure and deviation from the community's *kalām*.[10]

The social cohesion and unity of the community was opposed by the schisms (*firaq*) that developed in the caliphates of 'Uthman and 'Alī. The groups that initiated a split in the unity of the community in the political realm are the Khawarij and Shi'a. Yahya Huwaidi considers that the emergence of *kalām* began with the problem of political leadership after the death of the Prophet (ṣ) (*Imama* and *Khilafa*) between the Khawarij and Shi'a and the doctrine of Islam and *Iman* subsequently followed and are interrelated. He contends that the political debate between the two rival sects is interrelated and connected to the doctrine of 'Islam and *Iman*'. He claims that it was not only a theological issue but was more of political in nature. He argues that since the Khawarij would declare the Shi'a disbelievers (*kuffar*) and vice versa, and thereby ineligible for political leadership of Muslims, the first theological discourse (*kalām*) emerged i.e. what is *Iman* and Islam? The result of this dialectic (*jadal*) resulted in determining the relationship between faith (*iman*) and deeds ('*aml*) He concludes that despite the political nature of this theological issue both the Khawarij and Shi'a considered deeds ('*aml*) to be a part of faith (*iman*).[11]

Fazlur Rahman contends that the doctrine of '*Islam* and *Iman*' and its relationship between *Iman* and '*Aml*, resulted in the practical attitude of political pacifism (*Irjā*'). He agrees with Goldziher's view that the community became pacifists (Murji) practically and under the political influence of Abdul Malik b. Marwan the doctrine of *Irjā*' was formulated.[12] Hasan al-Shaf'i argues that there is no definitive evidence that the community became Murj'i by supporting and protecting Umayyad rule.[13] Fazlur Rahman contends that al-Shafi'i reacted in formulating his doctrine of Hadith which he considers to be uncreative, static and literal. He concludes that the combined effect on the community's *kalām* content – theological Hadith, was a product of the community's deviation from the Qur'an and the 'prophetic *Sunnah*' and their inability to correctly formulate the 'living *Sunnah*' of the Prophet (ṣ).

The Shi'a and Murjī'a were brought into conflict over the doctrine of *qadar*. Fazlur Rahman argues that the link between the doctrine of *qadar* and the doctrine of 'Islam and faith (*iman*)' is the doctrine of 'faith and works'. In the same vein, the doctrine of 'human freedom and divine omnipotence' logically was affected by the doctrine of 'faith and works' and this brought about a significant development of a new schism, the Mu'tazila. The action-reaction or interaction between the Mu'tazila and the community bore forth *kalām* as theology proper. The community at this stage refused to base theological doctrines on the basis of reason at all, whereas the Mu'tazila refused to accept the *content* of tradition (*Hadith*) not tradition as a *source*.

Fazlur Rahman considers that the early schools of dialectical theology (*kalām*) emerged in the 2nd century Hijri through the action of foreign ideas – particularly Greco-Christian – on certain fundamental moral issues raised within the Islamic community. Abu Rayyan also considers that foreign cultural attacks (*ghazw al-Thaqafi al-Ajnabi*) were factor that influenced the emergence of *kalām*. [14] These moral issues clustered particularly around the problems of the freedom of the human will, God's omnipotence and justice, and God's relationship to the world. Fazlur Rahman considered that there were two theological schools: (1) Mu'tazila (2) Orthodoxy (*Ahl ul Sunnah wa'l Jama'ah*). Abu Rayyan states that another important factor that influenced the emergence of *kalām* which Fazlur Rahman does not highlight to be the ambigious verses (*ayat al-Mutashabihat*). Abu Rayyan argues that a significant proportion of *kalām* literature is dedicated to interpreting (*ta'wīl*) of these Qur'anic verses. [15]

The Mu'tazila school maintained the freedom of the will, insisting that right (*husn*) and wrong (*qubh*) are knowable through reason independently but confirmed by revelation, and claimed that God's attributes are identical with his essence and that God cannot do what is unreasonable or unjust. However, the Mu'tazila posed and solved all these problems theologically, not philosophically; their entire thought was theo-centric. Their opponents, the orthodoxy, (*Ahl ul Sunnah wa'l Jama'ah*), who came to constitute the orthodoxy, accused them of stark humanism and opposed them on all these major questions. The orthodoxy, after a long, hard struggle, completely routed the Mu'tazila as a theological school, but the spark of the Mu'tazila kindled the purely rationalist movement in philosophic thought.[16]

Fazlur Rahman considered Al-Ash'arī's synthesis between reason and revelation as a deviation from the *élan* of the Qur'an. Al-Ash'arī establishing reason as the foundation of theology and rendering theology as the crown of the religious sciences turned Islam upside down *viz.*, Shari'ah is established on *Din*, not *Din* is established on Shari'ah. Further, this developed a contradiction between the *élan* of the Qur'an, Qur'anic worldview and theology's connection to law. Ash'arīsms influence upon the interpretation of the Qur'an which was one-sided entirely further became more intellectually sophisticated when it came into contact with philosophy.[17]

Companions of the Prophet (ṣ)

The Companions of the Prophet (ṣ) (*sahaba*) had experienced the unfolding of the Qur'an on the socio-historical plane and would not quote individual verses unless these had a direct bearing on the problem under question. It was, in fact, more to the point on their part to quote a concrete precedent from the Prophet's (ṣ) life, if one was available. However, in the case of the two subsequent generations after the companions they had not experienced the historical unfolding of the Qur'an and the Prophet's (ṣ) mission. This stage was the most crucial stage in the historical development of the *kalām* specifically and religious sciences generally, because it was during this period that an appeal to individual verses of the Qur'an and texts of Hadith began to be made in order to resolve issues legally. This was significant also in the realm of theological matters as Ibn Taymīya approved this method for resolving theological matters. Fazlur Rahman considers that the proliferation of Hadiths resulted in the cessation of an orderly growth in legal thought in particular and religious thought in general.

Fazlur Rahman identifies a dislocation in the development of theological (*kalām*) doctrines and the Qur'an and states that the upheavals and final assassinations of the two caliphs 'Uthman and Ali initiated a split from the Qur'an and *Sunnah* paradigm. The earliest sectarian proliferation in Islam initiated a radical change and brought about a crisis two-three decades after the death of the Prophet (ṣ). The nature of this crisis was both due to political and religious factors that played on both the sectarian and majority community side, the Umayyads. The sectarians threatened the integrity of the state and the solidarity of the community. On the other hand, the Umayyads brought about a duality in the relationship of state-community solidarity. The Umayyads were focused upon their political survival and no longer the instrument of Islam. The community faced the dangers of the proliferation of sectarian phenomena from the Khawarij and Shi'a which threatened the very nucleus of its belief and practice. This activity established the starting point of debates, arguments and counter-arguments to win over the sectarians. The Umayyad state lent its arm to the community to suppress the heresies to protect their political integrity. Under these new terms a relationship of mutuality or reciprocity of interests was developed. The relationship had changed from the unified identity of community-state to a dyadic reality. This new reality brought about dynastic rule. Fazlur Rahman criticized this development as governance, dynastic or other, falling short of Islamic requirements when it develops power-dynamics of its own which are autonomous *vis-á-vis* the ideals and the dynamics of the community, i.e., when governance becomes secular or quasi-secular.[18]

> "It is this dyad of state-religion phenomenon of interdependence, rather than identity that started effectively with the Umayyads and shaped the basic attitudes of the community through its early experiences with heresies and the nature of those heresies. These early attitudes – over the subsequent centuries – generated theological, legal and spiritual rationales have become so entrenched and permanently settled that they have provided an exceptionably unique framework for whatever future elaboration, alteration, development for centuries."[19]

Fazlur Rahman contends that the development of theology displays stagnation more dramatically than does legal thought. This theology (*kalām*) which took shape during the 10th, 11th, and 12th centuries C.E., came to claim for itself the exalted function of being the "defender of the bases of Islamic Law," in its most dominant and enduring form of al-Ash'arīsm. The Ash'arī doctrines:

1. Rejected causality

2. Efficacy of the human will in the interests of divine omnipotence (man was therefore only metaphorically an actor, the real actor being God alone)

3. Declared good and evil to be knowable only through the revelation (and not through natural reason),

4. Denied that divine commandments in the Qur'an had any purpose (they were rather to be obeyed solely because they were divine commandments).

General Survey of the Early Schisms

Shi'a and Khawārij

The first active schism in Islam was the Khawarij who attained their name to the fact they rebelled against Ali in 38/658. Nafi' b. al-Azraq (d.65/683-4) had supported the revolt against 'Uthmān b. 'Affān. He also supported 'Ali's caliphate, until the latter submitted his claim to arbitration after which the Khawarij denounced him and then fought against him. Since they had rebelled on religio-ideological grounds, while the majority of the community did not join them, they had to explain and justify their stand. They were the ones that started religio-theological speculation and since their political activism had been directed against what they perceived to be gross governmental injustice and misrule. This uncompromising attitude produced internal self-criticism and at times left many Kharijis unsure whether an error had occurred and the nature of its true import. Many resorted to *Irjā'* i.e., they left the decision or judgment up to God. Indecision with regard to a hypothetical question as to whether something is right or wrong but as soon as the question becomes real and ceases to be hypothetical, those present there must know decisively as to whose answer to it was right and whose was wrong.

Fazlur Rahman considers that the early political wars and dogmatic differences between the Khawārij and the Shi'a gave rise to a prominent type of Hadith known as the 'hadīth about civil wars' (*Hadith al-Fitan*) under the greater rubric of Murjite

Hadīth. These hadīths were given currency in order to steer a middle course between the two groups and this "policy of synthesis and mediation is, indeed, of the essence of the *Ahl ul-Sunnah*."[20] Fazlur Rahman considers that the "middle-path-majority", although certainly in its earliest phase born of political necessity, was bound to be applied in a theological-legal sense also as the political factions tended to create for themselves a theological-moral-legal basis. These two extreme positions of Khariji rebellionism and Shi'a legitimism, led to Sunnism advocating political pacifism. This was enshrined in Hadith that would ultimately save the community from dogmatic civil wars.

Murjia

Fazlur Rahman deems that the first moral-theological controversy to be: 'Islam and *Iman*', and '*Iman* and works' gave birth to the Murjia and their doctrine of *Irjā'* and existence of Murjite Hadith.[21] In their first appearance during the time of 'Uthman and 'Alī, the Murjia represented the mild and moderate opinion against the strong factions for and against 'Uthman and 'Alī. During the Umayyad period, however, this moderate attitude slowly sank to the level of pure determinism (*jabr*), thus falling in line with the popular moral laxity and becoming an instrument in the defense of the Umayyad regime which, in turn, encouraged the dissemination of their views. Thus the Murjia of the early period of Ali, who took a neutralist position in the political quarrel between Ali and his opponents and were therefore also called Mu'tazila (the neutralists) came to be called Jabriya, 'predeterminists'.[22] As a result of the painstaking and heart-searching Hadith activity amidst an atmosphere of interminable conflict, the Muslim orthodoxy – the *Ahl al-Sunnah* (i.e. the majority of the community) finally formulated – at the hands of al-Ash'arī and al-Maturidī and their successors – a catholic definition of Islam which silenced Kharijism and Mu'tazilism and saved the community from suicide.[23]

Irjā' is a position taken when it is not always decisively clear that a certain error has been committed and what the precise nature and the moral weight of a particular error may be and that therefore final judgment must be left to God. The position of *Irjā'* characteristically articulated the attitudes of the larger body of the community which, by its inner logic, must eschew extremes, hold on to that which is practical and practicable, and always avoid theoretical decision on polarities in the interests of practical compromises. Therefore *Irjā'* as a practical attitude, necessarily characterized the majority of the community who refused to take sides in the dispute between 'Uthman and his opponents or between 'Alī, on the one hand, and 'A'isha, Mu'āwiya, Talha and Zubayr on the other. The larger community was sure that Kharijism was in error, namely the attitude that arrogates to itself the self-righteous claim to know precisely who is doing what amount of wrong and with what moral consequences. A reaction to the view held by most Kharijis that those Muslims who are guilty of major errors (*kabā'ir*) become infidels, who must die in this world at the hands of God. *Irjā'* then, is a reaction to this position of "threat" (*wa'īd*) both in this life and the life after death.

Irjā' when formulated as a doctrine and no longer considered solely as a practical attitude, reached to extremes and tied into the doctrine of *qadar*. This doctrine states that human beings possess free will, or that God has endowed humankind with a free will and that this will is efficacious so that a person is completely free to choose and to act. First of all unlike

Kharijism, which was a practical phenomenon and only secondarily a doctrine, *qadar* is primarily the name of a doctrine, not of a practical attitude, although it may help a practical attitude. A distinction should be made in that all leaders of the Khawarij were Arabs – the *qadarīyya*, which was a school of thought, was predominantly, and primarily a non-Arab affair, and included Persians and Egyptians, many of them from a Christian background. The Khārijīs were *not qadarīs* – believing that God created human acts.

Irjā' and Qadarism – Political Pacifism and Predeterminism

Fazlur Rahman considers the coupling between political pacifism (*irjā'*) and predeterminism (*qadar*) to be a turning point in the theological history of Islam. For this he states it is imperative to understand the development of *qadarism* and *anti-qadarism*. The starting point of this *qadarism* or the doctrine of free and efficacious human will is from the infiltration of Hellenized Christian background in Syria and Iraq.[24] This was deemed to be highly dangerous by the Umayyads, starting with 'Abd al-Malik b. Marwan who, therefore, deliberately adopted *anti-qadarism* as a state policy.[25] He also pressed the services of certain highly important and influential religious leaders into the service of the state and created a climate of *anti-qadarism* and *irjā'* which was subsequently destined to be incarnated as the Islamic orthodoxy of the Ash'arītes.[26] At this point Hasan al-Basri wrote his famous pro-qadari *Risala* against 'Abd al-Malik b. Marwan.

Fazlur Rahman argues that with the background of *irjā'* whether one can indeed presume to pass judgment on human actions as the Khārijīs patently did, in view of the fact that nothing happens without God's all powerful will. *Irjā'* was thus a fertile basis for the rise of the question as to a person's autonomous power to act – let alone such action being subject to human judgment. It is also very natural for committed Murjites to resort, in turn, to pre-destinarianism. Thus *irjā'* at this point is in its crude doctrinal form and not just as a practical attitude. This would of course, provoke *qadarism* a doctrinal response on the part of morally sensitive persons who were afraid of pre-destinarianism weakening the moral fiber of the faithful. Both sides could, and in the course of time did, avail themselves of the pre-existing stock of ideas, but their genesis was to be explained in terms of the matrices of the moods of the community and the intellectual formulations of these moods. Thus, the emergence of *kalām* literature began with the *anti-qadarism and* was subsequently the response of Hasan al-Basri did not necessitate at this point 'writing in a dialectical (*jadali*) style' but a refutation of the pre-destinarian basis.

The Umayyad 'Abd al-Malik b. Marwan and 'Umar b. 'Abdul 'Aziz were both educated in Madinah. The Umayyads due to their departure from the piety of the first community were nonetheless tolerated by the Medinese stance taken on the issue of 'Uthman and his opponents and 'Ali and his opponents was political quietism and similarly was the response to Khariji extremism. Since Madinah was not just a center of piety, but also of learning and incipient religious thought, this *irjā'*, when it was theoretically grounded led to pre-destinarianism – most probably of different shades. Thus, political pacifism (*irjā'*) and pre-destinarianism (*jabr*) were combined.

It seems that Fazlur Rahman accepts Macdonald and Wesnick's assertions that *irjā'* was a predominantly political doctrine.[27] According to Fazlur Rahman *irjā'* developed into a theory and gives rise to predestinarianism whence it ceases to have direct touch with actual practical attitudes. Further, *irjā'* was a response by the Muslim community or its religious leaders, and ʿAbd al-Malik b. Marwan himself had learnt it from the community leaders.[28] For this *irjā'* was directly relevant, something that the community supported as the only viable practical alternative to mutual incrimination and civil wars. Fazlur Rahman argues that if *irjā'* is raised to the level of a theory of the moral value of human acts, it is liable to generate the added theory of the moral value of human acts it is liable to generate the added theory of pre-determinism. Here Fazlur Rahman on the free-will of human beings is for no sensible person can be really persuaded to believe that they cannot do anything at all of their "own free will" nor that they can do anything they want to – knowing full well that nobody ever "chose" to be born. However, that given their social, economic, and moral factors, pre-determinism and its opposite can contribute to the development of relevant attitudes of life, but the inherent limitations of their effectiveness must be duly recognized."[29]

Fazlur Rahman argues that the opposite of *irjā'* is *wa'īdism*, meaning the 'unconditional threat of infidelity and the promise of hell for those guilty of serious error'; the opposite of *qadarism* is *jabrism*, the doctrine of predestination. The former polarity primarily represents a practical attitude; the latter *qadr-jabr* (free will-predestination) polarity is primarily a doctrinal affair, not a practical one. Thus, it is not necessary that a *qadarī* must be active or activist in actual life or even that he should preach activism. Nor is it true that activists, like Khārijīs, must necessarily hold *qadarī* views. In fact, they did not although one would expect otherwise. It is true that logically at least *jabr* and *irjā'* ought to go together as should *qadar* and *wa'īdism* – as is the case with Mu'tazilism.[30] The salient *qadari* doctrines are the following:

1. That God is one unique being, unlike any creature, possessing activity but no substantive attribute. Thus, He is living but has no substantive attribute of life; He knows but has no substantive attribute of knowledge. Because they denied the attribute of speech (*kalām*), they declared that the Qur'an – as God's speech – was not an eternal attribute of God but something created (*makhlūq*).

2. That humankind is endowed with free will and the responsibility to create autonomous actions. God neither wills nor creates evil. Therefore, the evil that materializes occurs without and despite His will.

3. That a Muslim who commits a grave wrong or sin ceases to have faith (*iman*), but does not become an infidel either as the Khārijīs insisted, but comes to occupy a "middle position" unless he or she repents. Deeds are, therefore, a part of faith.

4. That God's activity is for the sake of the good (*maslaha*) of His creation. Therefore, the laws that God has ordained for humankind have a purpose the good of humanity.

5. That good and evil or right and wrong are discoverable by human reason unaided by revelation but that the ritual institutions of religion, such as daily prayers and fasting, cannot be known by pure reason but are known only through revelation.

6. That God's justice demands that just as He *must* reward good people for their good deeds, so must He punish people for their evil deeds, otherwise a distinction between the effects of good and evil deeds will disappear. Hence they denied God's forgiveness for sinners. Divine justice is a *more or less equivalent* for every act, although of course, a grave sin wipes out all effects of good deeds, even of great good deeds.

The main theses of the *qadariyya* in their developed form of the Mu'tazila school which comes to prominence with Wāsil b. 'Aṭā' with the exception of their denial that God will be seen by the faithful on the Day of Judgment as their opponents, the Sunnīs insisted.[31] Outside the Hijaz, however, and especially in Iraq, this attitude of practical religiosity became subjected to severe philosophical speculations by outside influences *viz.*, Hellenism, Hellenized Christianity, Gnosticism, Manichaean dualism and Buddhistic elements provided the stock ideas for philosophical, religious and moral speculation.[32] And although the initial reflexive impulse to moral issues was generated by events within Islam, these were soon to be transformed in the great cities of Iraq into speculative issues.[33]

Fazlur Rahman considers the the first significant figure of Islamic religious thought and politics is Hasan al-Baṣrī (d.110/728) in Basra, Iraq in the late 1st/7th and early 2nd/8th. Fazlur Rahman argues Hasan al-Baṣrī as the representative of Medinese piety. Fazlur Rahman highlights Hasan al-Baṣrī's strong rejection of determinism and human freedom because it is in consonance with Fazlur Rahman's strong rejection of Ash'arī determinism. Whereas Fazlur Rahman is strongly motivated by philosophical discernment he contends that Hasan al-Baṣrī was more interested in pietistic morality that speculation.[34]

Fazlur Rahman contends that on the basis of the doctrine of the intermediate state of a grave sinner (*manzila bayn al-manzilatayn*) the Mu'tazila 'neutralists' received their technical name. He further alleges that it distinguished them from the old political neutralists i.e. Murjī'a. He rejects the generally accepted Sunni tradition that the reason for their name was when Wasil Ibn 'Aṭā' (80/131-699-749) 'broke off' (*i'tazala*) from the circle of Hasan al-Basrī.[35] Fazlur Rahman argues that because the majority of intellectual half of the community were political neutralists, the Mu'tazila were by and large (including their leaders) pro-Ali although some of them did not declare for their party in the earliest civil wars. Abu Rayyan concurs with Fazlur Rahman that both political and religious factors resulted in the technical name of the Mu'tazila.[36]

Fazlur Rahman contends that the factors that shaped Mu'tazilite thought were (1) internal: systematic thinking out of dogma which made them pursue ratiocination; (2) external: Their unmitigating struggle against Manicheanism, Gnosticism and Materialism. Fazlur Rahman argues that the combination of these factors rendered the creed untenable in the eyes of the community. He argues that the Mu'tazila became staunch advocates of Hellenistic rationalism in the face of the orthodoxy. On the subject of the attributes and especially with regard to the Word, they were undoubtedly influenced by Hellenistic ideas especially in their Christian formulations about the Logos. But since they held reason to be the essential constitution of God, a purely Greek idea, the net result was to put reason above revelation.[37] Abu Rayyan rejects the Hellenistic influence *in toto* arguing that the inter-action between the Mu'tazila movement and Greek thought occurred in the Abbasid period.[38]

Fazlur Rahman identifies a pivotal point in Islamic thought to be dialectical idealism voiced between the Orthodoxy and Mu'tazila. He argues that the Orthodoxy developed a spirit of integrative, broad and stabilizing catholicity, however they maintained an aggressive reaction against the proud and hollow rationalism of Mu'tazila. He concludes this phase in Islamic thought that is Islam was launched on a career where its dynamic formulations had only a partial and indirect relationship to the living reality of the faith. In the 4th/10th century the Sunni orthodoxy defined by Abu'l Hasan al-Ash'arī (d.324/935), which was prevalent throughout medieval Islam, and influenced by his contemporary Abu'l Mansūr al-Māturīdī (d.333/944) can be viewed as the culmination of a process that was an immediate reaction against the Mu'tazila and to some extent against the Shi'a.

In the second and third centuries, the second major theological difference which threatened the unity of the community was the problem of the freedom of the human will versus divine determinism. The first arising from the Khawarij and the second at the hands of the Mu'tazila who are in a sense the theological inheritors of the Khawarij.[39] The solutions presented by the Mutazilite rationalism appeared to the religious minded to be a form of gross humanism, an imposition upon God what a certain number of men regard as truth and justice. Fazlur Rahman posits that the affect of this theological controversy led to the emergence of Ḥadith that dealt with divine determinism at different levels – of intention, motivation and act; and thus deterministic Ḥadith are given birth. The *Ahl ul Sunnah wa'l Jama'ah* remained focused towards developing doctrine-content that would attempt to synthesize extremes, to stabilize and stick to the middle path. It was this practice which Fazlur Rahman refers to as *"Tasannun"* that explicitly formulated the content and an "orthodoxy" had come into existence through the progressive formulation and elaboration of the Ḥadith and the legal system brought about social equilibrium and cohesion. These conditions created a positive environment for the development in the intellectual, spiritual, scientific and cultural fields. However, Fazlur Rahman considers that this growth was relatively short lived because the content of the structure was invested with a halo of sacredness and unchangeability since it came to be looked upon as uniquely deducible from the Qur'an and the Prophetic *Sunnah*. This is due to the crass formalism and lack of interpretative thought that led to the stagnation of the Muslim community.

Fazlur Rahman personal modernizing project took heed of the fact that the content of the *Ahl ul Sunnah* was not progressive but stagnant. Further that Islam has always been subjected to extremisms, not only political but theological and moral as well. The *Ahl ul Sunnah wa'l Jama'ah* whose very genesis had been on an assumed plea of moderation, mediation and synthesis – which is an on-going process – and who, indeed actually functioned as such a force in the early stages, they became, after the content of their system had fully developed, authoritarian, rigid and intolerant. Instead of continuing to be a synthesizing and absorbing force they became transformed into a party among parties with all its rejecting and exclusivist attitudes. The result of the Hadith movement helped the formulation of certain important politico-moral tenets of the orthodoxy which, in turn, affected directly the spiritual and intellectual life of the community. All these results had, in the final analysis, come to be sanctioned by the *Ijmāʿ* or consensus of the community.

In the middle of the second century, the Hadith movement launched by the Orthodoxy had become fairly advanced and although most Hadith was still attributed to persons other than the Prophet (ṣ) – the companions and especially the generations of the companions – nevertheless a part of legal opinion and dogmatic views of the early Muslims had begun to be projected back to the Prophet (ṣ). But still, the Hadith was interpreted and treated with great freedom at this time.[40] However, it is the legal and dogmatic Hadith i.e., that concerning belief and practice which must, "strictly speaking" belong to the Prophet (ṣ).[41] The majority of the Hadith corpus is nothing more than the *Sunnah-Ijtihād* of the first generation of Muslims, an *Ijtihād* which has its source in individual opinion but which in course of time and after tremendous struggles and conflicts against heresies and extreme sectarian opinion received the sanction of *Ijmāʿ* i.e. the adherence of the majority of the community.[42]

In the religious history of Islam a crucial point must be born in mind and that is as the political, theological and legal differences threatened the integrity of the community, the idea to preserve its unity asserted itself. The agents of producing this structure of the orthodoxy are the *Ahl ul Hadith*.[43] These doctrines which had originated in the "living *Sunnah*" as a product of Islamic history acting on the Qur'an and the Prophetic *Sunnah*, were transformed through the medium of the Hadith, into immutable articles of Faith.

Fazlur Rahman states that in the second and third centuries the two major contending groups – the Mu'tazila and their opponents – found themselves developing their theological worldviews' and doing so in the abstract only one term of the concrete moral tension strongly advocated by the Qur'an. The Mu'tazila asserted that the Qur'an had emphasized the potentialities and the accountability of man – and the strict justice of God. The *Ahl ul Hadith* asserted the other tension in the Qur'an that in order to assert the absolute supremacy of the moral law, the Qur'an had equally emphatically stressed the Power, Will and Majesty of God. The result was the former appearing as denuding God of all godhead and substituting a naked humanism for the essentials of religion; and the latter, accentuating the Will and Power of God and proffering determinism as an unalterable part of the orthodox creed. Again, Fazlur Rahman criticized the orthodoxy that it was maneuvered into an extreme position. In place of the living, concrete and synthetic moral tension of the Qur'an and the Prophetic *Sunnah* the "orthodoxy" came into existence on the very plea and with the very program of installing the omnipotence of God and impotence of man into a dogma. Further, the orthodoxy developed pre-deterministic and (counter) free will Hadiths' in preponderance. Orthodoxy having to face the twin extreme positions of the Khawarij and the Mu'tazila asserted uncompromisingly the Will and Power of God. The Mu'tazila derived their doctrine and then sought to formulate it in terms of the current stock of philosophical ideas of Greek origin. The orthodoxy in the hands of Ibn Hanbal the emphasis on the power and majesty of God was a simple assertion of the religious impulse, the latter theologians like al-Ash'arī, al-Maturidi and especially their successors transformed it into a full-fledged theological doctrine. But their intellectual tools were no better than those of the Mu'tazila and thus the doctrine developed one-sidedly in favor of determinism. A little later, during the 4th and 5th centuries, the Muslims philosophers, being pure rationalists, developed determinism still further and, by an identification of causal, rational and theistic forms of determinism, produced a truly imposing deterministic structure of the universe – and of man. Fazlur Rahman considered the problem of human freedom and accountability connected to the problem of how faith is related to acts and with the definition of a Muslim. This problem had political consequences and the Ummayad's preferred that faith and actions were separate and determinism for maintaining their political stronghold.

Theological – Legal Doctrine of Good and Bad (Al Husn wa'l Qubh)

Fazlur Rahman criticizes the theological-legal doctrine of 'good (*husn*) and bad (*qubh*)' for being revelatory (*naqli*) and not rationally (*'aqli*) established.[44] He argues that the orthodoxy had established the foundations of good and bad upon revelatory foundations and despite the Mu'tazila establishing it in reason the Mu'tazila practice was authority based in law as their opponents.[45] The result of this failure has led to the 'absence of the emergence of a self-concious and independent ethics in the history of Islam'.[46] The Islamic philosophers also failed in producing a moral philosophy. He attributes this failure to the orthodox theologians failure to develop a rational investigation of good and bad (*al-nazar fi amr illah*), whereas they stressed the true and false (*al-nazar fi ma'rifat Allah*).[47] The underlying reason for Fazlur Rahman's critique is his idenfication of moral decadence to be chiefly responsible for the moral decadence of the Muslim community in the 20th century.[48]

It is necessary to understand the historical development of the theological doctrine of good (*husn*) and bad (*qubh*) and its interconnection with the doctrine of pacifism (*irjā'*) and the doctrine of prederterminism (*qadar*). Fazlur Rahman considers that at the outset the origins of *kalām* in Islam are not connected with *fiqh* but belonged purely to a theological circle of considerations. As we have stated above Fazlur Rahman considered Abu Hanifa as a Murjite.[49] On this basis he argues that Abu Hanifa's classified matters pertaining to creed as *al-fiqh al-akbar* and those matters relating to legal matters as *al-fiqh al-asghar*. He states that it is wrong to assume that there is a an organic relationship between *kalām* and *fiqh* on the contrary it implies that *kalām* is a higher and nobler science – not because it proves the logical assumptions of law but because its subject matter is higher and nobler, *viz.*, God, His attributes, and prophethood, than of that law whose subject matter is human action in relation to the Divine Command.[50] Thus, Fazlur Rahman draws this conclusion that Abu Hanifa's classification resulted in an alteration in the emphasis placed in the the Qur'an and *Sunnah* upon the establishment of a moral order.

Fazlur Rahman traces a second source for the inculcation of *irjā'* and *qadari* views to Hasan al-Baṣrī's epistle to 'Abd al-Malik b. Marwan in which he defends the freedom of the human will and attacks the doctrine of determinism. Again Fazlur Rahman attempts at deducing Hasan al-Baṣrī's aim not to protect the assumptions of law and justify *fiqh* but to protect the concept of God from attribution of injustice and impropriety. In other words, his was primarily a theological concern, not a moral one. He also considered that the Mu'tazila's primary concern was not with man but with God despite championing freedom of the human will and grounding of good (*husn*) and bad (*qubh*) in reason as distinguished from revelation:

> "...their self-entitlement as "People of Justice and Unity"
> clearly means that they are concerned with the vindication of

God's justice and unity, not with man's justice and responsibility."[51]

Nor does al-Ash'arī, envisage an internal organic
relationship between *kalām* and *fiqh*:

> "Indeed, he conceives of them as two different genres of
> knowledge and insists that the two must not be mixed up with
> each other."[52]

Under the impact no doubt of preexisting ideas in Iraq and
Persia some amount of reflection took place about this attitude.
As soon as this intellectual activity reached the reflective stage
and the predestinarians (*jabaris'*) and free-willers (*qadarīs'*)
formulated their doctrinal strands, human free will and divine
omnipotence became directly antithetical to each other. This
resulted in the power of God and the choice and efficiency of the
human will becoming mutually exclusive concepts. The
theological schools became more polarized in a theoretical sense
whereas the lawyers adopted the Murji'a school.[53] Fazlur
Rahman opines that this inherent contradiction later was not
considered to be antithetical to each other and was considered as
sound religious dogma.[54]

Fazlur Rahman elaborates that subsequently there was also a
development in the concept of *irjā'*. He argues that in the
beginning it meant the adoption of a 'neutral' attitude towards
the participants in the earliest disputes and a refusal to decide
who was in the right and who was in the wrong: 'the decision on
this issue was left to God'.[55] This proposition was then extended,
naturally enough, to a Muslim who professes Islamic faith but
may be guilty of serious sins; thereby this theological doctrine
that originated from political influences now influenced legal
thought more significantly at a later stage. In addition, a later

development was that there was a 'gap' between faith and works, which became the position of the Murji'a school. This is because the Murji'a actually came from otherwise very different, indeed conflicting, doctrinal schools – when the original attitude reached a formulation. It is in this sense that Abu Hanifa was a Murji'ī i.e., the idea that there is no necessary and organic relationship between faith and acts. The 'status of a sinning Muslim' (*murtakib al-Kabira*) is thus responsible for the entire religious and theological development of early Islam.[56]

The position of the Murji'a in the second century is as follows:

1. A person cannot know and is thus unable to make a moral judgment as to whether there was a right and wrong position among the early disputants – 'Uthman, 'Alī, 'A'isha, Talhā, Zubayr and Mu'āwiya.

2. If one could know how to make a judgment as to which person was right and who was wrong.

3. Those who were wrong were so wrong as to loose their faith altogether.

For this reason God in His wisdom must finally judge these matters and this is predominantly an anti-Kharijite position. From this position it soon followed logically, as it were, that a Muslim guilty of heinous sins still has faith and is a Muslim and is to be treated as such until God finally decides on the Last Day. Fazlur Rahman agrees with Wensinck and theorizes that based upon this stand there arose a specific genre of Hadith that sought to create a clear distinction between faith and acts. In response the orthodoxy formulated Hadith that supported the doctrine of the intercession of the Prophet (ṣ) on the behalf of the sinners of his community.⁵⁷ Also Hadiths' referring to the punishment in the grave surfaced which the Khawārij and the Mu'tazila rejected.

The primary meaning of *Irjā'* in its first phase was to leave the final decisions on sinners to God. From this followed a secondary conclusion that sinners nevertheless continue to be Muslims. In the second century, this meaning comes to predominate and a sharp distinction is made between faith and acts. The Murji'a held that works lie outside faith, and that faith neither increases or decreases; or that it increases but does not decrease.⁵⁸ Jahm b. Safwān believed that faith is the recognition of God and His prophets by the heart and that such a person is a believer (*mu'min*) even if he may verbally reject this. Others, such as Muḥammad b. Karrām (d. 255/869) and his followers, held that a person professing faith only by the tongue while rejecting it from the heart is a true believer. Most of the Murjia, however, believed that faith comprises both the act of the heart (belief, love and esteem) and its declaration by the tongue. This view is held by Abū Ḥanīfa (d.150/767). Fazlur Rahman argues that influential figures like Abu Hanifa advocated the doctrine of *Irjā'* which is historically contradictory to Abu Hanifa *Risala Abi Hanifa ila Uthman al-Bati* in which he addresses al-Bati's and informs that the allegation of him being a Murji is false. In the letter Abu Hanifa provides this argument that "when Muhammad (ṣ) was made a prophet and the people of Makkah were polytheists, the Prophet (ṣ) invited them to Islam and following that the obligatory deeds (*fara'id*) were revealed upon the people who attested Muhammad's prophethood (*Ahl ul-Tasdiq*). On this basis, he argues that deeds are not a part of faith because faith is attesting and testification only and deeds (*'aml*) are not a pillar of faith (*iman*)."⁵⁹ It seems that Fazlur Rahman judgment of Abu Hanifa is based upon the connotation that Murj'i means to be faith exclusive of deeds but disregards the basis of Abu Hanifa's argument. However, the majority of the heresiographers do consider a Murj'i to be someone who believes that faith is exclusive of deeds but the failure of Fazlur Rahman to evaluate Abu Hanifa's argument denotes weak scholarship.

The elitist Ash'arītes held that a Muslim cannot claim to be a true Muslim without understanding the basis of Islam rationally.[60] For the populist Ḥanafī-Māturīdīs 'the Islam of the common Turk is perfectly good,' even one who knows nothing about the rational bases of Islam. This is the essence of *irjā'* in its new form in the 2nd/ 8th century a rich crop of predestinarian *aḥādīths* arose.

The relationship between law and theology and the implications of each for the other are that law assumes that a person is the locus of legal-moral obligation and hence is charged with the responsibility of making a free choice and acting freely. The issue which Fazlur Rahman seizes is that eminent theologians such as Ahmad b. Hanbal express predestinarian views in their theology and deny any organic relationship between faith and action, there are two possibilities in this regard:

1. Theological views were of a quite different provenance to that of their legal assumptions; therefore the two were not synchronized. In other words, they held contradictory doctrines about humankind.

2. They saw no contradiction between the predestinarian theology and the moral foundations of their law.

The fact is that the legal activity of these jurists was geared to needs of action (*'aml*) pertaining to practical life. Its theoretical foundations were simple enough, God has sent down the last revelation through the last prophet on earth disclosing the way human beings should conduct themselves in the various spheres of life and it is their duty to obey. This obedience must however, be facilitated for the Muslim by elaborating and systematizing the divine imperative into actual legal rules. As for theology, this is a matter of belief (*iman* – *'aqida*). The *qadarī* freewillers, surely pushed their thesis to anti-Qur'anic extremes when they denied any role to God whatsoever in the sphere of human moral action. Similarly, they pushed their thesis of divine justice of such extremes that they denuded God of the power to forgive sinners. Therefore, *qadarism* had to be rejected, irrespective of whether it had any relevance to the bases of law and action.

Fazlur Rahman concludes that the effect of *kalām* a temper is certainly introduced where the sense of human initiative is dulled. And in conjunction with other factors the human initiative may gradually become almost smothered. Further, the motivation to raise the level and quality of one's action and preserve the sense of correcting one's conduct is weakened both by the doctrine of (predestinarianism – *irjā'* – intercessionism) – a moral trend does set in which runs counter to the Qur'an and its living – vibrant mission that aims at intensifying human moral energy.[61]

Ash'arīsm, Maturidism and Sunnism

The right wing of orthodox traditionalism was represented by Ibn Hanbal and his school. Fazlur Rahman attributes an expansive all embracing catholic spirit of Islam to be attributable to the Hadith compilers (*muḥadithūn*). By a fairly broadminded exercise of their orthodox insight, these men allowed to fall within the scope of the acceptable Hadith a body of authoritative material that allowed for latitude and integration of points of views and opinions that could not be fitted into one mold. It exhibits no external or superficial wisdom but an impeccable scrupulousness and an inner and genuine insight into the spirit of the prophet's teaching and the early community's understanding of it. The Hadith was opposed by the Mu'tazila who nevertheless slowly lost ground by the latter half of the 3rd/9th century; on no other hypothesis than this can we really understand the absolute success of the Hadith in that century.

From the 3rd/9th century onwards, the practice of moderation and catholicity of spirit which had created the *Ahl ul-Sunnah wa'l Jama'ah* 'the people of the middle path and unity', i.e. the orthodoxy, changed into a *theoretical and doctrinal* principle. The charge of conformism against the Ulama' as a whole seems, therefore, justified and the principle of 'obedience even to a tyrant' was often carried to its extremes. It is nevertheless, true that this political wisdom of the Ulama' has done a fundamental service to the community which goes all too often unrecognized.[62] Yet, the success of the Hadith was not due to the fact that it was, in its formulations and content, a possibly valuable amorphous mass, but because at bottom it expressed a definite spirit of religious realism that had characterized both the Qur'an and the early community. It brought under the aegis of the *Sunnah* all the necessary religious elements that were implicit or explicit in the Qur'an. Side by side with the coming to fruition of the Hadith, a widespread movement of dissatisfaction had started with the *clichés* of the rationalist school. Their newer views began to shape on the basis of their acquaintance with tradition and their gradual acceptance of it.

The most celebrated name in this newer movement, which turned the tables on the Mu'tazila by their own dialectic, is that of Abu'l Hasan al-Ash'arī (d. 330/442) who broke from his Mu'tazilite master Abu Ali al-Jubba'ī (d. 303/916). Al-Ash'arī's formulation of dogma essentially represents an attempt at a synthesis of the hitherto largely unformulated orthodox position (*mawqif al-salaf*) and that of the Mu'tazila. This is, as we have pointed out the very ethos of orthodoxy (*al-salaf*). But his actual formulas unmistakably show the character of a reaction of orthodoxy to the Mu'tazilite doctrine, a reaction from which he was unable to escape completely. The net result is therefore a partial synthesis and a partial reaction. On the question of human free will (*huriyat wa'l ikhtiyar*) he erected, on the basis of certain Qur'anic texts, his doctrine of 'acquisition' (*kasb*).[63] According to this doctrine, all acts are created and produced by God but attach themselves to the will of man who thus acquires them. Abu Rayyan agrees with Fazlur Rahman that the Asharites attempted to reach a middle position between the Jabariyah and Mu'tazila-Qadarites but in the end attribute all human actions to God himself. He states that the Jabirites rejected that humans could produce their own acts (*Ihdath al-F'il*) or acquire them (*kasb al-F'il*). The Mu'tazila affirmed the opposite. The Ash'arītes rejected that humans could produce their own acts but affirmed that they could acquire them. However, they invalidate this acquisitive power to humans by their atomism in which they affirm that God intervenes in every human action continuously and in every movement directly leaving no room for metaphysical or natural for human freedom. He argues that despite the Ash'arīte claims that they have adopted the middle position between the two groups and affirming that human beings possess free will the implications on the one hand of their origination of the world (*huduth al-'Alim*) and continuous creativity and on the other hand their explanation for human action – there is no room for any justification except that they are Jabirites.[64]

Fazlur Rahman identifies another dimension that al-Ash'arī set out to resolve was not so much a psychological as a moral one: how to reconcile divine omnipotence with human responsibility. And if man's consciousness (*wujdan*) of owning his acts is itself created by God, as al-Ash'arī believes then man acquires neither the one nor the other. The principle that seems to be at work here is that all power is referred to God while responsibility must remain with man. The principle itself, although it has a metaphysical form, is religious and moral in its essential character.[65]

On the problem of God, al-Ash'arī taught that God has real, eternal attributes, but attempted to safeguard against anthropomorphism (*tashbih*). Al-Ash'arī interpretation of God's attributes such has His hands and face (*sifat al-khabanyah*) were interpreted away from their literal and anthromorphic implications to which the Hanbali scholars responded bitterly. God knows by virtue of His Attribute of Knowledge, wills by virtue of His Attribute of Will, etc. They are neither identical with His Essence nor different from it. They are real although we do not know their 'how', and in this connection al-Ash'arī makes use of the negative dialectic of the Mu'tazilites which ultimately comes from Neoplatonism.

As regards to rewards (*al-wa'd*) and punishments (*al-wa'īd*), he emphasizes both the absolute Power of God and His absolute Mercy and Grace: He may punish or reward as He will. This is done not to uphold any caprice and arbitrariness on the part of God but again in order to express the religious attitude of humility and fear. Like all Attributes, God's Speech is eternal and uncreated. But the Qur'an as we know it, a definite text of a certain length, *etc.*, is only an expression although an expression par excellence of the Eternal Speech of God which in itself is a 'Mental Word'.

Thus, al-Ash'arī confirmed the absolute Power and Grace of God as orthodoxy had maintained it. All acts take place by the Will and 'good pleasure' (*riḍa*) of God, whether good or evil. Ash'arī reacting in opposition to the Mu'tazila and in support of Ibn Hanbal took the absolute Power of God and further supported it by the atomistic theory of nature denying causation and potentialities in natural bodies and providing for the direct efficacy of God for the production of events, whether physical or mental.[66]

Contemporaneously Abu Mansur al-Maturidi (d.333/945) of Samarqand had a similar outlook to Ash'arīsm but differed on certain points. Al-Maturidi, like al-Ash'arī, holds that all acts are willed by God, but unlike him, maintains that evil does not occur 'with the good pleasure of God'. More important, Maturidism, while emphasizing the omnipotence of God, allows the efficacy of the human will and, in some of its later developments, the absolutely free human production of acts was unequivocally stated. In these later developments, indeed, there is a free interaction between the two systems, and the doctrine of the absolute inefficacy of the human will generally lost its force although the Ash'arīte dogma, backed by some important Hadith, still retained it.

Fazlur Rahman argues that the theological issue of 'degrees of faith' was connected with the question of faith and works and later came to be connected with the idea of the omnipotence and grace of God. Those who held, like the Mu'tazila and the

Kharijites, that acts were an essential part of the faith, also held that faith increases and decreases i.e., is quantitative – and could reach a zero degree, despite the profession of the faith by the agent. The Murjī'a, on the other hand, believed that faith was something qualitatively unanalyzable and simple, not admitting either degree of measurement.[67] The Sunni *kalām* as was its tendency was between the two in principle, but on the whole inclined to the tenets of the Murjī'a. The Ash'arites would attempt to resolve theological issues by a middle course approach and this led to the majority of Muslims adopting the Ash'arī creed.[68] Abu Rayyan argues that the Maturidites attempted to adopt a middle course approach similar to the Ash'arītes *viz.*, the orthodoxy (*al-salaf*) and Mu'tazila but in reality they adopted a middle course between the Mu'tazila and the Ash'arītes with a latent tendency towards the Mu'tazila.[69] Fazlur Rahman argues that both the Maturidites and the Ash'arītes adopted the Murjite position in order to check fanaticism and persecution, and the Sunnis, accordingly, maintained that, with a genuine profession of faith, an irreducible amount of faith came into existence which was incapable of being eliminated by almost any external behavior, although it could increase or decrease beyond that point. The Qur'an repeatedly affirms the increase of faith and incessantly urges acts born of genuine faith; and the Hadith speaks of an intimate connection between acts and intentions, although certain Hadiths, which apparently counseled moderation and were to the effect that none shall be eternally damned with a 'grain of faith' were seized upon by theologians in this connection. Abu Rayyan argues that the Ash'arītes did not tend entirely towards the Murjites. He contends the Ash'arīte uprising against the Mu'tazila in the 5th century Hijri all but crushed the latter. Similarly, the Hanbali uprising against the Asharītes in 469 AH/1076 CE to destroy their attempts at joining their ranks resulted in the Ash'arītes crushing the former.[70]

Fazlur Rahman seems to argue on the same lines that a split occurred within the orthodoxy itself. The main continuation of the old traditional school of Madinah, the 'People of the Ḥadith', not only opposed Ash'arī solutions of dialectical theology but rejected the dialectical theology itself. The main continuation of the old traditional school of Madinah, the 'People of the Ḥadith', not only opposed al-Ash'arī solutions of dialectical theology but rejected the dialectical theology itself. The Qur'an and the *Sunnah*, they contended, must not be defended by a 'reason' that lies outside these, but the true 'reason' is to be found rather within them.[71] They accused the Mu'tazila, in effect, of betraying the true spirit of the Qur'an and the *Sunnah* in the process of defending them by rational formulas. Nevertheless, Ash'arīsm, as a system of dogma, slowly overcame opposition and finally won recognition in the East in the 11th/17th century through the efforts of the great Seljuq waẓir Nizam al-Mulk and the brilliant theologian and religious reformer al-Ghazālī. But the friction between the religious spirit of the *Ahl ul Hadith* and the rationalizing tendencies of the *Ahl al-Kalām* continued and culminated in the 7th/13th and 8th/14th centuries in a vigorous reassertion of puritanical activism in Ibn Taymīya and his school. But before that the *kalām* had to face a more thorough-going rational movement of the Muslim philosophers.[72]

Fazlur Rahman argues that al-Ash'arī's primary motivation was to uphold the uncompromising omnipotence and absolute will of God. The basic fault of the Mu'tazila in the eyes of al-Ash'arī is that they defined the God-human relationship that

God's power and will became compromised. On this point al-Ash'arī unconditionally agreed with Ibn Hanbal even though he differed with him over the role of reason in religious thought. Once this happens, God's existence may well become superfluous at least for humankind, if not for nature. Islamic theologies, like theologies of other religions, show clear signs of action and reaction. Thus, on the subject of free will (*qadar*), the Mu'tazila were all agreed that in the sphere of volitional activity God did not actually play any role and that humanity was central in all. The Mu'tazila were of course divided among themselves as to whether God had the *power* to act in these spheres.

Al-Ash'arī in turn defined his extreme position by rejecting the idea that humanity can be validly said to act at all, let alone act freely. Humankind can be said to be an "actor" only metaphorically (*bi'l-majāz*). God creates all human acts and man only "acquires" them. Ash'arī opting for the term "acquiring" instead of "doing", according to him, is based on the Qur'anic verse, al-Ṣāffāt: 96, that God creates human acts: "He [God] has created you and what you make [as handiwork]". This is part of Abraham's speech to his idol-worshiping people. Fazlur Rahman argues that Ash'arī failed to understand the verse correctly. The verse is preceded by "Do you worship that which you [yourselves] have carved?" (al-Ṣāffāt: 95).[73] It is clear that this verse is also saying that it is God who has created you and those idols that you have made. But al-Ash'arī replaces the words "what you make" with "what you do". The Arabic *wa ma ta'malun* allows for both translations but the context is clearly against al-Ash'arī's interpretation. Tāhir b. Al 'Āshūr in his *al Tahrīr wa'l Tanwīr* states that the reasoning used by the Ash'arī's to adduce from this verse the basis for the God creating the acts of mankind is weak because the verse allows for both grammatical possibilities – connective (*ma mauṣūla*) or infinitive (*ma maṣdarīya*). ʿĀshūr argues that the connective (*ma mauṣūla*) outweighs the infinitive *ma maṣdarīya* because: "and that God has created them is apparent in meaning, and it is meant *wa ma tʾamalūn* that God has created the material i.e., the stone or wood, from which you construct your idols. And this is because it is brought together in this verse reference of creation to God and the reference of their work (*ʿaml*) to their action (*fʾil*)".[74]

Fazlur Rahman avers that the vibrant message of the Qurʾan, inviting human beings to action, ended up three centuries later in the hands of the intellectual formulators of the creed of the mainstream of the Muslim community. This divergent view introduced a new temper into the community. Nevertheless, they were quite compatible with the bases of the law and were not necessarily injurious to moral action, since they represented pre-determinism only in a general sense and were not action-specific. But with Ashʿarism a totally new era of belief dawned upon Muslims. From then on, they could not act in reality; human action indeed became a mere metaphor, devoid of any real meaning. Al-Ashʿarī explicitly stated that even a waking person cannot speak in reality. This is certainly in stark contradiction to the very assumptions of law that humans can choose and act freely, and therefore are responsible. It is true that this particular Ashʿarī doctrine of human action is in the nature of a formula and, as such, has little direct bearing on real life. These formulas after a long period of time fail to affect the level of human activity, human initiative, and above all the frontiers of human imagination upon which these formulas must have a deadening effect.

The Justice of God (al-ʿAdl ul-Īllahīya) & Nature of Divine Law

The Muʾtazila had evolved a theory of rational ethics on the ground that good and bad are known by natural reason without the aid of revelation. The primary or "general" ethical truths about right and wrong are rationally discoverable by intuitive reason, but for actual obligations of "secondary" ethical truths, humanity needs revelation. Humans, by reason alone, cannot determine those acts that must be done or avoided in order to come closer to pursuing a truly ethical life. The Muʾtazila did not hold that determination of actual do's and dont's is possible without the aid of the prophetic revelation. Firstly, they held that general ethical truths are purely rational and universal. Secondly, they believed that the practice of revealed obligations helps us to rise to the cultivation of those universal truths. This also shows why the Muʾtazila did not create a school of law: they did not hold that positive law was possible through pure reason alone.

But al-Ashʾarism responded by insisting that no right or wrong could be known, general or specific, through pure reason. The al-Ashʾarītes held that without revelation, no act could be said to be good or bad. In a natural state the only law was self-interest. And, because human beings will deem all such things that promote their self-interest as bad, therefore God has to declare through revelation, what is good and what is evil. That pure reason yields no obligations or "reason is not a legislator" (*inna l-ʿaql laysa bi-shariʿ*) became the juristic axiom with all Muslim jurists. It is true that the Muʾtazila had given to the revelation only a secondary, though essential, place in their ethical theory. Fazlur Rahman opined that an effective procedure would have been to erect a system of universal ethical values on the basis of an analysis of the moral objectives of the

Qur'an. Instead he argues, the jurists were content to apply their legal principle of analogical reasoning (*qiyās*) quite unsystematically and in an *ad hoc* manner. He recommends that modern Muslim wishing to derive workable Islamic law from the Qur'an would require them making a fresh start by working out a genuine ethical value system from the Qur'an.[75]

But the Ash'arī anti-rationalism culminated in the assertion that God sends down laws through this revelation thanks to the sheer fiat of His will. The implication is that God does not thereby intend the well-being of His creation, as the Mu'tazila had contended. The real motivation of the Ash'arīs, no doubt was to counter the excesses of the Mu'tazilite rationality. In terms of the latter's view of God cannot do injustice and hence He can neither punish the virtuous nor forgive the evildoer. For in that case the distinction between virtue and evil would evaporate. To the Ash'arīs it seemed, and with good reason, that the Mu'tazila rationalism was imposing its own categories upon God who must do this and must not do that.

To this they replied with their own extreme formulation. They claimed that if God sent all virtuous persons to Hell and all evil persons to the Garden all this would be perfect justice because He owed nothing to anything. He is not under the will or command of anyone else. So contravening these commands on His part cannot be deemed to be wrong or a violation of the law. On the contrary, being the sole and absolute owner of His creatures, none of which had any claim to be created, He can do with them anything that He likes. And whatever he likes to do with them would be justice. Therefore, to search for ends and purposes in His laws is not only meaningless, but also grave disobedience to Him. This doctrine, of course is purely theological.

The general spiritual and intellectual atmosphere created by the orthodoxy and infinitely strengthened by al-Ash'arīsm effectively militated, through long centuries, against the development of a new comprehensive and systematic attempt to interpret the Qur'an into a really meaningful ethical and legal system. Ash'arīsm which succeeded only slowly in gaining general acceptance – thanks mainly to influence of certain outstanding men such as al-Ghazālī (d.505/1111) – held sway mainly in the Middle East. In the East, in Central Asia, and the Indian Subcontinent, the theology of Abū Mansūr al-Māturīdī was predominant in these regions. Al Māturīdī, on some crucial points, was close to the Mu'tazila and stands generally between the Mu'tazila and Ash'arītes. Thus, on free will (*qadar*), he held that humanity was not devoid of power, as al-Ash'arī declared. Before the act, a human being has a certain power, which includes the physical power with which he or she is endowed. But at the time of the actual act this natural power is consummated by another power, so that the act necessarily and immediately follows. The second power is created by God in the agent at the time of the action, as al-Ash'arī held. He also held the Mu'tazila view that right and wrong are natural realities and are discoverable by natural human reason, although he believed that revelation gives further moral strength to the agent to pursue good and avoid evil. He also affirmed that divine commands have purposes that are for the good of humankind. Although to an extent these views did remain alive among the Hanafī school of law, the spread of al-Ash'arīsm through the teaching of towering personalities such as al-Ghazālī and others to a large extent dampened the influence of Māturīdīsm. The affects of the Ash'arī creed on Sufism subsequently obliterated human will and efficacy entirely.

Post-Formative Stage in *Kalām*

Hasan al-Shaf'i states that *kalām* in its later stage was influenced by *falsafa* which began in the sixth century upto present times. From the 6th century to the 9th century Hijri he denotes as a period of prosperity (*izdihar*) and maturity (*naduj*) and describes this stage as follows:

1. *Kalām* underwent an evolution in its themes, methodology, classification of its topics, terminologies and was denoted as post-formative theology (*kalām al-muta'khirin*)[76] in distinction to its formative period (*kalām al-mutaqadimin*)

2. Substance: The addition of Muslim philosophers views on philosophical theology (*Illahiyat*) and natural theology (*Tabi'yat*) in order to refute them. This necessitated in the need for the complete development of metaphysics specific for *kalām* to present the Islamic perspective. The pioneers of this period were al-Razī, al-Amidi and Nasir al-Din al-Tusi. Ibn Taymīya is the strongest voice in this period that opposed this development.

3. Methodology: The introduction of Greek Logic to formative *kalām* which they had appropriated from the *fuqaha* and *usulis'*. Ibn Hazm, al-Juwayni and al-Ghazālī were instrumental in introducing it to *kalām*. It was opposed by Ibn Taymīya, Ibn Wazir al-Zaydi and al-Suyuti.

4. Classification of topics: Post-formative *mutakallim* organized their treatises in a different manner than formative *kalām*. Thus, the treatises would begin with

'general issues' (*al-Umūr al-'Āmma*) – which comprised of the traditional topics of *kalām* followed by topics related to metaphysics.

5. Terminology: Due to the introduction of philosophical and logical terms into *kalām* new terminologies were introduced specific to the post-formative *kalām*.

The impact of *falsafa* upon the traditional *kalām* schools resulted in:

1. Decline of the Mu'tazili school however the methodology of the Mu'tazili theologians found its place in Ash'arī and Shi'i *kalām*

2. The relocation of the Maturidis from Samarqand to Khurasan, Sub-continent and Asia Minor. The Hanafis' in general adopted the Maturidi *kalām* and wrote extensively in it.

3. The Ash'arīs influence was predominant over the Arab and Persian Muslim world. Fazlur Rahman argues that during the medieval period the Sunni orthodoxy – Ash'arīsm collided with the 12th century philosophical schools who erected their thought system on Greek philosophy that nevertheless made serious efforts to accommodate Islamic orthodoxy, the former crushed the latter by its sheer weight. Subsequently, philosophy took refuge and developed in a Shi'i intellectual-spiritual milieu or was transformed into intellectual Sufism. Despite the inner weaknesses of the orthodox system itself – particularly the Ash'arīte theology, which, in its cardinal tenets of the 'inefficacy of the human will' and 'purposelessness of the divine law', was in conflict with

the Qur'an – it was not difficult for an al-Ghazālī or an Ibn Taymīya to locate the inner discrepancies in an Ibn Sīna metaphysics or an Ibn 'Arabī theosophy. Resulting in a truncated Islamic intellectualism – non systematic, non-unified Qur'an approach.

4. The Ash'arī school dominated the Sunni religious institutions and politically the ruling classes belonged to. During the medieval period Muslim society, changes but they were not orderly or controlled. Law and theology formed the central part of the medieval higher educational system of Islam imparted in the *madaris*. The bare bones of Sunni theology as formulated by al-Ash'arī and his followers were further elaborated into systems by Fakhr al-Din al-Razi (d. 1209), al-Iji (d. 1355) and others by incorporating certain philosophical themes like: (1) Essence and existence; (2) Causation; (3) Nature of God's attributes. The Muslim *mutakallimun* developed counter-theses of *kalām* against and in place of Muslim philosophical doctrines advocated by the *falasifa* like Ibn Sīna. Similarly, the historically less important, although more reasonable theses of the Sunni *kalām* system founded by al-Maturidi were elaborated further by writers like al-Nasafī (d. 1310) and his commentator al-Taftazani (d. 1389).[77]

5. Once the *madaris* were organized, it was these legal and theological systems that were administered to students. Early on a distinction surfaced between the universal (*kullī*) and "particular" (*juz'ī*), sciences.[78] By the theoretical and practical sciences was generally meant theology (also called *'ilm al-tawhīd* – science of the unity

of God – or *uṣūl al-dīn* – principles of faith – or, later on, *ilāhiyat* – the science of theology on the one hand, and law (called *fiqh*, later Shari‘ah) on the other. The other distinction was between the "religious sciences" (*‘ulūm shar‘īya*) or "traditional sciences" (*‘ulūm naqliya*) and the "rational or secular sciences" (*‘ulūm ‘aqliya* or *ghayr shar‘īya*).

6. The revival and reform movement of Ibn Taymīya left an indelible mark upon Sunni *kalām*. His criticism attempted unsuccessfully in his time but became extremely influential in the subsequent pre-modern and classical modern period in routing the influences of Greek philosophy and removal of the Mu'tazila methodological influence upon the Ash'arīs.

7. Both Sunni and Shi'a treatises began to receive extensive treatments of commentaries and supercommentaries to the extent an "Islamic scholasticism" seems to appear at this stage.[79] Fazlur Rahman states post-formative *kalām* is both in spirit and content scholastic: with all its subtle reasoning, it expressly formulated and, in the very process of this formulation, exhibited a fundamental lack of confidence in human reason.[80]

8. Islamic intellectuallism suffered as the spread of Sufism because of its inimical attitude toward all intellectualism. Influential theologians like al-Ghazālī considered the philosophical works of al-Fārabī and Ibn Sīna harmful and pleaded therefore their scientific works should also be rejected. After the fourteenth century the science of rhetoric (*‘ilm ul balāgha*) took precedence over theology, philosophy and logic. A major development that

adversely affected the quality of learning in the later medieval centuries of Islam was the replacement of the original texts of theology, philosophy, jurisprudence, and such, as materials for higher instruction with commentaries and supercommentaries. The view that the mind is creative in knowledge is essentially a characteristic of modern theories of knowledge.[81]

Hasan al-Shaf'i contends that the influence of this development in *kalām* were overall negative however it did not fail to present new currents of thoughts (*tayyarat*) and trends (*itijahat*) in traditional (*al-salafi*) circles. The overall state of Islamic thought was strong and vibrant.[82] In the second half of the post-formative period of *kalām* can be described as one of laxity, imitation, reproduction and rumination of the past. He characterizes this period of *kalām* as follows:

1. Focus upon commentaries and supercommentaries of *kalām* texts from the 6th to the 9th century.

2. Stability and dominant influence of the Ash'arī and Shi'i twelver school in Egypt, Africa and the Islamic world through the establishment of *madaris*. The Maturidi School dominated over Turkey and the Subcontinent but unlike the Ash'arī school did not establish *madaris*. However, due to the state endorsement of Maturidism it experienced a greater influence than in its formative period.

3. The influence of Ahmad Sirhindī and Shah Wali Ullah introduced new and critical thought upon medieval *kalām*.

4. The introduction of Sufi themes and topics into Ash'arī *kalām*. In Shi'i *falsafa*, Mir Damad and Mulla Sadra introduced *kalām* and Sufi topics and themes into it. According to al-Shafi'i this occurrence was a factor that led to the Muslim world's backwardness and isolation.

5. European colonialism instigated political, economic and cultural subjugation of the Muslim world.

Philosophical Movement and Its Relationship with the *Kalām* Movement

In Islam the development of philosophical thought succeeded earlier schools of dialectical theology (*kalām*) – Mu'tazila and *Ahl ul Sunnah* – that begun to arise in the 2nd/8th cemtury through the action of foreign ideas – particularly Greco-Christian – on certain fundamental moral issues raised within the Islamic community. The legacy of philosophy in Islam has been that it was "sporadic and individual and never took the form of a movement or a tradition expressing itself through established schools of thought."[83] Fazlur Rahman considers that the most fundamental and palpable reason is the fact that the orthodoxy, after the attack upon philosophy by al-Ghazālī, proscribed it completely and did not allow it to grow any further, or rather destroyed the very conditions for its growth. The orthodox treatment of philosophy is strongly reminiscent of their treatment of the doctrines of the Mu'tazila. Just as the Ulama' had founded the science of *kalām* to counter Mu'tazila rationalism, so now they expanded the contents of *kalām* to reckon with the theses of the philosophers. In face of the philosophical theses impinging on religion, the scope of *kalām* was further enlarged to include formal treatments of those theses

– such as prophethood, resurrection of the bodies, creation etc. Henceforward the doctrine of atomism in physics became a part and parcel of Muslim *kalām* since it was thought that atomism does not require causation and hence allowed for the direct Finger of God to interfere in every event.[84]

Philosophy when attacked by the orthodox Ulama' went underground and, so far as much of its content was concerned, it found a spacious home within theosophic Sufism. Since the 12th century, the best and most creative minds of Islam drifted away from the orthodox system of education to Sufism. The Ulama' were left with little more than dry bones, the real currents of life having escaped their system and taken their own way – far more dangerous than that of the Mu'tazilites or the philosophers. But within the religious system, which came to constitute both the entire scope and the sole preserve of the *madrasas*, there remained curious fundamental inconsistencies both among the Sunnis and the Shi'a – inconsistencies which Fazlur Rahman believed could have been removed only by further growth through a critical and constructive free thought.

Fazlur Rahman identifies six doctrines that characteristically shape the post-formative period of *kalām* which he refers to as systematic theology as well: (1) uncompromising transcendalist picture (*tanzīh*); (2) denial of trust in natural properties; (3) denial of immanent processes of nature; (4) denial of freedom of human will; (5) Omnipotence of God; (6) absence of an Islamic moral philosophy; (7) lack of confidence in human reason; and (8) religious consciousness (*wujdan*). He contends that modern scholars of Islam have found that these doctrines were fundamentally against the Qur'an and the prophetic model. He considers that the post-formative *mutakalimin* offered a real service to Islam with its: (1) doctrine of being; and (2) theory of knowledge. The worldview that develops on the basis of this *kalām* is an overwhelming theistic determinism. The *falasifa* argued for a pure rational determinism whereas Sufism's particular interpretation of the theological doctrine of the Unity of God advocated a monistic determinism. Further Rahman argues that these forces coupled with the political despotism of the time sustained Determinism (*jabariya*) and this is the paradigm which medieval Islamic thought cultivated.[85]

Fazlur Rahman's modern theological thought definitively argued for the freedom of human will. He relied upon Ibn Taymīyah's criticism of the post-formative *mutakallimin* doctrine of determinism and the designating *kalām* as the 'crown of the religious sciences'. Approving of Ibn Taymīya's criticism he argues that *kalām* is supposed to be an intellectual defense of the creed and *fiqh* should be designated as the 'crown of the Shari'ah sciences'. With regards to the doctrine of determinism Ibn Taymīya argues that the obligation of the Shari'ah injunctions become artbitary:

> "one and the same person, when he is a theologian, believes in
> a rigorous determinism and impotency of the human will, but
> when he behaves as a Faqih, either in the capacity of a Qadi or
> a *Mufti* he has to assume freedom and efficacy of the human
> will."[86]

Fazlur Rahman attributes this anomaly that intellectualism was never owned by the religious masses or Ulama' and integrated into the religious system. Indeed, it was spurned under the claim of the self-sufficiency of the Shari'ah sciences, especially of their crown. It is indeed, a curious phenomenon of Muslim religious history that even the Mu'tazila who claimed to derive moral imperatives good and bad (*Husn wa qubh*) directly from reason did not differ in legal matters at all from the rest of the community, although law is no more than application of morals to a society. Fazlur Rahman categorically states that for us, a rational understanding of the Qur'an and the *Sunnah* is the only reliable method for arriving at moral imperatives and legal enactments.[87]

Fazlur Rahman states that the most fundamental fact about the religious thought of the philosophers – especially Ibn Sīna whose doctrines have been historically the most important (because they were for the first time elaborated into a full-fledged system) – is that on all the points where the frontiers of religion (*din*) and rational thought (*falsafa*) met, the two neither reached utterly different results nor yet were they identical but seemed to run parallel to one another. This point occurred on all points along the line where the traditional theology and philosophy faced one another. From this fact of systematic parallelism, the philosophers made the fatal leap and concluded (1) that philosophy and religion were ultimately tackling exactly the same questions, dealing with exactly the same questions, facts and methods (2) that the Prophet (ṣ) was therefore, primarily a philosopher, but (3) that since the Prophet's addresses were not the intellectual elite but the masses who could not understand the philosophic truth, the prophetic revelation naturally catered for their needs and "talked down" to their level in terms intelligible to them. The perilous belief, therefore, became firmly implanted in his mind that religious and philosophical truths are identically the same; only religion, since it is not limited to the few but is for all, necessarily accommodates itself to the level of mass intelligence and is, therefore, a kind of philosophy for the masses and does not tell the naked truth but talks in parables.

Al-Ghazālī's Reformist Synthesis

According to Fazlur Rahman the Islamic philosophical movement from the point of view of its amplification of Islamic doctrine, was an outgrowth of the Mu'tazila *kalām*. Al-Ghazālī (d.505/1111) represented the first great reaction against the rationalist systems of the philosophers, monumental in the depth and durability of its influence. In his early life he became disillusioned with the traditional *kalām* because of its formalism and externality. In his search for truth, he studied philosophy but found it not only far from orthodox Islam in its teachings but above all lacking in certainty in its proofs. In religious convictions he searched for a type of mathematical certainty. This as the balance of religious forces in the structure of Islam stood at that time, he found only in Sufism.[88]

Fazlur Rahman argues that Muslim theologians and jurists, beginning with al-Ghazālī, generally asserted that since Islamic theology is a science that elaborates and defends the metaphysical assumptions of law, it is therefore, the "highest" and the "noblest" of religious sciences and since religious sciences have an absolute primacy over other branches of knowledge, theology becomes the crown of all knowledge.[89] Fazlur Rahman states that the first time the relationship between theology and law is made by al-Ghazālī who distinguished knowledge into two categories (1) religious sciences (*al-'ulūm al-dīnīya*) (2) purely rational sciences (*al-'ulūm al-'aqlīya*) is in his *al-Mustaṣfā*. Al-Ghazālī characterizes theology as the most general and the highest of the religious sciences. He terms the rest of religious sciences like *fiqh*, *hadīth*, *tafsīr*, and the like, "particular sciences". These sciences are made possible only by the prior science of *kalām* which establishes the theoretical foundations of the religion like God's existence, His attributes, the world as creation of God, and prophethood. Once the *mutakallim* has done this, his task is completed and the sphere of the activity of pure reason in the religious field ends. Thus, *kalām* evolved into a metaphysical science in the time of al-Ghazālī.

Fazlur Rahman argues that this post-formative *kalām* had distinguished itself from *fiqh* entirely in content, method and principles. He agrees with Ibn Taymīya's evaluation of 'post-formative development in *kalām*' (*kalām muḥdath*) as being distinct from the principles of Shari'ah themselves which are based on traditional authority just as is the detailed content of the Shari'ah; the principles of theology, are squarely based on reason. According to Fazlur Rahman he considered this to be a dislocation from the Qur'an and prophetic model. This resulted in a transformation of the Islamic teachings for al-Ash'arī the net legacy of the Qur'an therefore, is to resolve theological matters rationally and not traditionally. It is here where Fazlur Rahman demands that the essence of the Qur'an which is its ethics and is also the link between *fiqh* and *kalām* be formulated in modern times.[90]

Al-Ghazālī finally adopted a position from the philosophers' point of view, which was in harmony with the Sufi ethics, that man is soul alone to the exclusion of the body.[91] Al-Ghazālī in Fazlur Rahman's opinion affirmed an agnosticism about the ultimate and absolute nature of God and maintained that He was knowable only in so far as He was related to and revealed Himself to man. This revealed and relational nature of God is constituted by the Divine Names and Attributes. Mysticism reveals these to man in their true nature. He, therefore, rejected the extreme Sufi claims of absorption, union and incarnation. He was in pursuit not of religious aesthetics and artistry but of religious morality. The religious certainty he sought did not consist of security, safety and calm repose, but of moral purification and the war against vice that degraded man. Thus it was that he came to substitute for the 'Prime Mover' of the philosophers and the 'Essence of Essences' of the Sufis, the ultimate 'Commander' of the Qur'an. The *kalām* formulates that command: mysticism reveals it to man in a way that his whole being is transformed into its receptacle and organ. And although there may be found unconcealed contradictions in al-Ghazālī's intellectual aspect, the spiritual integrity and organic unity of his personality is beyond a shadow of doubt.[92] The synthesis thus achieved by al-Ghazālī between Sufism and *kalām* was largely adopted by orthodoxy and confirmed by *Ijmā'*. Its strength lay in the fact that it gave a spiritual basis for the moral practical *élan* of Islam and thus brought it back to its original religious dimensions. But the balance was delicate and could be maintained only within the limits of a strictly moral ethos. Within orthodoxy, there were two groups which did not adopt al-Ghazālī's synthesis: one the *Ahl ul Hadith* and the other more rationalist *mutakallimun*.[93]

A century after al-Ghazālī's *kalām* was used in a new direction with a purpose wholly alien to *vis-à-vis* Sufism developed itself into a speculative system which turned the moral doctrine of the Unity and Omnipotence of God of the *kalām* into a monistic pantheism of mystic philosophy on the basis of the philosophical doctrine of emanation. In this theory, the scholastic Ghazālīan names of God are transformed into a network of hierarchal manifestations or epiphanies of the Divine Essence through which the mystic progressed to be united with the Being of God.[94] Ibn 'Arabī, Mir Damad and Sadr ul-Din al-

Shirazi incorporated into their *falsafa*, the former in his theosophy and the latter in their *Irfan*.

The main stream of *kalām* however, could not reject reason in favor either of pure mysticism as al-Ghazālī had done, or of simple traditionalism like the majority of the *Ahl ul Hadith*. The rationalist challenge, whose first phase began with the Mu'tazila became far more systematic and formidable with the advent of the philosophical movement, and left a permanent legacy. Therefore, Islamic dogma had to be restated equally systematically and with a corresponding vigor with the same logic as the philosophers had used.[95] The greatest and most incisive formulator of the new systematic theology is Fakhr al-Din al-Razi (d.606/1209). Later, the results of this systematic theology were set forth by al-Iji (d. 756/1355) in a work entitled *al-Mawaqif* which attracted commentators for several centuries.[96]

All the relevant philosophical disciplines were studied and elaborated by the new systematic theology known as *Illahiyat*. Greek logic, especially its theory of knowledge, was assiduously cultivated. This together with physics (theories of nature) and metaphysics formed the basis of theology. In each of these fields, the theories of the philosophers were elaborated, modified or rejected according to what was seen as implicit in the dogma. In the theory of knowledge, cognition was declared to be non-essential, external relation between the knowing mind and the known object. This was the Islamic answer to the philosophical epistemology which, at the level of pure cognition, declared the identity of the subject and the object in the act of cognition and which, despite the efforts of Ibn Sīna to safeguard it against any pantheistic suggestion, or incarnationism, was, nevertheless, being manipulated by many Sufi theorists in terms of a final identity between God and man.

In the field of natural philosophy (*tabi'yat*), controversies continued between the atomism of the *kalām* and the Aristotelian philosophical theory of matter and form, which was the basis of the philosophers' theory of causation. The *mutakallimun* rejected the Aristotelian doctrine of matter and form as a prerequisite for rejecting natural causation and restated the early Ash'arīte atomism with fresh arguments until affirmation of atomism and denial of natural causation came to be looked upon as almost a cardinal religious dogma regarded as a necessary step to prove the temporal creation of the world and the Islamic eschatology.

Fazlur Rahman's conceptualization of *kalām* was that it was an intellectual artifice whereby theologians defended the fundamentals of the faith against objections, innovations, and intellectual doubts. *Kalām* did not and could not establish faith; it presupposed the truth of faith and defended it, with disputation (*jadal*) as its weapon and method. Secondly, al-Ghazālī had attained belief in God, prophethood and the Last Day without the *kalām* propositions had they caused him to attain belief, he would not need to resign from his post at the Niẓāmiyyah. Fazlur Rahman acceptance of Ibn Taymīya is whole sale, and accepts his criticism of al-Ghazālī that his faith was an "undifferentiated faith" (*īmān mujmal*).[97]

Fazlur Rahman argues that al-Ghazālī was seeking a correct and effective method of realizing and appropriating the truth in a new and deeper way. At the intellectual and spiritual level, it helped him realize and reappropriate the ultimate religious truths with a new depth and meaningfulness. He rejected theology and philosophy not in content but in the method that they employed – dialectical and logical rationality. In fact, he re-appropriated basic *kalām* propositions through mystical experience. Al-Ghazālī retained much of a philosophical-speculative outlook through Sufism, particularly through Ibn Sīna's philosophy. Sufism reinvigorated al-Ghazālī's Ash'arism. Ash'arism had taught that human beings could not be said to act in a real sense, but only in a metaphysical sense, since God was the real 'actor'. Sufism proclaimed that only God exists. Both Ash'arism and Sufism taught passivity *vis-á-vis* God, since both subscribed to inanity of natural and human voluntary causations. Further the wedding between Sufism and Ash'arī *kalām* makes al-Ghazālī proclaim that, "indeed, there is nothing in existence except God and His acts, for whatever is there besides Him in His act". In fact, Ash'arism, just like Sufism, had rendered God a concentrate of power and will, just as the Mu'tazila had made Him a concentrate of justice and rationality. However, Sufism also brought to the fore the element of universal divine mercy, which the Mu'tazila practically denied and the Ash'arī's ignored. Al-Ghazālī's Sufism thus enabled him to supplement his Ash'arism in an important way.[98]

Al-Ghazālī's works can be divided into three categories. The first period he devoted to the teaching and writing on traditional *kalām* and *fiqh*. In the middle period, he was devoted to Sufism and regarded the "science of the hereafter" as being the truly religious science and possessing absolute value, while he assigned an instrumental value to *fiqh*, sometimes even condemning it as "a science concerned only with this world." He criticized the *fuqaha* as corrupt men of this world. He wrote a separate work, *Iljām al-'Awām min 'Ilm al-Kalām* where he characterized the *mutakallimūn* as immature children to whom spiritual truths must never be divulged. Positively, he wrote

'Moderation in Creed' (*al-Iqtiṣād fī 'l-I'tiqād*), where he strongly advised avoidance of the extravagances of the *kalām* but where he inserted basic *kalām* formulas as true creed but as interpreted through a very moderate Sufism. But it is in his *Jawāhir al-Qur'an* (Gems of the Qur'an) that he makes repeated and highly interesting attempts to give a religious evaluation of *kalām* and *fiqh*. He says that the importance of *fiqh* stems from the need of society for law. *Kalām* is needed to combat those who innovate and sow doubts in the minds of others. Al-Ghazālī contended that he jurists are to be regarded as the builders of hospices and other facilities on the way to Makkah for the sake of pilgrimage, while the position of the theologians (*mutakallimūn*) is like that of the guides to the pilgrimage and guardians along the way.

This parallelism was confirmed on many other theological points as well, for example the doctrine of the physical resurrection of the Day of Reckoning. The philosophers rejected the physical resurrection but firmly believed in the survival of the soul and therefore in a spiritual hereafter with its psychic pleasures and pains. Ibn Sīna having confirmed the afterlife concluded that religion had to affirm physical resurrection because it was aimed at the masses of "dullards". Fazlur Rahman felt that philosophers were consciously engaged in their approach to religion. Al-Ghazālī failed to present sufficient focus upon this religion (*din*)-philosophy (*falsafa*) parallelism and instead focused upon the philosophical doctrine of the eternity of the world. After al-Ghazālī's attack on philosophy, it went underground and returned in the form of theosophic intuitionism.[99]

Fazlur Rahman considered that the rigid psuedo-philosophic body of knowledge that constituted *kalām* constricted intellectual activity and expression. The orthodoxy that placed *kalām* as the crown of the sciences had thus placed a body of knowledge that represented its creed which was victim to inner inconsistencies, extreme tendencies and failure to portray the doctrines of the Qur'an and *Sunnah* correctly. The formulation of *kalām* doctrines during the fourth century – at the hands of al-Ash'arī and al-Maturidi – crystallized the orthodox point of view thanks to the *Ahl ul Hadith* who had projected back views to the Prophet (ṣ). As a result, this development, remarkable for the cohesion of its internal structure, resulted in creating a sense of equilibrium and balance that is probably unique in the history of mankind in its gigantic dimensions. It was this fact that was responsible for the sudden flowering of the brilliant Muslim civilization.

Fazlur Rahman states that the basis on which this equilibrium had been built did not allow further growth and development. His emphasis upon social change did not take a one-sided tendency towards change but conservatism as well. However, the state of affairs brought about by the *mutakallimun* stifled pure thought, rationalism and scientific thought which constitute the elements of change itself and instated conservatism.

Later Medieval Reform – Ibn Taymīya and Ahmad Sirhindī

In contradistinction to al-Ghazālī's personalism Fazlur Rahman's finds in Ibn Taymīya a form of Islamic positivism.[100] His was a concern with the two central disciplines of the Shari'ah tradition in the form of theology and law, as well as the community that is the bearer of this kerygmatic tradition and a serious attempt to reform that tradition. He notes that while al-Ghazālī's influence was almost immediate, Ibn Taymīya message lay dormant through the centuries. And even when it was "discovered" by Muhammad b. 'Abdul Wahhāb and his followers in the eighteenth century Arabian peninsula, it was miserably truncated. The Wahhābī version totally lost the vision of an integrally reconstituted Muslim community, which was at the center of Ibn Taymīya's entire endeavor, even though, in its own right, it became seminally influential in modern Islam. Fazlur Rahman's thought can be said to be strongly influenced by Ibn Taymīya however Fazlur Rahman severely criticized his political thought because of its strong *irjā'ist* elements in his thought.

Ibn Taymīya's aim was to rediscover and intellectually reconstitute the early normative community of Islam which was based on the teaching of the Qur'an and the *Sunnah* as he saw it. He did find fault with members of the early normative community. After the fourth century, Islamic developments in all fields – *fiqh*, *kalām*, sufism and politics – began running riot and became increasingly uncontrolled. Ibn Taymīya terms these "*neo-fiqh*", "*neo-kalām*", "*neo-Sufism*" and "*neo-politics*" and declares them to have become chaotic and irresponsible.[101] The state of chaos, innovation, and radical change within Islam was due the weakening of the caliphal center and the ascendancy of the Buyīds over Baghdad. This resulted in the loss of Islamic frontier lands in northern Syria and elsewhere accompanied by the spread of the Qarmatians and Bātinites. Hence Ibn Taymīya insisted strongly on the unity and solidarity of the community, in fact, the *jamā'a-Sunnah* (community-tradition) equation is the exact reverse of the *bid'a-firqa* (innovation-sectarian) equation.[102] He reversed the position of al-Ghazālī, who had regarded *kalām* as superior to *fiqh*, and denounced the former as a sheer distortion of Islam. Thus, according to Ibn Taymīya *kalām* particularly as pursued as later theologians (*mutakallimun*) after the third century of Islam, has absolutely no basis in the Qur'an and the *Sunnah*.[103]

This opposition between theology, based on reason (*'aql*), and law, based on revealed authority (*Shari'ah*), was first formulated by the Mu'tazila and then inherited and taken over by al-Ash'arī in his work on the defense of theology. Ibn Taymīya approvingly attributed the opposite position to al-Ash'arī. For according to him, al-Ash'arī held the assertion of the dichotomy of reason (the basis of *kalām*) and revelation (the basis of *fiqh*) propounded by the *mutakallimun* was, indeed, false because revelation itself contains reason. Revelation not only invites the exercise of reason, but actually has many rational principles.[104] Ibn Taymīya accused them of robbing the laws and commandments of God of all certainty and claiming it for their own pseudo-science. They assert in matters of theology "only one of several alternative opinions can be right. As for the science concerning details [of the law – *al-furū'*] everyone who asserts himself to find an answer in a given case is correct (*kullu mujtahidin muṣīb*)."[105] Finally, that there is certainly far greater agreement and certitude in law than there is in dialectical theology.[106]

Ibn Taymīya's opposition to and disdain for traditional *kalām* was relentless. He not only regarded it as worse than degraded *fiqh* but as a singularly unfortunate development in Islam. Ibn Taymīya in his criticism of al-Ghazālī's opting for Sufism, opined that he should have taken the path of the Qur'an and the *Sunnah* of the Prophet (ṣ). One of the main charges brought by Ibn Taymīya against mainstream Sunni *kalām*, Ash'arīsm, was that it declared humankind to be impotent in the interest of "saving" God's omnipotence and absoluteness. He held that any law worthy of the name requires that when an accused is brought before a judge, he/she is assumed to have the power to act, and it is for this reason that human beings are regarded as responsible. Ibn Taymīya not only denounced *kalām* – "the science of the principles of the faith" (*'ilm uṣūl al-dīn*) – but also assailed the "science of the principles of law" (*'ilm uṣūl al-fiqh*).

Fazlur Rahman describes Ibn Taymīya's methodology and approach to understanding Islam up until his time as well as his reformist orientation – as being *Irjā'ist* and synthetic. In fact, the middle of the road is a syntheses of various and, indeed, divergent developments within Islam. None of these developments are without a genuine basis in the Qur'an and the *Sunnah* of the Prophet (ṣ). And yet all have erred in varying degrees once they abandoned the Qur'an-*Sunnah* anchoring point and became undisciplined by becoming a law unto themselves. Ibn Taymīya genuinely accepted all of them in their early stages when they were close to the Qur'an. But he condemned them, particularly *kalām* and Sufism, in their later development. His denunciation of later *kalām* is harsher, than that of Sufism. *Fiqh*, despite its vagaries is the most reformable since it is tied to action.

Ibn Taymīya posited that theological questions based on transmitted reports (*khabar*) [i.e. Qur'an and *Sunnah*] can be treated as practical questions of law, even thought the fore are called "questions of principles" (*masā'īl uṣūl*), while the latter are called "questions of details" (*masā'īl furū'*). These are terms invented by certain jurists and dialectical theologians. These terms are particularly associated with the dialectical theologians (*uṣūliyyūn*), especially when they discuss questions [that involve a judgment] of right and wrong. The truth of the matter is that between theology (*uṣūl*) and law (*furū'*), the basic issues are "questions of principles" (*maṣa'il uṣūl*), while derivative ones are "questions of detail" (*masā'īl furū'*).

Ahmad Sirhindī – Renovator of the Second Millenium

Fazlur Rahman evaluates the significance of Ahmad Sirhindī's criticism upon Ash'arī theology and identifies that he focused upon his doctrine of determinism (*jabr*).[107] He states that Sirhindī's creative act of God brings into existence the entire diversity of the universe. The creative command has no diversity of relationships, although, again, from the human point of view, every new thing or event must appear to demand a fresh relationship. But in reality, the multiplicity of the world is not the act of God as such but effects of His eternal act. Sirhindī criticizes that Ash'arī failed to understand the matter when he described the creative activity of God as something originated (*hadith*) and thus relegated creativity from the realm of the eternal attributes of God to the realm of contingency and change.

Fazlur Rahman contends that Sirhindī addresses the relationship of God's act and human action and according to him is 'vital for the moral outlook of Islam'. Sirhindī critiques the essential point in the Sunni creed on the question *viz.*, that every human voluntary human act must be construed that it should be attributable morally to man and ontologically to God. According to his formulation of the solution, the human will has no direct efficacy with regard to the act; it is God who produces the act entirely – although He does so after man has willed the act and not before it. Sirhindī goes on to argue that despite Ash'arī's insistence that the attribution of the act to the human agent is real, nevertheless, his denial of the efficacy of human will in the production of the act is really a doctrine of moderate determinism (*al-jabr al-mutaswassit*).

Sirhindī addresses God's act as the efficacy of Divine Power and Decree (*Qada*) and man's volitional efficacy are collaborative. Fazlur Rahman identifies the importance of this doctrine as providing meaning and content to the orthodox formula and a basis for Muslim ethical thought.[108] Sirhindī states that the Sunni's believe in the Divine decree and say that all good and evil, sweet and bitter is by Divine Determination (*qadr*). For Determination (*qadr*) means production and bringing into existence and it is obvious that the producer and originator of everything is God. The Mu'tazilites and Qadarites reject this doctrine and advocate the full efficacy of human will; Sirhindī, on the other hand, argues the Divine Decree does not take away the power and choice of man. He has decreed that it shall be up to man to choose to act or not to act (in a certain way). In brief, God's decree itself is the cause of human free choice; it has brought about the power of choice in man (*muhaqqiq al-Ikhtiyar*) rather than removed it.

Fazlur Rahman concludes that Ash'arī formulation renders God a 'puppet master', in reality God has provided for man the world stage to act freely therein. This seems to coincide with God designating man as the (vicegerent of God) *khalifat-ullah*. He states that God and man are not two actors coordinate with one another nor is the divine power a co-runner with man on the course of world history. This evidently contributes to Fazlur Rahman's historical method which removes the attribution of historical events to God. Its acceptance reforms and modernizes the traditional concept of history and essentially brings to light the focus of modern historical methods used in Oriental scholarship. Further this elicits the modern approach Islamic scholarship should appropriate. He states that the divine power provides the conditions for free human activity; its collaboration with man is in the sense that it behaves like a matrix, a conditioning, maturing, formative agency for the human will, purpose and endeavor. He contends that it is up to man to recognize this situation. In this sense God's power is the supreme power, the condition is indespensible and essential of man and in this manner everything that man does is attributable to him. He argues to regard God as Man annulling man and substituting Himself for the human race is ethically the most dangerous misreading of reality. It seems that the influence of Ibn Taymīya and Abdul Wahhab's upon associating partners with God (*shirk*) is subconsciously operative in Fazlur Rahman's interpretation of Sirhindī. Also, his emphasis upon Divine Power (*qadr*) does not emphasize or distinguish with the Divine Decree (*Qada'*). He seems to combine the two and not separate the two. The implication of not treating Divine Power and Divine Decree as mutually exclusive terms is that the Divine Will is restricted and rendered inoperative. Further, by interpreting the Divine Decree under the rubric of *Sunnat ullah fi al-Kawn* God's decree becomes determinable through scientific research and analysis. This interpretation (*ta'wīl*) renders the doctrine of Divine Providence (*al-'Inayat ul-Illahiya*).

Classical Modernism

In the 18th century the Muslim world became firmly aware of their failing and deteriorating conditions under the European colonial and imperial rule which led to various movements calling for regenerating Muslim society. The leaders of these movements believed that a return to pure Islam, removal of un-

Islamic accretions (*bid'at*) and an emphasis on *Ijtihād* was the necessary approach required to be undertaken. Fazlur Rahman considered that the most influential and significant reform movement during this period was the Wahhabi movement which he labels had achieved the status of 'good orthodoxy'. He criticizes the policy of these movements that believe if the Muslims were to follow, i.e. repeat and reproduce exactly what their 7th century forefathers did, they would recover their rightful position with God, i.e., both in this world and the next. He asserted that this simple return to the Qur'an and the *Sunnah* was unsound as it would constitute to him a return to the graves – moreover, he advocated a true understanding of them that would give beneficial guidance today.[109]

Fazlur Rahman opines that there have been two basic approaches to modern knowledge by modern Muslim theorists: (1) Puritanical traditionalism[110]: that the acquisition of modern knowledge be limited to the practical technological sphere, since at the level of pure thought Muslims do not need Western intellectual products. Indeed, that these should be avoided, since they might create doubt (*shubuhat*) and disruption in the Muslim mind, for which the traditional Islamic system of belief already provides satisfactory answers to ultimate questions of world view; and (2) Modernism: that Muslims without fear can and ought to acquire not only Western technology but also its intellectualism, since no type of knowledge can be harmful, and that in any case science and pure thought were assiduously cultivated by Muslims in the early medieval centuries.[111] Fazlur Rahman contends that the former attitude will lead to a dualism and will eventually result in a 'secularist' state of mind, that is, a duality of loyalty to religion and to 'worldly affairs'.

In the latter half of the nineteenth century four prominent Muslim modernists formulated and expounded a positive attitude of Islam toward science and an unhampered investigation of nature Sayyid Ahmad Khan and Sayyid Amir 'Ali of India, Jamal al-Dīn al-Afghanī and Shaykh Muhammad 'Abduh. Amir 'Ali was the youngest of these; among the rest, it is difficult to say who was the earliest. All these men, who were contemporaries, enthusiastically preached the cultivation of science and appropriation of the scientific spirit of the West. The integral constituents of their reasoning are (1) that the flowering of science and the scientific spirit from the 9th to the 13th century among Muslims resulted from the fulfillment of the insistent Qur'anic requirement that man study the universe the handiwork of God, which has been created for his benefit; (2) that in the later medieval centuries the spirit of inquiry had severely declined in the Muslim world and hence Muslim society had stagnated and deteriorated; (3) that the West had cultivated scientific studies that it had borrowed largely from Muslims and hence had prospered, even colonizing the Muslim countries themselves; and (4) that therefore Muslims, in learning science afresh from the developed West, would be both recovering their past and refulfilling the neglected commandments of the Qur'an.

Aziz Ahmad opines that Ahmad Khan had introduced a modern apologetic approach in the second phase of his writings.[112] In this phase, he responded to the works of Christian missionaries and British civil servant historians' aggressive approach to Islam *viz.*, Sir William Muir and Sir William Hunter.[113] Muir's work deeply affected Sir Sayyid because his judgment was based on Islamic civilization, regarding it as contrary to human values as generally accepted by liberal thought in Britain. He initiated the genre of modernist "apologetic" by sponsoring Davenport's "*An Apology for Muhammad and the Qur'an*" and in his own *Khutbat-i-Ahmadiyya*. Chiefly Sir Sayyid was interested in defending traditional Islam, through pioneering polemics. Similarly, Afghani wrote an answer in the *Journal des Débats* to a lecture on Islam and Science by Ernest Renan.[114] Aziz Ahmed contends that both Afghani and Khan agreed on one point: both believed Islam to be capable of an evolutionary process within the present and future history of mankind and in accord with it. The difference between them is that Khan was interested in the concrete, the particular and the detailed; while his adversary was concerned with the general, the generalized and the emotionally surcharged abstract.[115] Wilfred Cantwell Smith argues that Amir Ali is closer to Afghani in intent, quality and influence than Khan.[116] They both endorsed the Tunisian Khayr al-Din Pasha's assertion that Western influences could be addressed by encouraging freedom of expression amongst Muslims. He believed that by promoting freedom of expression would revolutionize the ideas and minds of Muslim peoples. Both Afghani and Khan promoted *Ijtihād* and urged the Ulama' to abandon *Taqlid* which they failed to achieve. It is to this task *viz., Ijtihād* that Khan committed himself to this intellectual project named *Jadid 'ilm ul-Kalām* – which was to adjust Western knowledge with the basic values of Islam, otherwise it would threaten to produce an uprooted generation. Khan in his lectures argues that the scholastic method which the Mu'tazilites and the earlier *mutakallimun* had used for defence against and compromise with the Greek thought was no longer valid for creating a *modus vivendi* (an agreement to disagree) with the empiricism of the modern physical sciences. According to Khan a modern *'ilm al-Kalām* is necessary by which we may either demonstrate the principles of modern sciences to be erroneous or else show that the principles of Islam are not opposed to them.[117]

Khan employed the service of two mediums to fulfill this intellectual project: (1) *Tahzib al-Akhlaq* and (2) His naturalist commentary of the Qur'an. Aziz Ahmed argues that in both the entire structure of his argument is based on what he regarded as two basic Qur'anic principles: one of approach, of "speaking to people according to their powers of comprehension"; the other a scholastic criterion: "Islam is Nature, and Nature is Islam". These two principles served as premises for his modernization project and concluded in Hali listing fifty-two points of divergence from the traditionally accepted Sunni Islam. In his *Al-Tahrir fi usul al-Tafsir* he states his four main theses on which his modern *kalāmi* interpretation of the Qur'an are based: (1) God is true, and His word is true; no science can falsify the truth; it can only illustrate its truthfulness. (2) Between the Word of God and the Work of God there can be no contradiction. (3) The "law of nature" is God's manifest covenant, and His promise of reward or retribution is His verbal covenant; between these two, again there can be no contradiction. Fourth, whether man has been created for religion or religion for man, in either case man must possess something which other animals lack, in order to shoulder the burden of religion; this something is reason.[118]

Aziz Ahmad contends that the constructive affect of Khan and Afghani's struggle was a common objective: the revitalisation of Islam by reorientation of the study of the Qur'an and Hadith, Afghani did not attempt to formulate a modern *'ilm al-Kalām*. He pointed out the necessity of a new approach to the consensus of the Ulama'; and his *protegé* Muhammad 'Abduh showed more caution and greater respect for the consensus than Khan. Afghani attached no importance to such questions as the real substance of angels or the validity of miracles. Afghani's path intersected with Khan's not in the latter's complex project of modern *'ilm al-Kalām* but in political Islam.[119]

Fazlur Rahman criticizes the implications of Muhammad 'Abduh and Khan's acceptance of modern science, promotion of reason (*'aql*) and freedom of expression (*Ijtihād*) upon the traditional *weltanschauung* and realm of faith. He argues that for Muhammad 'Abduh, although the medieval Muslim cosmology and world view can be challenged by science, faith as such cannot; for faith, by its very nature, cannot be touched by science: the two have separate orbits and each must keep within its own. 'Abduh attempts to reintroduce a Mu'tazilite type of rationalism into orthodox Islam and can even defend the medieval Muslim philosophers' rejection of physical resurrection.[120] Sayyid Ahmad Khan established a criterion that the modern scientific spirit or the laws of nature must set the criteria for judging the acceptability of a certain faith. So judged, Islam turns out to be, among the religions of the world, most in conformity with the laws of nature, and of all religious documents the Qur'an is the most rational. Since Muslims have grossly misunderstood and misinterpreted the Qur'anic world view in the past, and since the orthodox Muslim theology is no longer valid, a fresh theology must be created from the Qur'an in the light of modern experience. In attempting this, Sayyid Ahmad Khan utilizes the arguments not only of the Mu'tazila but, indeed patently, those of the Muslim philosophers. Thus, his personal theological stance becomes that of a naturalist deist.[121]Thus, the endorsement and advocacy of a modern interpretation of *kalām* in the light of modern science and

Western knowledge was interpreted differently by Ahmad Khan and Muhammad 'Abduh.

Fazlur Rahman argues that their interest in general in the re-evaluation of the past, both Islamic and local (national), historical and valuation and additional interest were exerted towards modern scientism. He believes that this interest brought modern Muslims an orientation towards to the contemporary West. He contends that the awareness of modern Muslims towards their history and value system coupled with their understanding of the contemporary West engendered a critical attitude towards their local and national traditions.[122] Moreover, their awareness of the affects of Western colonialism upon their idenitities – politically, intellectually, economically and morally – fostered a heightened sensitivity towards nationalism and religion i.e. Islam.[123] Thus, Khan and 'Abduh had developed a reformist ideology of Islam at whose center was the creation of a modern *'ilm al-Kalām* that would be compatible with the *weltanschauung* born of the new 19th century scientism and the Qur'anic teaching at the same time. [124]

In Muhammad 'Abduh's work theology is minimal, although he did much to resurrect Mu'tazila type rationalism; Sayyid Ahmad Khan called desperately for a new *kalām* (theology) consonant with the requirements of the age and felt sure that, unless theology was reformulated afresh, Islam would be in real and grave danger like all other religions. At his instance, Muhammad Shibli wrote two books in Urdu a history of theology in Islam called *'Ilm al-Kalām*, and a systematic theology called *Kalām* wherein he attempted to restate arguments for God's existence, prophethood, revelation, and such, relying heavily, like Sayyid Ahmad Khan himself, upon medieval Muslim philosophers' like Ibn Sīna.

Fazlur Rahman contended that Muhammad Iqbal essayed a new approach to Islamic theology in his *The Reconstruction of Religious Thought in Islam.* He finds that Iqbal was keenly aware of modern Western philosophy, Persian Islamic mysticism but he did not regard him as a scholar of the Islamic theological tradition or of the Qur'an. Iqbal rightly perceived that the basic impulse of the Qur'an was dynamic and action oriented, seeking to direct history, on a spiritual value pattern and attempting to create a world order – two metaphysical principles of *Hazirat al-Quds* and *al-Mala' al-A'la* advocated by Shah Wali Ullah. Fazlur Rahman considered Iqbal's *The Reconstruction of Religious Thought in Islam* as a point of departure for building a new Islamic theology. He believes that Iqbal's work represents an attempt by a Muslim modernist to address the need that Khan identified.

However, Fazlur Rahman criticizes Iqbal's attempt for proffering a universe free from causality. He avers that Iqbal did not carry out any systematic inquiry into the teaching of the Qur'an but resorted to subjective selecticism of verses and traditional material that tallied with his interpretation to suit the contemporary needs of a stagnant Muslim society. He then expressed these theses in terms of such contemporary evolutionary theories as those of Bergson and Whitehead.

Fazlur Rahman argues that he does not disagree with Iqbal's concept of God as the ultimate source of creative energy that can be appropriated by individuals and societies in certain ways-but with his formulation of this concept and the method by which he attempts to deduce it from the Qur'an. Further, he points out that to couch the Qur'anic message in terms of a particular theory, no matter how attractive, sensational, or popular it may seem in fact, the more topical a theory is, the less suitable it is as a vehicle of expression of an eternal message. It cannot be denied that any such interpretation will necessarily be influenced by contemporary modes of thought; this is also required in the sense that only in this way does the message of the Qur'an become relevant to the contemporary situation.[125]

Notes

[1] Fazlur Rahman, *Islam and Modernity*, p.23.

[2] Fazlur Rahman, *Islam and Modernity*, p.25.

[3] Fazlur Rahman, *Islam*, p.3.

[4] Fazlur Rahman, *Revival and Reform in Islam*, p.30.

[5] Fazlur Rahman, *Islam*, p.4.

[6] Fazlur Rahman, *Islam*, p.5.

[7] Fazlur Rahman, *Islamic Thought in the Indo-Pakistan Subcontinent and the Middle East*, Journal of Near Eastern Studies, vol. 32, no.1/2, Jan-Apr 1973, pp.194-211.

[8] Fazlur Rahman, 'The Thinker of Crisis, Shah Waliyullah', Pakistan Quarterly, VI, 2, Karachi, 1956, p.2.

[9] Fazlur Rahman, *Revival and Reform in Islam*, p.30.

[10] *Ibid*, p.138.

[11] Yahya Huwaidi, *Darasat fi 'ilm ul-Kalām wa al-Falsafat ul-Islamiya*, Dar ul-Thaqafa, (Cairo, 1979), pp.95-97.

[12] Ignaz Goldziher, *Introduction to Islamic Theology and Law*, trans. Andras & Ruth Hamori, co-ed., Charles Issawi and Bernard Lewis, (Princeton University Press, New Jersey, 1981), p.76.

[13] Hasan al-Shaf'i, *Madkhal ila darasat 'ilm ul-Kalām*, p.54, See Ali Sami al-Nashshar, *Nash'at al-Fikr al-Islami*, vol.1, p.245.

[14] Muhammad Ali Abu Rayyan, *Tarikh al-Fikr al-Islami*, Dar ul-Marifat ul-Jami'iya, (al-Azarita: Egypt, 2000), pp.221-222.

[15] *Ibid*, p.223.

[16] Fazlur Rahman, *Encyclopedia of Philosophy*, Paul Edwards, vol. 4, 1967.

[17] Fazlur Rahman, *Islam*, p.67.

[18] Fazlur Rahman, *Revival and Reform in Islam*, p.32.

[19] *Ibid*.

[20] Fazlur Rahman, *Islamic Methodology in History*, p.58.

"the fundamental characteristic of the *Ahl ul Sunnah* in its genesis as consisting in an effort to synthesize extremes, to stabilize and stick to the middle path."

[21] Fazlur Rahman, *Islamic Methodology in History*, p. 60.

[22] Abu Rayyan states that opponents of the Mu'tazila had been labeled by the *jabariya* as the *qadariya* in order that the Hadith"the *Qadariya* are the Magians of this community". The Mu'tazila bitterly opposed the *jabariya's* attempts at defamation. See *Tarikh fikr al-Islami*, p.228.

[23] Fazlur Rahman, *Islamic Methodology in History*, p.61.

[24] Abu Rayyan states that the majority of the Muslim heresiographers trace the origin of this school of free-will to be Christian. See *Tarikh al-Fikr al-Islami*, p.231.

[25] Anti-qadarism or *jabariyah* that human acts have been Divine predetermined (*azaliyyan*). See Abu Rayyan, pp. 228-229.

[26] Abu Rayyan supports Fazlur Rahman's interpretation that the Umayyad's supported Jahm bin Safwan and his anti-*qadari* stance for political benefit. See Abu Rayyan, pp. 229-230; Hasan al-Shafi, p. 57.

[27] See Abu'l Wafa al-Taftazani, *'Ilm ul-Kalām wa mushkilatuhu*, Dar ul-Thaqafa, (Cairo), n.d. pp.40-41; Duncan B. Macdonald,

Development of Muslim Theology, Jurisprudence and Constitutional Theory, (Charles Scribner's Sons, New York, 1903), pp.124-125; A. J. Wensnick, *The Muslim Creed: Its Genesis and Development*, (Barnes and Nobles Inc., New York, 1873), pp.53-56.

[28] Al-Shahrastani that from amongst the companions that resorted to political quietism in the Caliphate of 'Uthman to be: 'Abdullah Ibn 'Umar, Sa'ad Ibn Abi Waqqas, Muhammad Ibn Maslamat ul-Ansari, Usama bin Zayd bin Haritha al-Kalbi. He argues that due to their knowledge of the Hadiths about civil wars (*fitan*) they resorted to this theological standpoint. Fazlur Rahman rejects Hadiths about civil wars (*fitan*) due to their specificity. See al-Sharastani, *al-Milal wa-l' Nihal*, vol.1, p.138.

[29] Fazlur Rahman, *Revival and Reform in Islam*, p.49.

[30] Al-Shahrastani, *al-Milal wa'l Nihal*, Dar al-Ma'rifa, (Beirut), pp.582-583.

[31] Abu Rayyan states that the same factors which led to the emergence of *kalām* overall also led to the emergence of the Mu'tazila. He argues that the Mu'tazila developed from the *qadariya* in the Umayyad dynasty as a continuation of the early *qadariya* in the issues of human freedom and Divine attributes. See *Tarikh al-Fikr al-Islami*, p.236.

[32] Abu'l Wafa al-Taftazani states that foreign cultural and religious influences is one of the factors that initiated the *kalām* movement. He argues that Muslims began to learn Greek logic nearing the end of the Umayyad period to combat the Jewish and Christian dialectic against Islam which can be subsumed in five major issues: (1) *Tahrif*: Distortion of revealed texts; (2) *Naskh*: Abrogation; (3) Trinity; (4) Qur'an; (5) Prophethood of Muḥammad (ṣ). *'Ilm ul-Kalām wa b'ad mushkilatihi*, p.22.

[33] A. J. Wensinck, *The Muslim Creed: Its Genesis and Development*, (Barnes and Nobles Inc., New York, 1873), pp.58-82.

[34] Abu Rayyan states that Hasan al-Baṣrī argued that the perpetrator of

a major sin to be a hypocrite (*munafiq*) and would be punished for his deed, he does not have faith and does not enter into disbelief. The Murjia claimed that he remains a believer (*mu'min*) and prevented from punishment (*qisas*). The Mu'tazila claimed that he was an evildoer (*fasiq*), eternally damned in hell, he is between two stations of disbelief and belief (*manzilat bayn al-manzilat al-kufr wa'l-Iman*), so he is neither a believer or disbeliever; lastly, the considered deeds to be a part of faith (*iman*). *Tarikh al-Fikr al-Islami*, pp.239-240.

[35] Abu Rayyan states that the founders of the Mu'tazila movement were Wasil b. 'Ata' and 'Amr b. 'Ubayd, both born in 80 A.H. See *Tarikh al-Fikr al-Islami*, pp.237-238.

[36] Fazlur Rahman, *Islam*, p.88; See *Tarikh al-Fikr al-Islami*, pp.240-242.

[37] Fazlur Rahman, *Islam*, p.98.

[38] Abu Rayyan, *Tarikh al-Fikr al-Falsafi*, pp.236-237.

[39] A.J. Wensnick argues that the Mu'tazila doctrine of *wa'id* responded to the Khariji doctrine of *murtakib al-kabira* and incorporated the *qadari* doctrine of human freedom. See A.J. Wesnick, *The Muslim Creed: Its Genesis and Historical Development*, pp.60-61.

[40] Fazlur Rahman, *Islamic Methodology in History*, p.34.

[41] Fazlur Rahman, *Islamic Methodology in History*, p.44.

[42] Fazlur Rahman, *Islamic Methodology in History*, p.45.

[43] Fazlur Rahman, *Islamic Methodology in History*, p.53.

[44] Fazlur Rahman, *Functional Interdependence of Law and Theology*, p.95.

[45] *Ibid*, p.89.

[46] *Ibid*, p.95.

[47] *Ibid*, p.95.

[48] See *Some Reflections on the Reconstruction of Muslim Society in*

Pakistan, pp.103-120.

[49] See entry Murjia, *Encyclopedia of Islam*, pp.605-607; In his *Risala ila 'Uthman al-Batti*, Abu Hanifa rejected the name Murjia for himself, asserting that it had been given by the innovators (*ahl ul-bida*) to those who were in fact the People of Justice (*'adl*) must be understood here as implying political justice and reform was not the Mu'tazili doctrine of free will. Abu Hanifa, was like the early Murjia in general, a strict predestinarian.

[50] Fazlur Rahman, *Functional Interdependence of Law and Theology*, p.90.

[51] *Ibid.*

[52] *Ibid.*

[53] See entry on Murjia, *Encyclopedia of Islam*, pp.605-607.

[54] Fazlur Rahman, *Funtional Interdependence of Law and Theology*, p.92.

[55] "The early Murjia affirmed unconditional solidarity with Abu Bakr and Umar and suspension of judgment with respect to Uthman and Ali." See entry on Murjia, *Encyclopedia of Islam*, pp.605-607.

[56] "This controversy that the definition of a *mu'min* or a Muslim and can a man continue to be regarded as a Muslim even if he commits a grave moral error"; See *Revival and Reform in Islam*, p.51; *Islamic Methodology in History*, p.59.

[57] See A.J. Wensinck, *The Muslim Creed*, pp.60-61.

[58] Ghassan al-Murjii, one of the three groups that comprised the Murjia considered faith to only increase and not decrease. Al-Isfaraini refers to the three groups to be the *yunusiya, ghassaniya, tawmniya, thawbaniya* and *marisiya*; See *al-Tabsir fi al'Din*, al-Isfaraini, pp.97-101.

[59] Ali Abdul al-Fattah al-Maghrabi, *al-Firaq al-Kalamiya al-Islamiya:*

Madkhal wa Dirasat, Maktaba Wahba, (Cairo 1995), pp.339-340.

[60] Sawi lists five opinions: (1) That he is a believer and it is correct but he is a sinner for having not reflected and studied (*nazr*) at all – having the ability to perceive the general proofs (*dalil ijmali*) or not; (2) that he has the ability to perceive and is possible for him to attain knowledge about it; (3) if blindly follows the Qur'an and *Sunnah* then he is not a sinner (*'aas*); (4) that perceiving the proofs for oneself is forbidden; (5) that it is only for perfection (*kamal*). *Al-Jawhara*, pp.108-109.

[61] Fazlur Rahman, *Revival and Reform in Islam*, p.66-68.

[62] Fazlur Rahman, *Islam*, p.169.

[63] Surah al-Ṭūr: 21

$$وَٱلَّذِينَ آمَنُواْ وَٱتَّبَعَتْهُمْ ذُرِّيَّتُهُم بِإِيمَانٍ أَلْحَقْنَا بِهِمْ ذُرِّيَّتَهُمْ وَمَآ أَلَتْنَاهُم مِّنْ عَمَلِهِم مِّن شَيْءٍ كُلُّ ٱمْرِىءٍ بِمَا كَسَبَ رَهِينٌ .$$

See Al-Ash'arī, *Kitab al-Lum'a*, Matba' Misr, 1955, pp.94-113.

[64] Abu Rayyan, *Tarikh al-Fikr al-Falsafi fi-Islam*, p.297.

[65] Fazlur Rahman, *Revival and Reform in Islam*, p.67.

[66] Fazlur Rahman, *Islam*, p.93.

[67] See note 178, for the five groups comprising the Murjia – not all groups were against the orthodox dogma of faith increasing or decreasing.

[68] Abu Rayyan, *Tarikh al-Fikr al-Falsafi al-Islami*, p.298.

[69] *Ibid*, p.299-300.

[70] *Ibid*, p.292, 298-299.

[71] It should be noted that the Medinese criticism against the Ash'arīs and the Mu'tazilis for attempting to develop doctrine outside the pale of revelation – is a principle stance of Fazlur Rahman's theological

thought; hence, his rejection of Ash'arī and Mu'tazila *kalām* and acceptance of Ibn Taymīya. Fazlur Rahman does not assess the intra-God question of His essence and attributes, God's attribute of "speech" as 'scholarly controversy', instead who partook interest in questions of God's justice, human free will, the nature of divine law, the definition of evil and the role of reason.

[72] Fazlur Rahman, *Islam*, p.94.

[73] Pickthall, *The Meaning of the Glorious Qur'an*: "When Allah hath created you and what ye make?"; Arberry, *The Koran Interpreted*: "and God created you and what you make?"; Asad, *The Message of the Qur'an*: "the while it is God who has created you and all your handiwork?".

[74] Tāhir b. Al 'Āshūr, *al Tahrīr wa'l Tanwīr*, pp.141-146.

[75] See his *Some Key Ethical Concepts of the Qur'an (Iman, Islam and Taqwā)*, pp.170-185.

[76] See al-Razī's, *Mahsil afkar al-Mutaqadimin wa al-Muta'khirin min al-Ulama' wa al-Hukama' wa al-Mutakalimin*.

[77] Fazlur Rahman, *Islam and Modernity*, p.27.

[78] Fazlur Rahman, *Islam and Modernity*, p.33.

[79] See Hasan al-Shaf'i, *Madkhal ila 'ilm ul-kalām*, pp.107-114.

[80] Fazlur Rahman, *Islam*, p.98.

[81] Fazlur Rahman, *Islam and Modernity*, p.36-39.

[82] *Ibid*, p.114.

[83] Fazlur Rahman, *Islamic Methodology in History*, p.126.

[84] Fazlur Rahman, *Islam*, p.95.

[85] Fazlur Rahman, *Islam*, pp.98-99.

[86] Fazlur Rahman, *Islamic Methodology in History*, p.137.

[87] Fazlur Rahman, *Islam and Modernity*, p.154.

[88] Fazlur Rahman, *Islam*, p.94.

[89] See *Revival and Reform*, pp.115-131.

[90] Fazlur Rahman, *Islam and Modernity*, p.154.

[91] Fazlur Rahman, *Islam*, p.100.

[92] Fazlur Rahman, *Islam*, p.95.

[93] *Ibid.*

[94] Fazlur Rahman, *Islam*, p.96; See also *Revival and Reform*, p.156.

[95] Fazlur Rahman, *Islam*, p.96.

[96] Fazlur Rahman, *Islam*, p.97.

[97] Fazlur Rahman, *Revival and Reform*, p.118.

[98] Fazlur Rahman, *Revival and Reform in Islam*, p.119.

[99] Fazlur Rahman, *Islamic Methodology in History*, p.115.

[100] Fazlur Rahman, *Revival and Reform*, p. 132.

[101] *Ibid*, p.133.

[102] *Ibid*, p.134.

[103] *Ibid*, p.134.

[104] *Ibid*, p.134.

[105] *Ibid*, p.135.

[106] *Ibid*, p.136.

[107] See *Selected Letters of Ahmad Sirhindī*, pp. 65-71.

[108] See *Selected Letters of Ahmad Sirhindī*, p.70.

[109] See *Islam and Modernity*, pp.43-84.

[110] See for a puritanist interpretation of *tajdid*: ʻAdnan Muhammad

Imamat, *Al-Tajdid fi al'Fikr al-Islami*, Dar Ibn ul-Jawzi, 1st ed., 1424 AH, pp.131-137.

[111] See for modernist interpretation: Muhammad Iqbal, *The Reconstruction of Religious Thought in Islam*, ed.,: M. Saeed Sheikh, (Lahore: Institute of Islamic Culture, 1986), p.6.

[112] Aziz Ahmad, *Jamal al-din al-Afghani and Muslim India*, Studia Islamica, No. 13 (1960), p.57.

[113] *Ibid*, p.66.

[114] *Ibid*, p.58.

[115] *Ibid*, p.58.

[116] Wilfred Cantwell Smith, *Modern Islam in India*, London, 1946, p.55.

[117] Aziz Ahmad, *Jamal al-din al-Afghani and Muslim India*, Studia Islamica, No. 13 (1960), p.60.

[118] Sayyid Ahmad Khan, *Al-Tahrir fi usul al-Tafsir*, Agra 1892, pp.10-11.

[119] Aziz Ahmad, *Jamal al-din al-Afghani and Muslim India*, Studia Islamica, No. 13 (1960), p.63.

[120] Fazlur Rahman, *Islam and Modernity*, p.51.

[121] *Ibid*, p.52.

[122] Fazlur Rahman, *Islam and Modernity*, p.53.

[123] *Ibid*, pp.53-55.

[124] *Ibid*, pp.55-56.

[125] Fazlur Rahman, *Islam and Modernity*, pp.151-154.

Chapter III
Concept of God

The concept of God in the theological thought of Fazlur Rahman holds the position of representing the worldview or *weltanshuuang* of Islam. In *Islam* and *Islam and Modernity* he elucidated the approach that he personally advocated should be taken in order to correctly formulate the worldview of Islam. The sources of Fazlur Rahman's conceptualization are in Islam's normative sources and not in its historic sources. Fazlur Rahman believed that the Qur'an and the life of the Prophet (ṣ) working together displayed correctly the Islamic worldview. He states that:

> "The Qur'an is the divine response, through the Prophet's mind, to the moral-social situation of the Prophet's Arabia, particularly to the problems of the commercial Makkan society of his day ... The early ṣuras of the Qur'an make it abundantly clear that the acute problems in that society were polytheism (idol worship), exploitation of the poor, malpractices in trade, and general irresponsibility toward society (which there is good reason to believe the Qur'an perceived as interconnected). The Qur'an put forward the idea of a unique God to whom all humans are responsible and the goal of eradication of gross socioeconomic inequality.

> Qur'anic theology and moral and legal teachings then gradually unfolded themselves in the political arena: the Makkans' rejection of Muhammad's (ṣ) message, the protracted debates that followed, and later, in the Madinah phase of his life, the controversy waged against Jews and to some extent against Christians formed the backdrop against which the Qur'an was revealed".[1]

This quote succinctly illustrates Fazlur Rahman's conceptualization of the Qur'an and interrelationship with the Prophet's mind and actions. In general it can be viewed as the framework which he established in order to develop a rational model of the Qur'an and the prophetic mission. He considered that the Qur'an was the divine response to the *real* and *practical* problems of Makkan society. The concept of God has a definite utilitarian purpose which is to eradicate socio-economic inequality. The fixed points in this framework can be logically expressed in the following sequence. Firstly, that the 'élan of the Qur'an is moral', which implies that its spirit of the Qur'an is to rectify human action and this implies individual and social change. Indeed, the second point which logically follows from this is that the 'objective of Islam is to establish a socio-moral order'. Thirdly, the 'historical unfolding of the Qur'an' allows us to observe the themes that God has stressed upon in the course of the twenty three year period of revelation, stage by stage. Fourthly, the themes allow us to develop the worldview as projected by the Qur'an upon the Prophet (ṣ) and the first community. Finally, and to which this thesis is concerned with, Qur'anic theology develops under the shadow of this worldview. Thus, the Qur'anic worldview is an umbrella concept under which the essence of Islam i.e., its ethics resides.

Fazlur Rahman's theological thought is representative of two criteria: (1) fulfilling the demands of the Qur'anic message (2) satisfying the needs of a contemporary modern Islam. Fazlur Rahman believed that Qur'an was not studied as a unity and with the correct interpretative tools and methods to bring forth the true Qur'anic worldview. The orthodoxy had formulated doctrines in light of their political and sectarian positions and was unjust in representing the Qur'an's theological doctrines. Moreover, the orthodoxy and the Mu'tazila, especially, whom Fazlur Rahman considers to be the real theological schools, engaged in a one-sided and reactionary activity that gainsay was utterly ambivalent to the Qur'an. With regards to the second criterion, Fazlur Rahman contended that the greatest threat to Islam was communism. Further what was inherently a part of communism is atheism and secularism, whereas with regards to capitalism it is secularism and moral degeneration.

As we have stated in our introduction that Fazlur Rahman's personal philosophical thought was "modern" *viz.*, addressing the modern individual to be acquainted with American pragmatism, British and German philosophy. On the other hand his source of ideas are not entirely Western, moreover, we believe that there are not many at all. Actually, the ideas which he adopts and reformulates into a modern 'reworking' are ideas by Muslim thinkers. The concept of God in Fazlur Rahman's thought displays this pattern which he has harmoniously weaved. We shall attempt to demonstrate this intricate intellectual synthesis in order to attain a better appreciation of this concept.

As we have stated in the introductory chapter of this thesis that Fazlur Rahman's overall thought evolved and passed through different stages. Fazlur Rahman wrote about his concept of God in three separate publications. The first is in his book *Islam* published in 1966, the second in an article *The Qur'anic Concept of God, the Universe and Man* in 1967, lastly, in *Major Themes of the Qur'an*, Fazlur Rahman dedicates a chapter to the Qur'anic theme of God. His first two publications indicate the influences of the philosophical school of American pragmatism, the ideas of Shah Wali Ullah and some insights of Muhammad Iqbal. Fazlur Rahman enunciates that the Qur'anic concept of God is of a pragmatic, functional God.[2] His titled the *Qur'anic Concept of God, the Universe and Man* is entirely underneath the influence of pragmatism and its underlying thesis is the psychological benefit that Man attains from the concept of God facilitates success. Hence, the concept of God possesses a psychological and moral utility. Secondly, he develops the Qur'anic term of *Sunnat ullah fi al-kawn* into a behavioral theory of God which enacts itself in the processes of the nature. Fazlur Rahman explicitly states that as far as *factual content* goes, eliminate God and translate their statements into perfectly "naturalistic" ones without any loss whatsoever.[3] Both these publications were written in the fourth stage of his life where he was the Director of the Islamic Research Institute in Ayub Khan's regime. His last publication *Major Themes of the Qur'an* exemplifies his dedication to the Qur'an and his years of in-depth study. It seems that Fazlur Rahman attempts to formulate his concept of God based upon how the Qur'an presents certain ideas to establish the existence of God.

As we have illustrated in the previous section that Fazlur Rahman found Ibn Sīna's thought to have taken into consideration the demands of both philosophy and religion seriously and attempted to formulate a synthetic, scientific and systematic system of thought to cater to the two dominant cultures of his time: Orthodox Islam and Greek Hellenism. Fazlur Rahman incorporated Ibn Sīna's doctrine of the Necessary being and contingency into his own system of thought. However, Fazlur Rahman's system is not a blanket acceptance of philosophical doctrines from various philosophers it is, rather, a serious attempt at synthesizing the Qur'an and philosophical thought, where philosophy not only served as the "handmaid of theology" but it was also representative of the human intellect and its evolution since the Qur'an was first revealed. This is precisely what Iqbal said in his *The Reconstruction of Religious Thought in Islam*: "The more important regions of experience, examined with an eye on a synthetic view, reveal, as the ultimate ground of all experience, a rationally directed creative will which we have found reasons to describe as an ego."[4]

Fazlur Rahman's concept of God is not that of the Sufis' as the essence of essences or the commanding God of the jurists but the God of creativity, order and mercy. Further we see that there is an evolution in Fazlur Rahman's concept of God which can be probably attributed to his greater focus upon the Qur'an in the last phase of his life at Chicago. His earliest writings depicting his concept of God is in his book *Islam* (1971) that:

> "As the Qur'an gradually worked out its worldview more fully, the moral order for men comes to assume a central point of divine interest in a full picture of a cosmic order which is not only charged with a high religious sensitivity but exhibits an amazing degree of coherence and consistency. A concept of God, the absolute author of the universe, is developed where the attributes of creativity, order and mercy are not merely conjoined or added to one another but interpenetrate completely."[5]

In his *Major Themes of the Qur'an* (1980), Fazlur Rahman states that the concept of God is: "orderly creativity, sustenance, guidance, justice and mercy interpenetrate the concept of God as a unity."[6] Fazlur Rahman states that these are all 'relational ideas' that relate God to His creation. Fazlur Rahman argues that the Qur'an is not interested in speculative theology, although there is some theology, cosmology and psychology.[7] Fazlur Rahman in consonance with Iqbal believes that the Qur'an is concerned with man's moral practical attitude and not with speculative theology because the function of the Qur'an is to provide guidance to man. Thus, he states that the Qur'anic concept of God is 'functional'. The implications of the concept of God being functional is in definite response to the orthodox considering it be an end in itself and some kind of mathematical formula.

> "But the kinds of differences about the conception of God – whether he is the ground of being that manifests itself through every existent and is therefore to be contemplated, or whether he is the ultimate and transcendent principle that has simply to be established and "proved" like a mathematical formula, or whether he is the creator-commander who has to be worshiped and obeyed … should surely be capable of being sorted out for public and collective life, leaving scope for private idiosyncrasies.[8]

Another important aspect to bear in mind about Fazlur Rahman is that he believed that the orthodoxy failed to understand Qur'an as a unity on the one hand, and the Western students of Islam failed to read it without prejudice and ignorance. Fazlur Rahman states: "The immediate impression from a cursory reading of the Qur'an is that of the infinite majesty of God and His equally infinite mercy, although many a

Western scholar (through a combination of ignorance and prejudice) has depicted the Qur'anic God as a concentrate of pure power, even as brute power – indeed, as a capricious tyrant."[9]

One of the criteria that Fazlur Rahman attempted to fulfill was that the concept of God should be rationally acceptable. In his *Major Themes of the Qur'an*, Fazlur Rahman begins with the categorical question: "Why God at all?"[10] He specifies that "why not let nature and her contents and processes stand on their own without bringing in a higher being, which only complicates reality and puts an unnecessary burden on both man's intellect and his soul? Fazlur Rahman finds the Qur'an's declares this to be belief in the Unseen. In his previous two writings Fazlur Rahman does not explicitly speak about this 'belief in the Unseen' because of the intellectual milieu of the late nineteenth and twentieth century that any attempt to justify religion on the basis of revelation was considered old dogmatism on the other the newer dogmatists attempted to discredit religion once and for all by pointing to its disreputable origin in some curious bodily state.[11]

Fazlur Rahman addresses the difficulty and the method that God employs in order to bring His existence to full importance in human consciousness. He contends that God does not try to make man come to belief by giving lengthy and intricate "theological" proofs of God's existence, but how to shake him into belief by drawing his attention to certain obvious facts and turning these facts into "reminders" of God.

"The main points in this ceaseless, tremendous thrust for "reminding" man are (1) that everything except God is contingent upon God, including the entirety of nature (which has a "metaphysical" and a "moral" aspect); (2) that God, with all His might and glory, is essentially the all-merciful God; and (3) that both these aspects necessarily entail a proper relationship between God and Man – a relationship of the served and the servant – and consequently also a proper relationship between man and man. By a natural necessity, as it were, these normative relationships entail the law of judgment upon man both as individual and in his collective or social existence. Once we have grasped these three points, we will have understood the absolute centrality of God in the entire, system of existence, to a very large extent because the aim of the Qur'an is man and his behavior, not God."[12]

Functional Nature of the Concept of God

Fazlur Rahman considers the nature of the Qur'anic concept of God to be functional[13]:

"The Qur'anic teaching is entirely oriented towards practice: it provides *guidance* for man … to keep the proper attitude of man on correct lines, tuned to the proper moral pitch and geared to a certain purpose. The Qur'anic concept of God is – therefore, primarily, indeed, purely – *functional*. This is most certainly not to say that the Qur'an is indifferent to the truth value of its statements, but to affirm that the truth-value of statements – even about God – is subservient to and, in some vital sense, needs to be tested by their success in producing a state of affairs in the world. It should not, therefore, shock or surprise anyone that, although Allah (God) is mentioned in the Qur'an more than six thousand times (apart from other quasi-names of the Deity, like Fazlur Rahman – 'the Merciful' – and Rabb – 'the Sustainer'), *all* these statements are *actually* statements about man – the center of all interest in the Qur'an".[14]

"His existence, for the Qur'an, is strictly functional – He is Creator and Sustainer of the universe and of man, and particularly the giver of guidance for man and He who judges man, individually and collectively, and metes out to him merciful justice."[15]

Fazlur Rahman uses the term *functional* to describe the nature of the Qur'anic concept of God. Fazlur Rahman uses the term *functional* in one of three ways in which the concept of *Imago Dei* or the "Image of God" can be interpreted which he seems to have incorporated into his theological thought from Jewish and Christian theology. The concept of the Image of God is not present in Islamic Theology.[16] However, there are hadīths in Bukhārī and Muslim that enunciate the creation of Adam in the image of God or the creation of Adam in the image of Adam.[17]

In Christian theology *imago dei* or the "Image of God" is a theological term, applied uniquely to humans, which denotes the symbolic relationship between God and humanity. It is generally held to mean that people contain within their nature elements that reflect God's nature. Though we have a physical image, it does not mean that God has one. Rather, God is spirit (John 4:24), not flesh and bones (Luke 24:39). The term has its roots in Genesis 1:27, wherein "God created man in his own image. . ." This scriptural passage does not mean that God is in human form, but rather, that humans are in the image of God in their moral, spiritual, and intellectual nature. Thus, humans mirror God's divinity in their ability to actualize the unique qualities with which they have been endowed, and which make them different than all other creatures: rational structure, complete centeredness, creative freedom, a possibility for self-actualization, and the ability for self-transcendence.

It fundamentally refers to two things: (1) God's own self-actualization through humankind; (2) God's care for humankind. To say that humans are in the image of God is to recognize the special qualities of human nature which allow God to be made manifest in humans. In other words, for humans to have the conscious recognition of their being in the image of God means that they are the creature through whom God's plans and purposes can be made known and actualized; humans, in this way, can be seen as co-creators with God. The moral implications of the doctrine of *imago dei* are apparent in the fact that if humans are to love God, then humans must love other humans, as each is an expression of God. The human likeness to God can also be understood by contrasting it with that which does not image God, i.e., beings who, as far as we know, are without self-consciousness and the capacity for spiritual-moral reflection and growth. Humans differ from all other creatures because of their rational structure – their capacity for deliberation and free decision-making. This freedom gives the human a centeredness and completeness which allows the possibility for self-actualization and participation in sacred reality. However, the freedom which makes the human in God's image is the same freedom which manifests itself in estrangement from God, as the myth of the Fall (Adam and Eve) exemplifies. according to this myth, humans can, in their freedom, choose to deny or repress their spiritual and moral likeness to God. The ability and desire to love one's self and others, and therefore, God, can become neglected and even opposed. Striving to bring about the *imago dei* in one's life can be seen as the quest for wholeness, or one's "essential" self, as pointed to in Christ's life and teachings.

Erickson[18], a well-known Christian theologian states there are three common ways of understanding the manner in which humans exist in *imago dei*: Substantive, Relational and

Functional. The substantive view holds to the idea that there is some substantial characteristic of the human race that is like God. Some may argue that we are a mirror image of God's essential nature. Other substantive views suggest a spiritual commonality with God, God being a spirit and not having a physical body. Throughout the ages there have been different interpretations of substantive likeness to God. Irenaeus[19] put forward a distinctive difference between image and likeness. Humankind before the Fall (the moral and spiritual failure of its original progenitors) was in the image of God through the ability to exercise free will and reason. And we were in the likeness of God through an original spiritual endowment. Medieval scholars suggested that this was the holiness (or "wholeness") of humankind which was lost after the Fall, though free will and reason remained. Calvin and Luther agreed that something of the *imago dei* was lost at the fall but that fragments of it remained in some form or another.

The relational view argues that one must be in a relationship with God in order to possess the 'image' of God. Those who hold to the relational image agree that humankind possess the ability to reason as a substantive trait, but they argue that it is in a relationship with God that the true image is made evident. Later theologians like Karl Barth and Emil Bruner argue that it is our ability to establish and maintain complex and intricate relationships that make us like God. For example, in humans the created order of male and female is intended to culminate in spiritual as well as physical unions (Genesis 5:1-2), reflecting the nature and image of God. Since other creatures do not form such explicitly referential spiritual relationships, these theologians see this ability as uniquely representing the *Imago Dei* in humans.

The functional view differs from the previous two in that it argues that the image of God imprinted on us resides in function rather than in form or relationship, this function being primarily our task of ruling over earth. Genesis 1:26 speaks of humankind being made in the image of God and given the function of naming and ruling over the fish of the sea and the animals on land, reflecting God's rule over all the universe, ourselves included. This view sees this ruling function of dominion as best expressing the *imago dei*, or our likeness to God. It seems probable that Fazlur Rahman consistent mentioning of the divine trust between man and God (33:70), and Adam's vice-regency on earth (2:30) and his creative knowledge (2:31) are fundamental constituents in the Qur'an's concept of man.

God as the Necessary Being

Fazlur Rahman belived that Ibn Sīna's philosophical thought was a serious attempt at rationally interpreting religion. In general, Ibn Sīna's thought serves as a foundation for Fazlur Rahman's philosophical thought. Fazlur Rahman considered Ibn Sīna in particular had attempted to take religion seriously and attempted to formulate a rational system that would integrate philosophy and religion together:

> "Muslim philosophers, by a re-elaboration of the Greek tradition of philosophy, not only sought to build a rational system, but a rational system which sought to integrate the tradition of Islam."[20]

Specifically, Ibn Sīna's doctrine of the Necessary Being appealed to Fazlur Rahman because of its ontological soundness because it provided a resolute philosophical argument that was firstly true to the demands of the Qur'anic concept of God and modern scientific mind. Here it is important to bear in mind that Fazlur Rahman that Islam faced its greatest challenge from communism and, therefore, logically atheism and secularism. Hence, he attempted to present Islam in the most rationally acceptable manner while still being true to the Qur'an.

We shall begin tracing Fazlur Rahman's doctrine of the Necessary Being from Ibn Sīna himself. Ibn Sīna'a doctrine of being is emanationistic. From God, the Necessary Existent, flows the first intelligence alone, since from a single, absolutely simple entity, only one thing can emanate. But the nature of the first intelligence is no longer absolutely simple since, not being neccesary-by-itself, it is only possible, and its possibility has been actualized by God. This dual nature pervades the entire creaturely world, the first intelligence gives rise to two entities: (1) the second intelligence by viture of the higher aspect of its being – its actuality, and (2) the first and highest sphere by virtue of the lower aspect of its being – its natural possibility. This dual emanatory process continues until we reach the lower and tenth intelligence which governs the sublunary world and is called by the majority of the Muslim philosophers the Angel Gabriel.[21]

Muslim philosophers employed the Neo-Platonic theory of emanation in order to facilitate philosophically the passage from God the One, to the world, the many. However, the implications of this theory are that there is no "gulf between the Creator and the creation"[22]. This would either result in a pantheistic or an anthropomorphic worldview, where the created beings are reabsorbed into the being of God. Ibn Sīna addresses this issue and maintains the 'gulf between the creature and the Creator' by his theory of existence and essence.

The Greek concept of God considers that God and God alone is absolutely simple in His being; all other things have a dual nature. Being simple, what God is and the fact that God exists are not two elements in a single being but a single atomic element in a single being. What God is, i.e., His essence, is identical with His existence. This is not the case with any other being, for in no other case is the existence identical with the essence. It follows that God's existence is necessary, the existence of other things is only possible and derived from God's, and that the supposition of God's non-existence involves a contradiction, his existence is utterly unique.

Here it is important to identify Fazlur Rahman's personal conviction of the nature of essence and existence in his opinion resembles more the Liebnizian proof of God as the *ground* of the world, i.e., given God, we can understand the existence of the world.[23] This is exactly what Fazlur Rahman considers is meant by this distinction to which he further adds the attributes of meaningfulness, purposesiveness and reasonableness.[24] Similarly, Fazlur Rahman concurs with Ibn Sīna that God creates through a rational necessity.[25] On this basis of rational necessity, Ibn Sīna also explains the divine pre-knowledge of all events, as we shall see in his account of God. The world, as a whole is then contingent, but, given God, it becomes necessary, this necessity being derived from God. This is Ibn Sīna's principle of existence.[26]

From the metaphysical point of view, the theory seeks to supplement the traditional Aristotelian analysis of an existence into two constituitive elements as it were, *viz.*, form and matter. according to Aristotle, the form of a thing is the sum total of its essential and universalizable qualities consistuting its definition; the matter in each thing is that which has the potentiality of receiving these qualities – the form – and by which the form becomes an individual existent. Ibn Sīna's criticizes Aristotle's postulation on the basis form is universal and, therefore does not exist. Matter too, being pure potentiality, does not exist, since it is actualized only by the form. The second is the definiton or essence of a thing is its form and in his *De Anima* matter is also included in the essence of a thing, otherwise a partial definition will result. Therefore, if both form and matter are constitutive of definition, we can never arrive at the actual existence of a thing.[27] To this end, Ibn Sīna argues that with form and matter do not yield a concrete existent, but only the essential and accidental qualities. In his view, both form and matter depend upon God (or the active intellect) and, further, that the composite existent also cannot be caused by form and matter alone there must be "something else" or in other words, all creations are contingent upon God.[28] Hence, God being the Unity from which all other existents attain matter and form, Existence and Unity are the primary ideas and mark the starting point. Further, they do not have definitions since definitions involve terms and concepts which are themselves derived.[29]

According to Ibn Sīna, "accident" has an unorthodox philosophical meaning that "whenever two concepts are clearly distinguishable from each other, they must refer to two different ontological entities" and whenever two such concepts come together in a thing, Ibn Sīna describes their mutual relationship as being accidental. This is also the case between essence and existence and between universality and essence.[30] Thus if we regard essence as a universal, that concrete determinate existence is something over and above the essence; it is something added to the essence, or it is an "accident" of the essence.[31] Therefore there are two things that must be noted: (1)

that existence is something added not to the existent objects but to the essence. (2) the sole principle of individual existence is God – the Giver of existence; matter is the occasional cause of existence, supplying external attributes of multiplicity.

God is unique and He is the Necessary Being; everything else is contingent in itself and depends for its existence upon God. The Necessary Being must be numerically one. Even within this Being there can be no multiplicity of attributes – infact, God has no other essence, no other attributes than the fact that He exists, and exists necessarily. This is what is implied by Ibn Sīna's statement that God's essence is identical with His necessary existence. Since God has no essence, He is absolutely simple and cannot be defined. Fazlur Rahman here argues that if He is without essence and attributes how is He related to the world in any way?

Aristotle's conception of the deity, the world presented itself as a veritable other – it was neither the object of God's creation, nor of care, not even of knowledge. His God led a blissful life of eternal self-contemplation and the world organizes itself into a cosmos out of love and admiration for Him, to become like Him. The Muslim philosophers worked out under the influence of Neoplatonism that God's absolute simplicity is combined with God knowing things in an implicit manner the essence of things. The system is worked out and systematized by Ibn Sīna, who strives to derive God's attributes of knowledge, creation, power, will etc., from His simple unchanging being i.e., these attributes are nothing but the fact of His existence. The attributes are shown to be either relational or negative; they are, thus, absolutely simple. The Diety is, therefore, absolutely simple. That God is knowing, is shown by the fact that pure being from matter and pure spirit, He is pure intellect in which the subject and object are identical.

Ibn Sīna conceived that God's self-knowledge is by the fact itself knowledge of other things as well, since, knowing Himself, He also inevitably knows the rest of the existents which proceed from Him. But God can only know the essences and not the particular existents, since the latter can be known only through sense-perception and, therefore in time; but God, being supra-temporal, changeless and incorporeal, cannot have perceptual knowledge. Ibn Sīna devises an argument to show that although God cannot have perceptual knowledge, He nevertheless knows all particulars "in a universal way", so that perceptual knowledge is superflous for Him. He knows both these existents and the relations subsisting between them. Fazlur Rahman criticizes Ibn Sīna's conceptualization "that it cannot avoid the introduction of time factor, and therefore, change in divine knowledge."[32]

In Ibn Sīna's intellectualist-emanationist account of the Deity, will has no meaning. For Ibn Sīna, God's will means nothing but the necessary procession of the world from Him and His self satisfaction through this. Indeed, he defines it in purely negative terms, *viz.*, God is not unwilling that the world proceed from Him; this is very different from the positive attributes of choice and the execution of that choice.[33] Similarly, the creative activity of God means the eternal emanation or procession of the world, and since this emanation is grounded finally in the intellectual nature of God, it has the character of unalterable rational necessity. [34]

The world exists eternally with God for both matter and forms flow eternally from Him. But although this concept was abhorrent to Islamic orthodoxy, Ibn Sīna's purpose in introducing it was to try to do justice both to the demands of religion and of reason and to avoid atheistic materialism. For the materialists, the world has existed eternally without God. For Ibn Sīna, too, the world is an eternal existent, but since it in itself contingent in its entirety it needs God and is dependent upon Him eternally. Fazlur Rahman observes that the purpose of the doctrine of essence and existence unlike atheism requires God who should bestow being upon existents; and in order to avoid pantheism, it further requires that the being of God should be radically differentiated from the being of the world.[35]

Fazlur Rahman pinpoints two basic issues why the orthodox rejected Avicenna's theory of God and His relationship to the world than any Greek philosophical theory. One of these is its relentless theistic determinism. Although the world is not in itself necessary but only possible, it becomes nevertheless necessary when viewed from God's side, who operates by a rational dynamic necessity. The other issue concerns the philosopher's acceptance of the eternity of the world and his rejection of temporal creation.

The oft-questioned and perplexing philosophical issue of how the world was created and how it has been created in time was addressed by Ibn Sīna. He declared that (1) both the universe as a whole and everything therein derived its existence directly from God and (2) that the world as a whole was, nevertheless, eternal and was not "created" by God at any moment of time although it *depends* on God. He contended that the genuinely religious stake (which was absolutely rational) in this whole problem was not that the world should be "created out of nothing at a time" (*ḥādith*) but that the world should be contingent, dependent upon God (*mumkin*). Ibn Sīna had established that God is the "ground" of the Universe and *explains* the latter; without Him the world would be "groundless," unintelligible, irrational.[36]

Orderliness of the Universe & Unity in God:

Fazlur Rahman states that:

> "One of the main functions of the idea of God is to vindicate the orderliness of the universe – that there is no lawlessness in nature, that the whole cosmos is an organic unity. This is the reason behind the insistent emphasis on the unity of God".[37]

Fazlur Rahman believes that the actions that God performs are the greatest indicator and proof for belief in His existence. God's performance elucidates the function He operates in the Universe i.e., He provides order. Fazlur Rahman connects this rational proposition with another rational proposition of the Qur'an that had there been more than one God there would be pandemonium in the universe. Here Fazlur Rahman explicates a profound anecdote about the Nature of God:

> "The glory of Allah is that no matter what point you may imagine, He is there and yet to transcend every point is His very nature: otherwise the requirements of order cannot be met."[38]

Fazlur Rahman believes that the fundamental nature of God is that He is present and immanent at every point in the universe and His creation serves as the index (*āyāt*) to Him. Despite the numerous signs and indications that point to God, He is still transcendent and incapable of being comprehended. Fazlur Rahman argues that it is this inherent logic of the concept of God that He be beyond all imaginable perfection, although He is present at every point within the scale of perfection. Fazlur Rahman states that it is this immanence-cum-transcendence which constitutes also the logic of a growing and expanding order. Here we would like to illustrate systematically Fazlur Rahman's perspective on God's immanent-cum-transcendent nature.

God's Immanent-Cum-Transcendent Nature

In traditional *kalām* the doctrine of Transcendence or *tanzīh* is absolutely advocated by the al-Ash'arīs. The position is upheld against the doctrine of anthropomorphism or *tajsīm* purported by the *Ahl ul Hadīth*. The upholders of anthropomorphism have also being referred to as the *hashawiya*. The problem lies in the names and attributes of God that resemble the names and attributes of man. The al-Ash'arīs were referred in this particular area as the *sifātiyya* or *mushabbaha* or *Ahl ul Tamthīl*, all pointing towards the al-Ash'arī position on the Divine Names and Attributes of God being similar to that of man.

As we have elucidated earlier that a fixed point in Fazlur Rahman's point of view regardinng the traditional schools of theology is their one-sided presentation of Qur'anic doctrine, highlighting one side of and neglecting the other.[39] Fazlur Rahman does not address the traditional theological issues of God's names and attributes (*al asma' wa'l sifāt*). Neither does he address the anthropomorphic depiction of God in the Qur'an *viz.*, His hands, shins, feet, face, etc., He restricts himself to presenting a *natural theology* most probably to render the Qur'anic concept of God more intelligible and rationally acceptable:

> "A careful perusal of the Qur'an would reveal that it attributes all natural processes and events to God: from rains to the processes of the rise and fall of nations, from winning and losing in war and peace to the orderly revolution of cosmic

bodies, all is referred to God. This clearly shows that God is not just the most transcendent but also the most immanent."[40]

Fazlur Rahman is intimately aware and concerned that God is not to be conceived in any manner as being in conflict with nature because he wants to emphasize the orderliness of the universe due to His presence. On the other hand, Fazlur Rahman is aware that if God's immanence is overemphasized and a proper balance is not established with His transcendence then this will logically proceed to a pantheistic conception of God. By doing so, Fazlur Rahman believes that God's uniqueness is compromised because God uniqueness lies in Him being the Necessary Being from whom all other beings are contingent and dependent upon. Thus, God being the ground upon which all other creatures possess meaning and not vice versa necessitates that God's immanence is corrected by God's transcendence. Also, Fazlur Rahman accepts Ibn Sīna and Ahmad Sirhindī's affirmation of a duality in nature between mind and body. Fazlur Rahman avers that the door to Ibn Arabī's pantheism and Ash'arī determinism cannot be prevented unless a systematic reformulation of Islamic metaphysics is not maintained. It seems that Fazlur Rahman sees the need to emphasize the transcendental aspect of God because of the explicit statement of the Qur'an, that there is nothing comparable unto Him (*laysa kamithlihi*). Below we wish to present the balance that is established between immanence and transcendence and it is highlighted here as has been done persistently, that Fazlur Rahman always sought to locate the middle term[41] and attempted to establish a balance between the two.

> "The immanence of God, of course, does not, have the slightest implication that acts performed by nature or man are

really performed by God: God is not a rival of or a substitute for human or natural agencies in producing effects, nor does He interfere in any of the workings of these." [42]

To maintain this intricate balance between God's immanence and transcendence, Fazlur Rahman declares a principle of interpreting or *ta'wīl* Qur'anic verses with the objective of emphasizing the salient characteristics of the concept of God of meaningfulness, orderly creativity and purposiveness.

"Indeed in all the Qur'anic statements where God appears as the real subject, one can so far as the factual content goes, eliminate God and translate these statements into perfectly "naturalistic" ones without any loss whatever."[43]

Fazlur Rahman's Principle of Naturalistic Interpretation (*ta'wīl*)

Fazlur Rahman asserts that God is a creative, purposive will that provides meaningfulness, purposiveness and order. An important question, however, arises if his natural theology is absolutely deterministic? It should be highlighted that the predominant naturalistic theologies portrayed God as a clock maker and the universe as a clock and thereby advocating a mechanistic functioning of the universe; where He has created the universe and set into motion and distanced himself from the day-to-day running of the universe. The impression that is left on man is of an impersonal God, a God that has no psychological connection to man and therefore implies that man's prayers to God are in vain. If Fazlur Rahman were to advocate a thoroughly deterministic worldview his theology would be deistic and not theistic, which we believe is the demand of the Qur'anic concept of God. On the other hand, if the implication of God communicating through the universe signifies that God is dependent upon the universe for His expression, to this Fazlur Rahman argues:

> "the Qur'anic concept of God makes no demands either on nature or man ... God may and can upset nature, yet He does not do so for He has granted it autonomy."[44]

The autonomy granted to the universe is that which God has "ingrained" into it through his command or *amr* to which we shall discuss later. Another important point which is raised here by Fazlur Rahman is the picture presented by the orthodoxy of both God and the universe that He can willingly and unwillingly disrupt the orderly function of the universe is declared by him to be naïve because he firmly wants to root out the miracle-mongering attitude so prevalent and commonplace in the traditional orthodox view of God and the universe. Thus Fazlur Rahman emphasizes that the Qur'an tells us that the universe is the index (*ayah*) to God, that its laws are part of His behavior (*Sunnah*). He declares:

> "The universe is, therefore, related to God as character is related to man or, in a sense, as a whole is related to its parts. The two are neither identical with each other nor yet separate from each other. "[45]

So far it seems apparent that Fazlur Rahman considers God's actions to be deterministic and following a natural causality. However, the influence of Iqbal's conception of God as the superego shines through vividly. Fazlur Rahman states:

> "But just as man's self goes beyond his character (which certainly never exhausts that self at and up to any given moment) and is, in some sense, creative of it, so does God transcend the universe and is creative of it."[46]

Fazlur Rahman equates the Qur'anic term *sunnat ullah fi al-kawn* to a Divine form of natural causality behaving in the universe and in man. It seems that Fazlur Rahman equates the *Sunnah* of God to the *Sunnah* of the Prophet (ṣ) *viz.*, *Sunnah* is a behavioral concept, similarly the *Sunnah* of God is the behavioral aspect of God:

> "And thou shalt never find any changing the wont of God, and thou shalt never find any altering the wont of God." (Fāṭir: 43)

He analyses three examples from the Qur'an in which he attempts to illustrate and interpret verses of the Qur'an that depict God *directly* acting or intervening in matters of the universe or man. Fazlur Rahman contends that they illustrate the *contentual* (factual) equivalence of "naturalistic" statements and those wherein God appears as the subject. Verses in the Qur'an where God is apparently portrayed as the cause of people's going astray from the right path as well as going on the right path.

> "If God had willed, He would have made you one nation; but He leads astray whom He will, and guides whom He will; and you will surely be questioned about the things you wrought." (al-Naḥl: 93)

The issue of Divine guidance has been treated by the *mutakallimun* such as Abu Mansur al-Maturidi who considers that guidance is given and taken away by God as if it is the addition or subtraction of a thing.[47] Al-Farhārī argues that God himself has attributed guidance (*hidāyah*) to himself in many verses in the Qur'an. Many of the al-Ash'arīs have defined *hidāyah* as "the creation of obedience in the slave" and have defined misguidance as "the creation of disobedience in the slave". This is based upon the Ash'arī belief that all creation is to be attributed to God himself. The Mu'tazila opposed them, claiming that the "creation of obedience contradicts the necessity of reward" and "the creation of disobedience contradicts the necessity of punishment". Also, they have defined it as evil (*qabīḥ*) and have explained 'guidance' as the "expression (*bayān*) of the right and misguided path in the conscience of a slave". The Ash'arīs' attribute the creation of guidance to God because God creates the actions of his creatures regardless of whether they are in obedience or disobedience. Farhārī provides several linguistic equivalents to *hidāyah* and the most interesting which we find is that guidance is attributed to God and misguidance is attributed to the devil. Thus verses in the Qur'an that state that God gives guidance and misguidance is to be interpreted as God providing guidance and *metaphorically* it is implied that Satan misguides in reality. Another argument supplied by the latter day Maturīdī al-Farhārī is that misguidance must be appropriated by choice of an agent and vice versa. The al-Ash'arīs argue that God states that "as for the people of Thamūd We have them guidance, then they responded with blindness to Our guidance", so guidance is the creation of obedience. Farhārī retorts that Divine guidance is dependent upon the causes of guidance such as Prophethood, Revelation and Invitation. He then cites examples from the Qur'an that the verses referring to God providing guidance are metaphorical because there are other verses which state that "God sends down from the sky provision" which is interpreted by Farhārī to mean that God sends down rain which is a necessary cause for seeds to grow and eventually bear fruit.

In response to the Mu'tazila, Farhārī states their position as guidance referring to demonstrating (*bayān*) the correct path and not the creation of obedience as the Ash'arīs' hold, because the slave is the creator of his own actions. Farhārī rejects this on the basis of a verse in the Qur'an where God speaks to the Prophet (ṣ) revealing to him that "you cannot guide those whom you love (Abū Tālib, the uncle of the Prophet (ṣ)), however most certainly God guides whomsoever He wishes", thus if guidance meant demonstrating then those whom the Prophet (ṣ) preached by necessity should have become guided, however, they did not. Farhārī goes on to say that the Prophet (ṣ) had demonstrated the correct path but he was rejected and this is in response to the Mu'tazila, and he prayed for the disbelievers to be guided and some were guided and some were not.[48]

Fazlur Rahman states that "this issue of divine guidance where then lies the human responsibility? It is asked, construing these statements in the light of the philosophic problem of free-will and predestination, the Qur'an does not show the slightest interest in this philosophic problem and in fact, asserts both sides of the tension in order to keep human behavior on the right path, which is its central concern and not the nature of God."[49]

Fazlur Rahman's methodology in interpreting the verses of the Qur'an seems to be that he takes the *apparent* (*zāhir*) meanings of the words whereas the *mutakallimun* employ rhetorical tools such as the *ḥaqīqa*, *majāz* and *kināya* of a word or phrase. Farhārī rightly points out that the Ash'arīs interpret the verses in light of their doctrine that "God creates the actions of his creations"; whereas, the Mu'tazila interpret the verses in light of theirs that "man creates his own actions". Thus, the burden of responsibility for providing guidance in the former is God whereas in the latter it is man himself. Fazlur Rahman position considers that "man is God's coeval" and hence there is no *absolute* solution and a sense of indeterminism is present in his solution. Further, Fazlur Rahman's Western philosophical and scientific background and mindset cause him to scientifically interpret the Qur'anic *data* regarding guidance to be supporting both sides. He then turns to God's being (*dhāt*) and its relationship with man which to him is strictly a psychological affair much like Iqbal. He realizes that guidance is an action of God much like His other actions and is therefore connected to His behavior. Hence, Fazlur Rahman is pushed towards establishing an intuitive psychological explanation for the divine action of giving guidance. He recalls that God's behavior or conduct is encompassed in the Qur'anic concept of *sunnat ullah fi al-kawn.* He considers that this 'doctrine of *sunnat ullah fi al-kawn*' can be scientifically termed as a generalization for 'God's behavior' and the act of divine guidance must be interpreted with in it. Finally, he attempts to devise a 'scientific law' that can accurately describe the phenomena of Divine guidance. Here the subtly of Fazlur Rahman's concept of God come forth – the presence of God's *sunnah* or natural laws provides order to His creation i.e., the universe. Since, the universe does not behave in a haphazard manner, in other words, if one were to consider the universe a living creation like man, and noted the peace and smooth processes by which it conducts itself and not as a tyrant oppressing its subjects, then this is due to God being merciful to man that the universe does not harm him but unfortunately man harms himself by being an oppressor and corrupter in the land and this is precisely what Fazlur Rahman means, he states:

> "...the Qur'an never states that God *absolutely* leads people astray. A study of all the relevant passages shows that God leads evildoers, those who reject the truth, astray. What the

Qur'an is, in fact, saying is that whenever a man does an evil act, his chances of repeating that kind of act increases and the chance of doing good decreases proportionately until a time comes when, by consistently practicing evil, he apparently reaches a point of no return. That is where his "heart is sealed", his "ears deafened" to truth. This is also the case *mutatis mutandis* with the performance of good acts. This is a psychological law whose operations, like the operations of all laws are attributed to God by the Qur'an. Yet, even at that stage one may not say that a real or absolute point of no return has been reached. People confirmed in evil ways can always try to redeem themselves and utter hopelessness is never actually reached. Indeed cases of apparently sudden and surprising change – 'return' or 'conversion', where the moral personality is turned upside down are well established. To be sure these phenomena also occur according to laws – and are perfectly "natural" – but again, they are attributed to the mercy of God. At no point can the phenomena be closed to scientific investigation; and yet at no point does their attribution to God and God's relevance on them cease."[50]

The second case which Fazlur Rahman cites to present his principle of natural causality is based on the verses pertaining to God increasing or decreasing a person's wealth and straightens his circumstances. "When his Lord tests man, honors him and bestows bountifully upon him, he exclaims, 'My Lord has honored me.' But when He tests him and straitens his livelihood, he exclaims, 'My Lord has dishonored me.' Nay, (the fact is that) you do not honor (your) orphans, nor do you induce one another on feeding the poor ones (in the society); you devour inheritances wholesale and you are excessively attached to worldly goods" (al-Fajr: 15-20). Fazlur Rahman contends that the act, attributed to God, has been explained as a natural social process.[51]

The third case which Fazlur Rahman refers to is the Prophet's (ṣ) claims to prophethood. According to the Qur'an, his opponents asked him why God came to select him as a prophet out of all people in the two cities of Makkah and Ta'if . The Qur'an sometimes replies by saying, "God chooses whomsoever He wills as His Messenger" (e.g. āl 'Imrān: 175). But the following verse gives the reason, "God knows best where to place His Prophethood" (al-An'ām: 124). Thus, the apparent act of God's choice has been given a naturalistic grounding.[52]

Fazlur Rahman principle of *sunnat ullah fi al-kawn* is a central principle in his thought which is related to the dynamic, creative, purposeful and evolutionary nature of the Universe. This metaphysical principle relates 'God-Universe-Man' nexus with God's nature immanency-cum-transcendence on one end and axiology on the other. However, Fazlur Rahman argues the Qur'an prefers the religious idiom rather than the "naturalistic" idiom. This is because upon the factual structure of the universe there supervenes a value structure which is the peculiarity of religio-moral life. The essence of religious life consists in value-affections and value correspondence between the subject (man) and the objective reality (God). Fazlur Rahman believed that axiology is essentially where religious life inhabited. He quotes Iqbal affirming his position: "'Life is an endeavor for freedom' and a Muslim would need for salvation, private and public, a life according to *Din*."[53] Fazlur Rahman connects his axiological thought to the principle of *Tawḥīd* and states: "the Islamic principle of *Tawḥīd* has evolved a genuine universal outlook. The belief in the unity of God provides a psychological basis of society by restoring the essential unity of mankind, and by insisting that all mankind represents one brotherhood bound together by a spiritual connection."[54] Thus the ideal of general happiness or general human wellbeing can never be secured by any amount of theorizing about the psychological origin of values, unless a theory of value on a *a priori* ethics. In this connection Fazlur Rahman enunciates the acquisition of Western ideas to be: "the good of Plato, the *amor intellectualis dei* of Spinoza, the good will of Kant are the ideas that are fundamental in a genuine philosophy of value."[55]

As we have stated earlier in this chapter, Fazlur Rahman conceptualizes God as a functional, pragmatic concept. Further, he considers the existence of God to be *good,* as we have shown above under the influence of Plato, Spinoza and Kant. He states that value in the eyes of pragmatists and social thinkers to be that which is useful for mankind.[56] Where there is being rather than nothingness, God already exists for already the primordial value is realized. God is that which has, as His primary attribute, the propulsion to being out of an abysmal emptiness of non-being. Being is good and to exist itself implies purpose. Now, being with order completes the objective and existential conditions for a religio-moral response, God is be existing and his existence is of the nature of creative and purposive will.

Since nature is well-knit and working with laws that have been made inherent in it, there is undoubtedly "natural causation," and, as we shall see more fully in chapter IV, the Qur'an recognizes this. But this does not mean that God creates nature and then goes to sleep; nor, of course, does this mean that God and nature or God and the human will (as elaborated in chapter II) are "rivals" and function at the expense of each other; nor yet does it mean that God operates in addition to the operations of man and nature. Without God's activity, the activity of nature and man becomes delinquent, purposeless, and self-wasting. Things and humans are, indeed, directly related to God just as they are related to each other, and we must further interpret our statement that God is not an item among other items of the universe, or just an existent among other existents. He is "with" everything; He constitutes the integrity of everything: "Do not be like those who forgot God and [eventually] God caused them to forget themselves" (al-Ḥashr: 19). And just as everything is related directly to Him, so is everything, through and in relation to other things, related to God as well. God, then, is the very meaning of reality, a meaning manifested, clarified, and brought home by the universe, helped even further by man.

As we have shown above Fazlur Rahman's conceptualization of God is *good* because it is *useful* for mankind; this is strictly in agreement with the pragmatist's concept of God. Hence, for Fazlur Rahman God is a pragmatic or functional concept because it aids man in achieving good and happiness in life, which to him is freedom and salvation. He states that:

> "What the human situation is … the basic moral tensions of the human nature. The overall gain for a man or society generally imbued with such a faith is that they march ahead hopefully to conquer nature and to build a just, equitable, free and creative social order in harmony and unison with laws of God, and avoid the numbing frustration of a materialist or an agnostic whose hopelessness is the handiwork of the negative forces called the Devil."[57]

Pragmatic Arguments for Belief in God

> "This is most certainly not to say that the Qur'an is indifferent to the truth value of its statements, but to affirm that the

truth-value of statements – even about God – is subservient to and, in some vital sense, needs to be tested by their success in producing a state of affairs in the world. It should not, therefore, shock or surprise anyone that, although Allah (God) is mentioned in the Qur'an more than six thousand times (apart from other quasi-names of the Deity, like al-Rahman – 'the Merciful' – and Rabb – 'the Sustainer'), all these statements are *actually* statements about man – the center of all interest in the Qur'an".[58]

Fazlur Rahman believed that Islam in its contemporary modernist era was facing the daunting challenge of atheism and secularism. Primarily, Fazlur Rahman's theological thought attempted at providing a reasonable and rational basis for a belief in God. As we have shown above Fazlur Rahman reformulated Ibn Sīna's doctrine of necessity to address the intellectual mindset of his age. Thus, Fazlur Rahman employed pragmatic arguments to establish theistic belief. Theistic pragmatic arguments are not arguments for the proposition that God exists; they are arguments that believing that God exists is rational. The most famous theistic pragmatic argument is Pascal's Wager.[59] Pascal's Wager states that, "God is, or He is not":

1. A game is being played... where heads or tails will turn up.

2. According to reason, you can defend either of the propositions.

3. You must wager. (It is not optional.)

4. Let us weigh the gain and the loss in wagering that God is. Let us estimate these two chances. If you gain, you gain all; if you lose, you lose nothing.

5. Wager, then, without hesitation that He is. Not. There is here an infinity of an infinitely happy life to gain, a chance of gain against a finite number of chances of loss, and what you stake is finite. And so our proposition is of infinite force, when there is the finite to stake in a game where there are equal risks of gain and of loss, and the infinite to gain.

Pascal's Wager is the most commonly referred to example of a pragmatic argument for the establishment of belief. The wager proposes that in the face of extreme skepticism in the belief in God it is more pragmatic if the probability of their being a God turns out to be true. Hence on the basis of the probability and not surety or certainty is belief in God established. Further, belief is established with the objective of utility in mind. Thus, the decision to believe in God is with consideration to lack of certainty and possibility of gain in the future.

Pragmatic arguments are relevant to belief-formation, since inculcating a belief is an action. There are, broadly speaking, two kinds of pragmatic arguments that have to do with belief-formation. The first is an argument that recommends taking steps to believe a proposition because, if it should turn out to be true, the benefits gained from believing that proposition will be impressive. This first kind of pragmatic argument we can call a "truth-dependent" pragmatic argument, or more conveniently a "dependent-argument," since the benefits are obtained only if the relevant state of affairs occurs. The prime example of a dependent-argument is a pragmatic argument that uses a calculation of expected utility and employs the Expectation Rule to recommend belief:

"whenever both probability and utility values are known, one should choose to do an act which has the greatest expected utility."[60]

Among the various versions of his wager argument, Pascal employs this rule in a version which states that no matter how small the probability that God exists, as long as it is a positive, non-zero probability, the expected utility of theistic belief will dominate the expected utility of disbelief. Given the distinction between (A) having reason to think a certain proposition is true, and (B) having reason to induce belief in that proposition, taking steps to generate belief in a certain proposition may be the rational thing to do, even if that proposition lacks sufficient evidential support. The benefits of believing a proposition can rationally take precedence over the evidential strength enjoyed by a contrary proposition; and so, given an infinite expected utility, Pascal's Wager contends that forming the belief that God exists is the rational thing to do, no matter how small the likelihood that God exists.

The second kind of pragmatic argument, which can be called a "truth-independent" pragmatic argument, or more conveniently, an "independent-argument," is one which recommends taking steps to believe a certain proposition simply because of the benefits gained by believing it, whether or not the believed proposition is true. This is an argument that recommends belief cultivation because of the psychological, or moral, or religious, or social, or even the prudential benefits gained by virtue of believing it. In David Hume's *Dialogues Concerning Natural Religion*, for example, Cleanthes employs an independent argument, "religion, however corrupted, is still better than no religion at all. The doctrine of a future state is so strong and necessary a security to morals that we never ought to abandon or neglect it" (Hume, 1711-1776). Perhaps the best-known example of an independent-argument is found in William James's celebrated "Will to Believe" essay in which he argues that, in certain circumstances, it is rationally and morally permissible to believe a proposition because of the benefits thereby generated.

Unlike independent pragmatic arguments, dependent ones are, in an important sense, truth-sensitive. Of course, being pragmatic arguments, dependent-arguments are not truth-sensitive in an evidential sense; nevertheless they are dependent on truth since the benefits are had only if the recommended belief is true. In contrast, independent pragmatic arguments, yielding benefits whether or not the recommended beliefs are true, are insensitive to truth. Independent-arguments, we might say, are belief-dependent and not truth-dependent.

Here Fazlur Rahman locates the middle term between dependent and independent pragmatic arguments and opines that despite the truth value of the Qur'an's statements which he does consider to be true. The concept of God must also appeal to man in a vital sense i.e., not only intellectual but willingly as well. Here it becomes clear that Fazlur Rahman has attempted a synthesis between the voluntarism and evidentialism or will and intellect.

Moral Arguments for Belief in God

Having established that purpose of the Qur'anic concept of God and belief in it are squarely for the benefit of man Fazlur Rahman discusses the nature of the relationship between God's action *vis-a-vis* man's, he states:

> "It is because of the practical purposiveness of the Qur'an that
> it avoids all theoretical discussion on the nature of God ... the

interest of the Qur'an is to keep human conduct within ... tension".[61]

Fazlur Rahman argues that Qur'an does not possess a speculative approach to the concept of God but rather a moral approach to the concept of God. Thus, the concept of God is not intended for the intellect to *understand* but it is for the self to *intuit*. In other words, the Qur'anic concept of God affects the psychic nature of man more than his intellectual nature and by doing so the message of the Qur'an becomes *universal* and not *particular* for the elite. As we have stated above, Fazlur Rahman considered the God of the Qur'an to be a functional being, a being who is to be estimated according to what He does."[62] Thus, the Qur'an does not provide clear arguments for the problem of Divine power and how it affects human freedom.[63] It is more concerned with maintaining man in a state of moral tension to rectify the attitude of man and make it resolute in order to achieve a specific purpose – the establishment of a good moral order.

Kant's Moral Imperative is an anchoring point in Fazlur Rahman's moral theology. The Moral Imperative is a principle originating inside a person's mind that compels that person to act. It is a kind of *categorical imperative*. Kant interpreted the imperative to be the dictate of pure reason in its practical aspect. Not following the moral law was seen to be self defeating and thus contrary to reason. Later thinkers took the imperative to originate in the conscience, as the divine voice speaking through the spirit. The dictates of the conscience are simply right and often resist further justification. In other words, the experience of the conscience is the basic experience of encountering the right. Fazlur Rahman believes that when the Qur'an speaks about the *fitra*[64] or innate nature and *shākila* or innate propensity of man, it is referring to God's imprinting the moral imperative from which man is incapable of escaping from, 'God has ingrained in it a discernment of good and evil' (al-Shams: 8). This imprinting of the moral imperative – Fazlur Rahman uses the Qur'anic term of *amr*. We shall address the Qur'anic term *amr* in the following section:

God's Relationship to the Universe

The fundamental teaching of the Qur'an about the universe is: (a) that it is a cosmos, an order; (b) that it is a developing, dynamic order; (c) man should study the laws of the universe which constitute part of the behavior of God (*sunnat ullah fi al-kawn*); (d) the Universe is the domain in which man fulfills purposeful activity.

Iqbal defines Nature as:

"Modern science regards Nature not as something static, situated in an infinite void, but a structure of interrelated events out of whose mutual relations arise the concepts of space and time. And this is only another way of saying that space and time are interpretations which thought puts upon the creative activity of the Ultimate Ego."[65]

The doctrine of the power of God subsumes the Qur'anic terms of creation-measuring out-command *khalq-taqdīr-'amr*. This power issues forth in the merciful creativity of God, in terms of "measuring" things, producing them "according to a certain order or measure," not haphazardly or blindly. It should be noted here that in Arabic the term for both power and measuring out is *qadar* and the Qur'an uses *qadar* in both senses. In pre-Islamic Arabia, this term, more often in its plural form *aqdār*, was used to mean "fate," a blind force that "measured out" or predetermined matters that were beyond man's control, in particular his birth, the sources of his sustenance, and his death. It was a pessimistic belief, but it was not a belief in fate's predetermination of all human acts.

According to the Qur'an when God creates something, i.e., brings it into being and gives it external form, at the same time he invests it with laws of its being and inlays it with potentialities and dynamics of its development. The first (i.e. bringing something into being and giving it a form) is called *khalq*, while the second is termed by the Qur'an either *'amr* (which means Command) or *taqdīr*. The terms *'amr* and *taqdīr* call for some elaboration of their meaning. The expression *'taqdīr'* literally means 'measuring out,' something and *qadar* is a quantity or volume measured out. Additionally, *taqdīr* is to be understood in terms of powers, potentialities, dispositions-cum-processes rather than in terms of events and happenings i.e., predetermination of events as the orthodox theological schools believe. Fazlur Rahman contends that the orthodox opinion is in opposition to the Qur'an and regards it to be a foreign importation.[66]

Fazlur Rahman begins constructing the Qur'anic doctrine of creation by quoting from it: "Glory the name of thy Lord, the Exalted Who created (*khalaqa* i.e. gave form to things) and consummated (the forms) and Who (having created) inlaid the potentialities (of things: *qaddara*) and thus gave direction (*hada*)" (al-A'lā: 1-3). He adduces from these verses that when God creates or externally forms a thing, at the same time invests it with its inner, natural constitution, the dynamic law of its behavior, i.e., its *taqdir* which also constitutes its *hidāyah*, the direction or the goal towards which it tends.

In another passage in Surah Fuṣṣilat: "When He said to the heavens and the earth, 'Come hither willingly or unwillingly', they replied, 'We come in voluntary obedience (i.e., not despite ourselves)'... God then inspired every heavenly sphere with its peculiar *'amr* (i.e., taqdir) ... and this *taqdir* (investment with dynamic laws of behavior) was by the Mighty, Knowing God", (Fuṣṣilat: 11-12). The same phrase, "*taqdīr* by the Mighty, Knowing God" is used in Yā Sīn: 39, where the orderly revolutions of space bodies are described, which are said to "swim" each in its own orbit. The Qur'an's avid description of embryology in (al-Mursalāt: 20-23). Lastly, he cites another passage: "He created everything and invested it with *taqdīr* (i.e., determined its character by giving it a constitution)" (al-Furqān: 12).

Fazlur Rahman draws two important closely-connected points from these passages. First, events in the world are never predetermined or preordained by God (or indeed, by physical forces). Event A shall occur at a particular fixed time remains an open possibility, among other possible alternatives, until it is actually caused. This is because, secondly, what is determined are not events but potencies, powers and forces. Fazlur Rahman supports his argument with an example of chemical reaction between hydrogen and oxygen. He argues that the potencies of hydrogen and oxygen to turn into water if they are mixed under certain conditions. The actual event of their being so mixed at a definite space-time is never predetermined and depends on a host of factors. The fact, however, that things have definite, measurable natures, is also extended by the Qur'an into the further meaning of *qadr* as power. This is because everything which is measurable, is within grip, as it were, and does not have the quality of being absolutely free, or, rather, lawless. Thus, the term *qadr* or *qudrah* comes to mean 'power'.

With regards to the Qur'anic term *'amr* which we have rendered by the word 'command'. Fazlur Rahman modern interpretation of *'amr* is the law of behavior. In al-A'rāf: 54, the Qur'an speaks about how the sun and moon revolve, the Qur'an says, "To God belong both creation (*khalq*) and commanding (*'amr*, i.e., investing objects with dispositions, patterns of behavior, potencies)". Then in Yūnus: 3,31; the Qur'an concludes in identical terms "God systematically runs (*yadabbiru*) the Command". It is thus obvious that the concepts of *taqdīr and 'amr* are in this usage, identical with each other.

The universe then, manifests a primordial dynamic power which is purposeful and good. The fact that the universe exists at all, exhibits power and goodness for *viz.*, existence is better than non-existence. He argues that the existence of the universe affirmatively proves the existence of God and disagreement with this is pure disputatious.[67] Also, that his objective is to prove the existence of a power or will with these attributes we have ascribed to it. Since this will is purposeful, it follows that it is dynamic and ceaselessly creative.

Now that we have established that the universe has been created according to laws and runs on regular patterns and man is asked to discover these laws and locate these patterns so that he may conquer nature and harness it – not as a vain pursuit but to create goodness therein and to make it a vain pursuit but to create goodness therein and to make it subservient to his purposeful activity. The entire creation is laid at the service of man who may successfully exploit it for a good end. Although orthodoxy has presented a picture that God has created the universe for granted and man simply exists in it is deemed incorrect by Fazlur Rahman. He claims that man *with his efforts*, properly and constructively directed, man can harness nature for

His ever-unfolding good purposes. And this is, indeed his duty whose discharge constitutes "service" (*'ibādah*) on his part. This is based upon the divine trust God offered to the heavens and the earth and which they "refused" to accept, but which was voluntarily accepted by man. This "trust" is to discover the laws of, and thus get mastery over, nature – or, in the Qur'anic terminology, "to know the names of all things" – and then use this mastery, under the human moral initiative, to create a good world order.

God-Universe Relationship with Man

Fazlur Rahman considers man to be valuable and important because he occupies *the* central place in God's grand design. Since God is a necessary, purposeful and creative will, man is contingent upon God for his existence. As he has repeatedly, "existence is better than nonexistence" signifies two things to him, one which is primary and the other which is a result of its true nature. The primary significance of man being brought into existence is *goodness*. The other significance is because is inherently good his nature must be good as well, and therefore, he must serve a good purpose in God's ultimate wisdom. This is duly important because God's actions cannot be treated as arbitrary otherwise His Divine Intelligence and Wisdom is brought into question. Moreover, this line of questioning should push us towards investigating God's creation and trying to determine what it really *means*. Fazlur Rahman states:

> "The goal of man is to study the universe, the laws of his own inner psychic constitution and the process of history and then to this knowledge in the service of the good and that this purposeful activity – the *'ibādah* or 'service of God' – is the purpose of his creation and indeed, of all creation."[68]

Fazlur Rahman considered the acquisition of knowledge or education to be the primary step that man must undertake, thereafter the application of this knowledge to serve the goodness of humanity, to him served man's purpose of creation. Educating man or *teaching* man knowledge that is beneficial or detrimental is the purpose of revelation. God, therefore, taught man which he knew not in order to know himself and to help others. Albeit, this is an oversimplified explanation of Fazlur Rahman's central thrust but this is to underline the *common sense* approach he took to philosophy, theology and religion, in general.

He divides *all* knowledge into three broad categories, which he believes, and in consonance with Iqbal as well, that the Qur'an's teachings are divided into, namely three: (1) scientific knowledge of things (physical science) (2) man's inner constitution (psychological science) and (3) man's outer behavior as a continued process in time (historical science).[69] In the following section we are going to discuss the purpose of this knowledge which man above all creation is permitted to attain.

Doctrine of Man's Creative Knowledge

The doctrine of man's creative knowledge is not a doctrine that Fazlur Rahman formally enunciates as a doctrine *per se,* however he does repeat it and refer to it consistently in his writings about man's *true* nature. He adduces from Surah al-Baqarah: 30-33, when God informed the angels that He was going to create a vicegerent of His on earth to which the angels remonstrated that that creature "will work mischief and shed blood on earth". God implicitly accepting their criticism rejected their demands, saying, "I know what you know not". Then a test was given to the angels to "name" things, to which they were unable to. God's vicegerent, Adam, the archetypal of all mankind, "succeeds in giving names to things"; whereupon God said to the angels, "Did I not tell you that I knew better (why I created man)?". Fazlur Rahman emphatically believed that Adam's and mankind's ability in general which distinguishes him from the rest of creation is his capacity to "give names" to things.[70] Here it is highlighted Fazlur Rahman's interpretation of Qur'anic doctrines in the light of modern knowledge and requirements. He states:

> "Now, "naming"things implies the capacity to discover the properties of things, their interrelations and laws of behavior. That is to say, man is distinguished from the rest of the creation through his creative, scientific knowledge of things (physical science), of man's inner constitution (psychological science) and man's outer behavior as a continued process in time (historical science)."[71]

He reinterprets the Qur'anic *phrase* of 'naming of things' to 'discover the properties of things, their interrelations and laws of behavior'. This reinterpretation of the Qur'an's *dicta* is in consonance with his belief that the socio-historical demands of a time after the Qur'an's initial revelation necessitates. He also rejects the medieval conception of man as the 'microcosm'; contributing to his goal to render the worldview of Islam modern in all areas of knowledge. He conceives that naming in the modern world implies more than *just* naming i.e., its outward appearance, it is more concerned with its reality: the laws, theories and properties that govern any objective phenomena.

Fazlur Rahman conceives that the Qur'an's epistemological bases and all doctrines related to Islam as pragmatic and his conceptualization of man is no exception. The pragmatic school in epistemology contends that "truth is a matter of practical action and conceptual articulation" and this is precisely what he means by:

> "... partly man's essential task is to reconstruct a scientific picture of the objective reality and partly to proceed to interfere in it and create a moral order on the basis of this scientific knowledge."[72]

The second task that Fazlur Rahman discusses here addresses the pragmatic usage of scientific knowledge which he contends should be supervene on the first, i.e., the scientific structure. Further, he believes that the import of the verse in the Qur'an that speaks about the divine trust between man and God is signifying the task that man must perform.

Doctrine of Divine Trust (*Amanah*)

The Qur'an speaks of a divine trust taken between God and man when it says:

> "We offered this Trust to the heavens, the earth and the mountains but they declined to bear it and shrank back in fright, but Man bore it – he is, indeed, aggressively foolhardy."[73]

Fazlur Rahman considers that man being God's vicegerent on earth, vested by God with the intellectual capacity to generate a scientific understanding of the universe and then finally harnessing it and re-channeling it towards establishing a socio-moral order is the content of the divine trust that man volunteered to uphold. The Qur'an says in response to man's choice that he is "aggressively foolhardy."

The impact of this "Trust" being revealed and then realized by man should generate within a sense of responsibility and a need to honor this trust. This naturally should lead man to reflect upon how to fulfill the task given to him. Any outer action first requires an *inner* action or a state of mind that will allow a person to properly and successfully execute any task. Fazlur Rahman contends that the central brunt of the Qur'an's ethical teaching is to establish a delicate balance in a man's attitude to achieve this task. Here lies the *functional* aspect of God is revealed in the life of man. It provides purpose, meaning, duty and identity to man.

Fazlur Rahman argues that the antithetical extremes or poles in man come to constitute tensions in man's mental-moral life. The most basic and recurrent criticism the Qur'an makes of human character is that man is reckless, haughty, boastful, independent, and self-sufficient (in the sense that he considers himself to be the measure of all things) or his mood soon passes into that of abject desperation and hopelessness and a state of utter helplessness. There is hardly a creature who is both inflated and deflated so quickly. The basic purpose of the Qur'an is to create and maintain in man an attitude between these two extremes: If one of these extremes is reached *kufr* or rejection of the source of life whether he becomes devoid of hope or devoid of necessary humility, i.e., the necessity to submit to an order or a standard which is outside him. Thus, the Qur'an is concerned to bring about and maintain a state of between these two – a state of self-control and confidence. It is only by intensifying this state of mind that the creative energy and quality of man can be maximized which is the purpose of human life. This is the state of faith (*īman*), the opposite is *kufr*. Man at this point would deem it necessary to protect himself from *kufr*. This "protection" is denoted by Fazlur Rahman as *taqwā*. God then grants or gifts man a correct perception of things – intellectually and morally –

a perception which the Qur'an often calls "guidance" (*hudā*) and "light" (*nūr*).

Doctrine of Man's Actions and Divine Response

Fazlur Rahman formulates the doctrine of man's actions and divine response as logical extension based upon the doctrine of divine trust. The divine trust between God and man necessitates that man attain and develop a level of cognizance where he is intimately aware of his responsibilities and tasks that he has to achieve i.e., his duty to God. This level of cognizance Fazlur Rahman refers to as the "middle" state (*wasaṭa*), probably based on the Qur'anic verse (al-Baqarah: 143). He argues this state is a condition for this guidance and light, but nonetheless this guidance and light is a "gift" of God. He considers it a gift from God because man's actions are not a total cause for that response and God's will cannot be commandeered at will. Thus, man must apply his full faculties and abilities towards achieving a particular task but in no *absolute* terms will God respond in the manner that man desires. However, claims Fazlur Rahman, God generally does reward man's efforts with success.[74]

Similar to man's cognitive situations so is the case with man's moral situation Fazlur Rahman states:

> "It is for this reason that God is described as the 'Light of the heavens and the earth' (al-Nūr: 35), a Light which is definite and not vague in its functions and modes of operation ... the opposite condition is described as 'layers upon layers of darkness wherein one cannot see one's own hand if one were to stretch it out (al-Nūr: 40)'"[75]

Man actively gropes, God gives perception: man searches, God grants discovery, man prays, i.e., makes the effort, God brings the result. It is upon man to struggle, endeavor and fight:

to achieve goodness, to attain results is *conditional* upon man's proper endeavor but is likewise a gift of God. Hence, if man exerts his effort and displays the proper state of mind and attitude, God will be his comrade, his co-operative, his helper and friend.

Fazlur Rahman argues that the personal dimension of the effort and pretends to be able to treat it as a non-personal entity. A basic point about an effort or a struggle is the *personal* concern, the tension, the anxiety and hope which the agent experiences and without which no effort can be called an effort and no struggle a struggle and, in fact, it would be robbed of its hope. The idea of God gives him psychological strength and stability to carry out a task. This is the meaning of prayer. Prayer is an active, receptive attitude of mind, wherein the agent, while engaged in a cognitive or moral endeavor, seeks help from the source of life. Through this, new energies flow into the self of the one who prays. But it will be noticed that there must be a struggle or endeavor afoot on the part of the one who prays and it will be in the context of this struggle – that his prayers will have any meaning at all. This is why the Qur'an says, "Seek help (in your struggle, O Muslims!) from patience and prayers" (al-Baqarah: 45, 153). For, patience and prayer fortify the self so that it does not succumb to the weakening and corrosive influences of fears and temptations. It is through this renewal of strength and fresh infusion of energies that God becomes the friend and helper of the man of Faith: "This is because God is the comrade (*mawla*) of those who have faith but the *kafirs* (who negate the source of life and its implications have no comrade (Muḥammad: 11). For, in al-Furqān: 29;[76]

$$\text{لَّقَدْ أَضَلَّنِي عَنِ ٱلذِّكْرِ بَعْدَ إِذْ جَآءَنِي وَكَانَ ٱلشَّيْطَانُ لِلْإِنْسَانِ خَذُولاً}$$

This is, indeed, the crucial distinction between God and Satan, between men of faith fighting for good and their opponents, *viz.*, that whereas men of faith persevere, and as the struggle proceeds, become more and more energetic and full of conviction of the rightness of their cause, the opposite is the case with people who reject truth (*kafirs*).[77]

Fazlur Rahman's theological thought in general can be categorized into two major areas: (1) historical (2) normative. The historical component of Fazlur Rahman's theological thought studies the historical emergence, development and formulation of theological doctrines. The Mu'tazila and the *Ahl ul Sunnah wa'l Jama'ah* are considered to be the only significant theological schools that have influenced the course and content of Islam. On the other hand, the normative component of Fazlur Rahman's theological thought is his *Ijtihād* or new thinking in this area. This *Ijtihād* is based upon a religious philosophy stemming from the religious philosophical system of Ibn Sīna. Fazlur Rahman considers Ibn Sīna to be the first systematic thinker of Islam and believes that Ibn Sīna's work was the first attempt by any Muslim thinker to develop a religious philosophy of Islam.[78]

Fazlur Rahman's appreciation of Ibn Sīna can be attributed to his academic and scholarly occupation with him in the first phase of his intellectual and scholarly career, dedicating himself to: (1) *Avicenna's Psychology* (2) *Avicenna's De Anima* (3) *Prophecy in Islam*. Avicenna's philosophy was not solely an intellectual affair but was dedicated towards developing a scientific, purposeful and meaningful system of thought that represented Islamic philosophy. Further, Ibn Sīna represents to Fazlur Rahman as standing in the middle between two traditions – the Hellenistic and the Islamic.

Fazlur Rahman finds that Ibn Sīna is a citizen of two intellectual-spiritual worlds; the Hellenistic and the Islamic. Similarly, Fazlur Rahman deeply connected with the overall condition of the Muslims in his time also found himself as a citizen of two intellectual-spiritual worlds; the Western and the Islamic. Similarly, in both their minds they have intrinsically unified the two worlds that they are identical; the question of loyalty to either, therefore, does not arise for him at all. Under these circumstances, both traditional Islam and the heritage of Hellenism were inevitably interpreted and modified to a greater or lesser extent. This is apparent in the whole of his philosophy which enters into the technically religious field, but is most palpably so in his doctrine of prophecy. Fazlur Rahman himself considered himself to be standing in the middle between the Western and Islamic. The synthesis achieved by Fazlur Rahman and the system of thought that he developed incorporated many elements and the most significant are from Ibn Sīna, Ibn Taymīya, Ahmad Sirhindī, Shah Wali Ullah and Iqbal.

Fazlur Rahman argued that the correct methodology that needed to be followed in developing a creative and dynamic system of thought necessitated that the Qur'an be studied as a unity, after which the metaphysical foundations for the God-World-Man relationship be expressed in a systematic theological expression; thereafter, Islamic ethics and law. Now here it is important to understand the significance of how a prophet is an essential element of Islam. Firstly, because he is the human recipient of divine revelation, what is the nature of this interaction? Secondly, the prophet being a human being invested with a divine message and ordered to preach this knowledge – how is this knowledge distinct from other knowledge?

Notes

[1] Fazlur Rahman, *Islam and Modernity*, p.5.

[2] Fazlur Rahman, "The Qur'anic Concept of God, the Universe and Man", *Islamic Studies* Vol. 6, no. 1 (March 1967), pp.1-18.

[3] Fazlur Rahman, "The Qur'anic Concept of God, the Universe and Man", *Islamic Studies* Vol. 6, no. 1 (March 1967), p.3.

[4] Muhammad Iqbal, *The Reconstruction of Religious Thought in Islam*, p.29.

[5] Fazlur Rahman, *Islam*, p.33.

[6] Fazlur Rahman, *Major Themes of the Qur'an*, p.1.

[7] Fazlur Rahman, "The Qur'anic Concept of God, the Universe and Man", *Islamic Studies* Vol. 6, no. 1 (March 1967), p.1.

[8] Fazlur Rahman, *Islam and Modernity*, pp.144-145.

[9] Fazlur Rahman, *Major Themes of the Qur'an*, p.1.

[10] *Ibid*, p.1.

[11] Fazlur Rahman, *Islamic Philosophy, Encyclopedia of Philosophy*, p.780.

[12] Fazlur Rahman, *Major Themes of the Qur'an*, p.2.

[13] Jordan, Jeff, "*Pragmatic Arguments and Belief in God*", The Stanford Encyclopedia of Philosophy (Spring 2011 Edition), Edward N. Zalta(ed.).

[14] Fazlur Rahman, "The Qur'anic Concept of God, the Universe and Man", *Islamic Studies* Vol. 6, no. 1 (March 1967), p.1.

[15] Fazlur Rahman, *Major Themes of the Qur'an*, p.1.

[16] Encyclopedia of Christian Theology; Millard J. Erickson, *Christian Theology*, 2nd ed. (Grand Rapids: Baker Book House, 1998), p.51.

[17] Volume 8, Book 74, Number 246: *khalaqa Allahu Adam ʿala suratihi*, Ibn Hajr considers that the pronoun of *suratihi* is referring back to Adam not to God Himself.

خَلَقَ اللهُ عَزَّ وَجَلَّ آدَمَ على صُورَتِهِ طُولُهُ سِتُّونَ ذِرَاعاً، فَلَمَّا خَلَقَهُ قال: اذْهَبْ فَسَلِّمْ على أُولَئِكَ: نَفَرٍ مِنَ الْمَلَائِكَةِ جُلُوسٍ فاسْتَمِعْ ما يُحَيُّونَكَ فإِنَّهَا تَحِيَّتُكَ وَتَحِيَّةُ ذُرِّيَّتِكَ، فقال: السَّلامُ عَلَيْكُمْ، فقالُوا: السَّلامُ عَلَيْكَ وَرَحْمَةُ اللهِ، فَزَادُوهُ: وَرَحْمَةُ اللهِ"

[18] Millard J. Erickson, *Christian Theology*, (Grand Rapids, MI: Baker Book House, 1994), pp. 498-510; Millard J. Erickson, *Introducing Christian Doctrine*, 2nd ed. (Grand Rapids: Baker Book House, 2001), pp. 172-175.

[19] Saint Irenaeus (2nd century AD – c. 202) was Bishop of Lugdunum in Gaul, then part of the Roman Empire. He was an early church father and apologist, and his writings were formative in the early development of Christian theology.

[20] Ibn Sīna, *A History of Muslim Philosophy*, vol.2, p.482.

[21] *Ibid*, p.481.

[22] *Ibid*, p.482.

[23] *Ibid*, p.483.

[24] Fazlur Rahman, *Islam and Modernity*, p.145.

[25] Ibn Sīna, *A History of Muslim Philosophy*, p.483.

[26] *Ibid*, p.483.

[27] Fazlur Rahman, "Essence and Existence in Ibn Sīna: The Myth and the Reality", *Hamdard Islamicus* 4 (1981), pp.3-9.

[28] Ibn Sīna, *A History of Muslim Philosophy*, p.483.

[29] *Ibid*, p.485.

[30] *Ibid*, p.485.

[31] *Ibid*, p.486.

[32] *Ibid*, p.502.

[33] *Ibid*, p.502.

[34] *Ibid*, p.503.

[35] *Ibid*, p.503.

[36] Fazlur Rahman, *Islamic Methodology in History*, p.121.

[37] Fazlur Rahman, "The Qur'anic Concept of God, the Universe and Man", *Islamic Studies* Vol. 6, no. 1 (March 1967), p.2.

[38] *Ibid*, p.2.

[39] *Ibid*, p.2.

[40] *Ibid*, p.2.

[41] See Ibn Sīna, *A History of Muslim Philosophy*, p.480; Fazlur Rahman adopted Ibn Sīna's habit of locating the middle term. The former would avail this method as a means to attain a synthesis.

[42] Fazlur Rahman, "The Qur'anic Concept of God, the Universe and Man", *Islamic Studies* Vol. 6, no. 1 (March 1967), p.2.

[43] *Ibid*, p.2.

[44] *Ibid*, p.3.

[45] *Ibid*, p.3.

[46] *Ibid*, p.3.

[47] Al-Maturidi Abu Mansur, *Ta'wīlat Ahl ul-Sunnat*, vol. 4, Dar al-Kutub, (Beirut), Lebanon, p.320.

[48] Al Nibrās, pp.198-202.

[49] *Ibid*, p.3.

[50] *Ibid*, p.4.

[51] *Ibid*, p.5.

[52] *Ibid*, p.5.

[53] Fazlur Rahman, "Fundamental Ideas in the Philosophy of Value", *Pakistan Philosophical Journal* 8 (1964), p.13.

[54] *Ibid*, p.13.

[55] *Ibid*, p.13.

[56] *Ibid*, p.7.

[57] Fazlur Rahman, "The Qur'anic Concept of God, the Universe and Man", *Islamic Studies* Vol. 6, no. 1 (March 1967), p.5.

[58] Fazlur Rahman, "The Qur'anic Concept of God, the Universe and Man", *Islamic Studies* Vol. 6, no. 1 (March 1967), p.1.

[59] See Pascal, Blaise, *Encyclopedia of Philosophy*, 2nd ed., editor in chief by Donald M. Borchert, (Thomson Gale Publications, 2006). Blaise Pascal (1623-1662) French Philosopher devised an argument that came to be known as Pascal's Wager. Historically, Pascal's Wager was groundbreaking because it charted new territory in probability theory, marked the first formal use of decision theory, and anticipated future philosophies such as existentialism, pragmatism and voluntarism.

[60] Jordan, Jeff, "Pragmatic Arguments and Belief in God", *The Stanford Encyclopedia of Philosophy (Spring 2011 Edition)*, Edward N. Zalta (ed.).

[61] Fazlur Rahman, "The Qur'anic Concept of God, the Universe and Man", *Islamic Studies* Vol. 6, no. 1 (March 1967), p.1.

[62] *Ibid*, p.17.

[63] *Ibid*, p.1.

[64] *Encyclopedia of Islam*, entry: *fitra* "a kind or way of creating or of being created", pp.931-932.

[65] Muhammad Iqbal, *The Reconstruction of Religious Thought in Islam*, p.30.

[66] Fazlur Rahman, "The Qur'anic Concept of God, the Universe and Man", *Islamic Studies* Vol. 6, no. 1 (March 1967), p.6.

[67] Fazlur Rahman, "The Qur'anic Concept of God, the Universe and Man", *Islamic Studies* Vol. 6, no. 1 (March 1967), p.8.

[68] Fazlur Rahman, "The Qur'anic Concept of God, the Universe and Man", *Islamic Studies* Vol. 6, no. 1 (March 1967), p.10.

[69] *Ibid*, p.11.

[70] *Ibid*, p.11.

[71] *Ibid*, p.11.

[72] *Ibid*, p.11.

[73] al-Aḥzāb: 72.

[74] Fazlur Rahman, "The Qur'anic Concept of God, the Universe and Man", *Islamic Studies* Vol. 6, no. 1 (March 1967), p.13.

[75] *Ibid*, p.14.

[76] "Satan always (ultimately) leaves his men in the lurch" (al-Furqān: 29).

[77] Fazlur Rahman, "The Qur'anic Concept of God, the Universe and Man", *Islamic Studies* Vol. 6, no. 1 (March 1967), p.14.

[78] Ibn Sīna, *A History of Muslim Philosophy*, p.485.

Chapter IV
Concept of Prophethood

he Qur'an is the Word of God revealed to the Prophet (ṣ) implies that the Qur'an is uncreated and eternal attribute of God, insofar as it constitutes His Word (or Speech), or is it something created and not an eternal attribute? In the modern period as opposed to the medieval postulations related to this matter, the question took on a different form "how the Prophet's (ṣ) mind came into touch with a set of words which had divine and eternal origin?"[1]

Prophecy or prediction (*tanabu'*) is one of the functions of a prophet. *Tanabu'* or prophecy has been defined as a "miracle of knowledge, a declaration or description or representation of something in the future, beyond the power of human sagacity to foresee, discern, or conjecture."[2] Etymologically, *nubuwwat* is from the root word *n-b-a'* which literally means something elevated and *risalat* is from the root word *r-s-l* which means the one who is selected by God and follows that which is revealed to him. [3] *Al-Jawhari* records that *nubuwwat* means 'news of great benefit providing knowledge or overcoming doubt'.[4] Al-Fayumi defines to prophesize means 'to teach'.[5] Al-Isfahani states that *nabi* refers 'to a way' (*tarik*) and *rasul* is referred 'to as objects representing paths to guidance'.[6] Qadī 'Abdul Jabbār argues that there is no difference between the prophet (*nabi*) and messenger (*rasul*) in response to the historical theological debate on the issue: a prophet is someone who has received revelation (*akhbar*) and elevation from God over the rest of humanity; and a messenger is someone who is sent forth (*mab'uth*) by God. The prophets encounter confrontation (*mu'arada*) and dialectical argumentation (*mujadala*) from the people they are sent to. Muhammad (*ṣ*) was provided with miracles (*mu'jiza*) – primarily, the Qur'an and other physical miracles such as the splitting of the moon and water flowing between his fingers – to apodeictically demonstrate the truth and veracity of his argument and his anointed status before God.[7]

The Mu'tazila, Asha'rī and Maturidi theologians (*mutakallimūn*) such as Qadī 'Abdul Jabbār (d. 367 AH/978 CE), al-Ghazālī[8] (d. 506 AH/1111 CE) and Abu Mansur al-Maturidī[9] (d.333 AH/ 944 CE) unanimously hold that prophethood is rationally obligatory upon God. Qadī 'Abdul Jabbār (d. 367 AH/978 CE) categorizes prophethood under the principle of justice (*a'sl al-'adl*) and claims it to be rationally obligatory upon God. The Mu'tazilites contended that prophethood is necessary upon God because it represents God's divine grace (*lutf*) – God organizing affairs in order to bring about a beneficial state of affairs. Hence, it is in God's concern for what is 'in the best interest' (*silah wa al-asluh*) of mankind that God sends forth his prophets' and messengers' that they may follow God's divine commandments (*shar'iyat*). The agency of prophethood makes apparent that which is good (*husn*) and evil (*qubh*). Further, as we are unable to determine whether a particular act is rationally beneficial (*maslaha*) or harmful (*mafsada*) it becomes imperative upon God to protect human beings from harm (*daf* *al-ḍarar*).[10]

The Ash'arī Fakhr ul-Din al-Razi argues that it is imperative that every human being have a leader (*ra'is*): if the leader commands only exterior acts (*zāhir*) then he is only a king (*sultan*) and if he commands upon the interior acts (*batin*) then he is a scholar (*'alim*) however if he is both then he is a prophet (*nabi*). Al-Razī argues that the rational need of prophethood is to acquire for the rest of humanity the manner of worship acceptable before God, thereby eliminating disputations between them otherwise tribulations would befall them. Secondly, the intellect is habit or custom orientated (*'ibādat*) and the Divine Law (*sharī'ah*) is worship (*'ibādah*) and custom is not worship.[11]

Abu Mansur al-Maturīdī argues that the prophets were raised up amongst a people whose temperament, mentality and custom were well known to them in order to be able to establish the existence of God with the aid of revelation. Also, the prophets are given an ability to discern the consequence of the actions of their people and argumentatively defeat any opponents with the revelation that they have expressly received and to further substantiate a wise, omniscient and a God capable of proving His existence. Secondly, the prophets can inform their people about the commandments (*'awāmir*) and prohibitions (*nawāhi*) made obligatory upon them and the afflictions (*mihna*) that they will face if they do not abide by them. Thus, knowledge of the promise (*wa'd*) and threat (*wa'id*) associated with the commandments, prohibitions and afflictions should cultivate wisdom (*hikmah*) in them. Al-Maturidī rejects the Mu'tazila principle that the purpose of sending prophets is not for the 'attainment of benefit and prevention from harm', but for the 'witnessing of God's wisdom (*hikmah*) and self-sufficiency (*ghanī*)'. Lastly, the prophets generate an affinity towards truth and justice in their people and repulsion towards falsehood and injustice.[12]

Islamic theologians (*mutakallimun*) did not partake in any theological discussion on the nature and method of revelation and the process of prophecy itself, rather their discussions treated revelation *a posteriori* and based upon Hadīths. On the other hand, Fazlur Rahman and the Islamic philosophers (*falasifa*) were more interested in the *a priori* discussion related to the very nature and method of prophecy itself. Ibrahim Madkur (d. 1996) points out that the Islamic philosophers' paid specific attention to three areas: (1) Happiness; (2) Prophethood; and (3) Soul for this very reason. Madkur contends that the philosophers focused upon prophethood because it was the most significant attempt at achieving a concordance (*tawfiq*) between: Philosophy (*falsafah*) and Religion (*din*); and Law (*Shari'ah*) and Wisdom (*hikmah*).[13]

According to Fazlur Rahman, al-Farābī was the first to develop a theory of prophethood based on two factors: the prophetic imagination and the religious-social order established by the prophet through an imaginative handling of the philosophical truth. He argues that prophecy is a connection between the active intellect and prophetic imagination. Madkur contends that al-Farābī attempted a psychological interpretation of prophethood, which represented the connection between God and mankind. For al-Farābī, prophethood was absolutely necessary because it was necessary to establish a virtuous city, that did not restrict his significance at an independent level but affected the political, moral, ethical and social aspects as well.[14] Madkur opines that the two areas that influenced al-Farābī's conceptualization of prophethood is on the one side his philosophical adherence with Platonism – which provided the socio-political dimension to the prophetic mission, and on the other hand his mystical connection to Muslim Sufism.[15]

Fazlur Rahman summarizes al-Farābī point of view into the following three main issues:

1. Prophet: He is utterly unique and distinct from all other human beings. He is an individual gifted an extraordinarily intellectual ability and is not common.

2. Prophetic intellect: The prophetic intellect is distinct from the philosophic and sufi intellect. He does not require any outside source for his personal intellectual evolution. He attains complete intellectual maturity entirely independent of any other source except God himself.

3. Prophetic issues: Upon attaining complete intellectual maturity, his intellect is elevated to the station of the active intellect and thereby being capable of receiving prophetic knowledge.[16]

Al-Farābī and Ibn Sīna were bitterly opposed by the orthodoxy (*ahl ul Sunnah wa'l jama'ah*) particularly by al-Ghazālī in his *Tahafut al-Falasifa* for equating the prophet to a philosopher. In response, Fazlur Rahman took al-Ghazālī to task and made him the center of his devastating critique throughout the extent of his works most probably because of the reliance of the orthodoxy on al-Ghazālī particularly his *Tahafut* and *Maqasid al-Falasifa*. It is quite apparent from Fazlur Rahman's writings that amongst the movements advocating a revival of Islam's past intellectual heritage, he attempted to revive Islamic philosophy. However, Fazlur Rahman was not content in merely reviving the classical Islamic philosophic tradition; he endeavored to modernize it by incorporating additional elements into Islamic philosophy in general and the concept of prophethood in particular. Thus, Ibn Sīna represented that critical figure and point in the history of Islam's intellectual history that could usher in a modern conceptualization of prophethood.

Avicenna's theory of prophethood[17], though it occupies a central place in his religious thought, cannot be regarded as the starting point of his thought but is rather a development of his metaphysics and epistemology. If his speculation on the nature and content of prophecy had been the starting point of his religious philosophy a very different metaphysics, especially a very different theory of the God-World relationship, would have been the result. It would have been similar to Sirhindī and Dehlawī – of these two, the metaphysics and epistemology of the intellectual revelation, the latter is really, when taken alone, not only indifferent to religion but incapable of producing a religious epistemology. The moral insight and the religious inspiration of the Prophet (ṣ) cannot have their basis in a purely intellectual intuitionism. And in his general theory of intellection Avicenna offers us only an intellectual intuitionism. However, Fazlur Rahman's criticism of Avicenna is that there is no religious mode of knowledge *viz.*, the moral imperative or of conscience.[18]

After Ibn Sīna had developed his metaphysics, he developed the basis of prophetic epistemology on the theory of pure intellection. Next, he relied upon his concept of the mutual relationship of philosophy and religion, which he had gained from his metaphysics and its comparison with religious dogmas. It would, therefore, be vain to look for a genuine point of transition from philosophy to the doctrine of prophecy in the philosopher's epistemology.

The most fundamental idea in Avicenna's doctrine of prophecy is that the prophetic religion is related to philosophy as a figure or a symbol is related to a corresponding reality. According to Fazlur Rahman this idea arose and was adopted from Avicenna's basic metaphysical theory, *viz.*, that of the God-World relationship and nature of God would be the most proper place to give rise to such an idea. Thus, Avicenna's theory of prophethood[19], occupies a central place in his religious thought; however, cannot be regarded as the starting point of his thought but is rather a development of his metaphysics and epistemology. If his speculation on the nature and content of prophecy had been the starting point of his religious philosophy a very different metaphysics, especially a very different theory of the God-World relationship, would have been the result. Of these two, the metaphysics and epistemology of the intellectual revelation, the latter is really, when taken alone, not only indifferent to religion but incapable of producing a religious epistemology. The moral insight and the religious inspiration of the prophet cannot have their basis in a purely intellectual intuitionism. And in his general theory of intellection Avicenna offers us only an intellectual intuitionism. There is no hint of a specifically religious mode of knowledge, of the moral imperative or of conscience.

Fazlur Rahman contends in his *Prophecy in Islam* that Ibn Sīna took al-Farābī's conceptualization and further supplied a basis for an intellectual revelation and added a rational psychological explanation of the orthodox doctrine of the prophetic miracles.[20] Ibn Sīna argued that the soul directly received knowledge from the heavenly sphere instead of searching for it in the lower worldly sphere. Thus, the prophetic nature is gifted with a miraculous intellect – with it he is able to acquire knowledge without the aid of any foreign source.

Ibn Sīna however, disagreed on two points between the prophetic intellect and the philosophic and sufi intellect:

1. Normal human intellect needs to persistently acquire more information and train all of his previous cumulative experiences. Thus, the human intellect is similar to a mirror that after the passage of time wear and tear begin to develop and the mirror loses its shine and beauty. On the other hand, the prophet's intellect does not need such refinement or acquisition of knowledge at all; he is bequeathed with an intellect that is pure and able to directly connect with the active intellect.

2. Normal human intellect receives knowledge partially whereas the prophetic intellect attains in the most complete, absolute and instant manner.

3. The critical point which distinguishes the prophetic intellect from the philosophic and sufi intellect is the prophet's extraordinary imaginative ability. Further, his ability to translate these symbolic images into verbal and physical expressions. [21]

Since the content of the prophet's faith is comprised of different objects so too is the prophet's faith the very object of a Muslims' faith. Hence, the objects of faith that a prophet professes are the same objects of faith in the faith of Muslims. Thus, the active intellect (*'aql ul-Fa'al*) and the world soul are objects of the prophet's faith and also for Muslims as well. Therefore, here lies the middle term or point of contact between his purely rational metaphysics and the phenomenon of prophethood.[22]

Fazlur Rahman pinpoints two basic issues why the orthodox rejected Avicenna's theory of God and His relationship to the world than in any Greek philosophy theory. One of these is its relentless theistic determinism. Although the world is not in itself necessary but only possible, it becomes nevertheless necessary when viewed from God's side, which operates by a rational dynamic necessity. The other issue concerns the philosopher's acceptance of the eternity of the world and his rejection of temporal creation. [23]

The doctrine of the God-world relationship, therefore, offers the most genuine point of transition to Avicenna's doctrine of prophethood. Prophetic religion states there is God, philosophy has established the first cause and the Giver of existence; religion asserts that God has created the world in time and through His will, philosophy has established an eternal dependence of the world on God. It is after this that religious attributes of God as formulated by orthodox theology are discussed and given new, philosophic interpretations.

The terms of Avicenna's approach to the problem of prophecy are squarely set by philosophy. The aspect of this theory of prophecy that is closest and most intimately related to the ethos of historic Islam is its teaching that the Prophet (ṣ), by virtue of his office, must function as legislator and must found a community state. Fazlur Rahman argues that the relationship between the state-shari‘ah relationship: "the shari‘ah and its imperatives are declared to be merely symbolic of a higher philosophic reality which is available only to the philosopher."[24]

Fazlur Rahman paid particular attention to psychology of the prophet and prophetic intellect and wrote two critical studies upon this matter. Firstly, his doctoral thesis at Oxford, *Avicenna's Psychology* focused upon psychology in general and the psychology of the prophet in specific and secondly, his *Prophecy in Islam* deliberated upon the prophetic intellection. In an article published in the *Encyclopedia of Philosophy*, Fazlur Rahman wrote: "Al-Kindī, however, simply asserted emanationism and creationism side by side without reconciling the contradiction between the two."[25] It was Avicenna (Ibn Sīna) who later attempted the reconciliation, but it was important to the development of Islamic philosophy that al-Kindī, far from giving up the Islamic requirements of the relationship of God and the world, juxtaposed both the Islamic and Greek doctrines. In his theory of intellection, al-Kindī was attracted by the idea of a form of knowledge that would do justice to the demands of reason and revelation, although in his extant works we do not find an elaborated theory of prophethood. This, again, was taken up later by al Fārābi and Avicenna, but it was al-Kindī who initiated development of the theory of intellection in Islamic philosophy".[26] Meaning that the relationship between prophethood and God-world were interlocked and prophecy represented both prophetic psychology and intellection, hence Fazlur Rahman's interest in prophecy lay in determining the nature and character of "prophetic knowledge". Prophetic knowledge served as the basis for revelation and prophetic reason served as its interpretation.

Al-Fārābi constructed a theory of divine inspiration that was to serve as a model for Avicenna. But apart from his original theories, the importance of al-Fārābi lies in his attempt to elevate philosophy to the place of highest value and to subordinate the revelation and the Shari'ah, or religious law, to it. In this also he served as a model for both Avicenna and Averroës (Ibn Rushd), but it was precisely this doctrine, in which the Shari'ah took an inferior place as a symbolic expression of a higher intellectual truth, that also ultimately responsible for the fatal attacks on the philosophical movement by representatives of the orthodoxy.[27] Fazlur Rahman critically evaluated the relationship between religion and philosophy and attempted to historically evaluate the origin of the supremacy given to philosophy over religion, and more specifically to Shari'ah. Fazlur Rahman found that the unique position was given by al-Fārābi and later fully developed by Ibn Sīna and Averroës. Once determining the source of this relationship Fazlur Rahman in his own writings attempted to reestablish the supremacy of Religion and Shari'ah by establishing that philosophy established the ungainly characteristic of intellectual elitism which caused the lost egalitarianism and universalism of religion.[28] Hence, Fazlur Rahman's philosophy reversed the relationship that the classical Islamic philosophers and established his modern Islamic philosophy where religion and philosophy were on a level ground and aided one another. Philosophy no longer served as the "handmaid" of theology but positively stood side by side with religion, one aiding the other. Although al-Fārābi gave no concrete examples of religions or names of prophets, there is little doubt that the prophet Muḥammad (ṣ) was fixed in his mind as a paradigm par excellence of a prophet and a lawgiver. This becomes clear in his insistence that the teachings of a prophet should not only be universal but should also be successful in history.

Fazlur Rahman's concept of prophethood is comprised of two main principles: (1) the moral *élan* of divine revelation (2) prophecy and divine revelation. The moral *élan* of the Qur'an and the previous revelations revealed upon prophets' are considered to be unanimous amongst all revelations. Subsequently, Fazlur Rahman develops his concept of prophecy and divine revelation based upon the doctrine of prophecy of Ibn Sīna.[29] Fazlur Rahman incorporated further elements from Shah Wali Ullah and Iqbal in order to describe the nature of revelation.[30] Lastly, as we have stated in the introduction, Fazlur Rahman explained prophecy and revelation in the light of American pragmatism and German phenomenalism.

According to Fazlur Rahman, prophethood is comprised of human beings that are specially elected by God to receive divine revelation. Prophethood is indivisible and necessary that prophets are not discriminated against each other. All prophets are not equal in qualities such as patience and steadfastness. The conviction that God's messengers are ultimately vindicated, saved or given success is an integral part of the Qur'anic doctrine.[31] All prophets are human and never part of divinity: they are simply recipients of revelation from God. Fazlur Rahman in consonance with the Mu'tazila, considers that God never speaks directly to a human being, He either sends a messenger (angel) or makes him hear a voice or inspires him, basing his position on al-Shūrā 42:51[32]:

$$\text{وَمَا كَانَ لِبَشَرٍ أَن يُكَلِّمَهُ اللَّهُ إِلَّا وَحْياً أَوْ مِن وَرَاء حِجَابٍ}$$

$$\text{أَوْ يُرْسِلَ رَسُولاً فَيُوحِيَ بِإِذْنِهِ مَا يَشَاءُ إِنَّهُ عَلِيٌّ حَكِيمٌ}$$

Ibn Sīna posits that the necessity of the phenomenon of prophethood and of divine revelation is established at four levels: (1) intellectual (2) imaginative (3) miraculous (4) socio-political. Rahman reinterpreted the intellectual component as the prophet's insight to be both creative of knowledge and values. Ibn Sīna's central philosophical theses that serve as the foundation for his doctrine of prophecy:

1. Theory of Being has led to the dependence of every finite being on God.

2. Doctrine of Mind-Body and the genesis and nature of knowledge have culminated in the religious conception of miracles in the one case and of creative revelatory knowledge in the other.

In this doctrine, Ibn Sīna proposes a different solution opined by the dogmatic theologians:

1. Qur'anic revelation is symbolic of truth, not the literal truth, but that it must be the literal truth for the masses. However, this does not mean the Qur'an is not the word of God. Indeed, literally it is the word of God.

2. Law: Although it is to be observed by everyone, is partly symbolic and partly pedagogical and, therefore an essentially lower discipline than philosophic pursuits.

Fazlur Rahman contends that this doctrine has been re-interpreted and modified Hellenism and in general, the elements of the Muslim doctrine of prophethood exist in Hellenism. Nevertheless, they exist in a nebulous and sometimes crude form; further they are scattered. He argues, there is no evidence of a Greek conception of prophethood and prophetic revelation as the Muslims knew it. In fact the Muslim conception of prophethood is new and unique in the history of religion. The Muslim philosophers' al-Fārābi and Ibn Sīna evolved out of these nebulous, crude and disjointed elements an elaborate, comprehensive, and refined theory of prophecy to interpret the personality of Muḥammad (ṣ), is nothing short of the performance of a genius.[33]

Fazlur Rahman in his *Avicenna's Psychology* argues that Ibn Sīna developed an entire doctrine relation on the necessity of the prophetic revelation is proved by an argument elaborated on the basis of a remark of Aristotle that some people can hit upon the middle term without forming a syllogism in their minds. Since, people differ vastly with regard to their intuitive powers both in quality and quantity, and while some men are almost devoid of it, others possess it in a high degree, there must be a rarely and exceptionally endowed man who has a total contact with reality.[34] This man, without much instruction from outside, by his very nature, becomes the depository of the truth, in contrast with the common run of thinkers who may have an intuitive experience with regard to a definite question or questions but whose cognitive touch with reality is always partial, never total. This comprehensive insight then translates itself into propositions about the nature of reality and about future history it is simultaneously intellectual and moral-spiritual, hence the prophetic experience must satisfy both the philosophic and the moral criteria. It is on the basis of this creative insight that the true prophet creates new moral values and influences future history. A psychological-moral concomitant of this insight is also the deep and unalterable self-assurance and faith of the prophet in his own capacity for true knowledge and accurate moral judgment: he must believe in himself so that he can make others believe in him and thus succeed in his mission to the world.

Fazlur Rahman reinterpretation and modernization of prophetic insight as being (1) creative of knowledge and (2) values is termed by Ibn Sīna the active intellect and identified with the angel of revelation. Now, the prophet *qua* prophet is identical with the active intellect; and in so far as this identity is concerned, the active intellect is called *'aql al mustafād* (the acquired intellect). But the prophet *qua* human being is not identical with the active intellect. The giver of revelation is thus in one sense internal to the prophet, in another sense i.e., in so far as the latter is a human being, external to him. Hence, Ibn Sīna says that the prophet, in so far as he is human, is "accidentally"[35] not essentially, the active intellect. God can and, indeed, must come to man so that the latter may develop and evolve, but the meaning of God can at no stage be entirely exhausted in man. Fazlur Rahman writes in *Islam*:

> "But, with all this, there were moments when he, as it were, 'transcends himself' and his moral cognitive perception becomes so acute and so keen that his consciousness becomes identical with the moral law itself. "Thus did we inspire you with a spirit of Our command: You did not know what the Book was? But We have made it a light" (al-Jumu'ah: 52). But the moral law and religious values are God's command, and although they are not identical with God entirely, they are part of Him. The Qur'an is, therefore, purely divine. Further, even with regard to ordinary consciousness, it is a mistaken notion that ideas and feelings float about in it and can be mechanically 'clothed' in words. There exists, indeed, an organic relationship between feelings, ideas and words. In inspiration, even in poetic inspiration, this relationship is so complete that feeling-idea-word is a total complex with a life of its own. When Muhammad's (ṣ) moral intuitive perception rose to the highest point and became identified with the moral law itself (indeed, in these moments his own conduct at points came under Qur'anic criticism), the word was given with the inspiration itself. The Qur'an is thus pure divine word, but, of

course, it is equally intimately related to the inmost personality of the prophet Muḥammad (ṣ) whose relationship to it cannot be mechanically conceived like that of a record. The divine word flowed through the prophet's heart."[36]

But although the intellectual-spiritual insight is the highest gift the prophet possesses, he cannot creatively act in history merely on the strength of that insight. His office requires inherently that he should go forth to humanity with a message, influence them, and should actually succeed in his mission leads the Muslim philosophers, although they admit the divineness of the leading Greek thinkers and reformers, to fix their minds upon Moses, Jesus, and above all Muḥammad (ṣ) who, undoubtedly, possesses the requisite qualities of a prophet to the highest degree. These requisite qualities are that the prophet must possess a very strong and vivid imagination, that his psychic power be so great that he should influence not only other minds but also matter in general, and that he be capable of launching a socio-political system.

By the quality of an exceptionally strong imagination, the prophet's mind by an impelling psychological necessity, transforms the purely intellectual truths and concepts into life-like images and symbols so potent that one who hears or reads them not only comes to believe in them but is impelled to action. This symbolizing and vivifying function of the prophetic imagination is stressed both by al-Fārābi and Ibn Sīna, by the latter in greater detail. It is of the nature of imagination to symbolize and to give flesh and blood to our thoughts, our desires, and even our psychological inclinations. When we are hungry or thirsty, our imagination puts before us lively images of food and drink. Even when we have no actual sexual appetite but our physical condition is ready for this, imagination may come into play and by stirring up suitable vivid images may actually evoke this appetite by mere suggestion. This symbolization and suggestiveness, when it works upon the spirit and the intellect of the prophet, results in so strong and vivid images that what the prophet's spirit thinks and conceives, he actually comes to hear and see. That is why he "sees" the angel and "hears" his voice. That is why also he necessarily comes to talk of a paradise and a hell which represent the purely spiritual states of bliss and torment. The revelations contained in the religious scriptures are for the most part, of the figurative order and must, therefore, be interpreted in order to elicit the higher, underlying, spiritual truth.

It is the technical or moral revelation, then, which impels people to action and to be good, and not the purely intellectual insight and inspiration. No religion, therefore, can be based on pure intellect. However, the technical revelation, in order to obtain the necessary quality of potency, also inevitably suffers in order to obtain the necessary quality of potency, also inevitably suffers from the fact that it does not present the naked truth but truth in the garb of symbols. The prophet expresses his moral insight into definite enough moral purposes, principles, and indeed into a socio-political structure, neither his insight nor the potency of his imaginative revelation can be of much benefit. The prophet, therefore, needs to be a lawgiver and statesmen *par excellence* – indeed the real lawgiver and statesmen is only a prophet. This practical criterion emphasizes the personality of Muḥammad (ṣ) in the philosopher's mind. The law (Shari'ah) must be such that it should be effective in making people socially good, should remind them of God at every step, and should also serve for them as a pedagogic measure in order to open their eyes beyond its own exterior, so that they may attain to a vision of the true spiritual purpose of the lawgiver. The law is not abrogated at any stage for anybody, but only the philosophic vision of truth gives to the law its real meaning and when that vision is attained, the law seems like a ladder which one has climbed but which it would still be unwise to discard. For those relatively unfortunate souls which cannot see through the law its philosophic truth, the technical revelation and the letter of the law must remain the literal truth.

The Qur'an states that revelation came to the prophet via the spirit or angel Gabriel is represented by the Qur'an, but the Prophet (ṣ) could sometimes see and hear him. According to early traditions the Prophet's (ṣ) revelations occurred in a state of trance when his normal consciousness was in abeyance. This state was accompanied by heavy sweating. The Qur'an itself makes it clear that the revelations brought with them a sense of extraordinary weight:[37]

$$\text{لَوْ أَنزَلْنَا هَذَا الْقُرْآنَ عَلَى جَبَلٍ لَّرَأَيْتَهُ خَاشِعاً مُّتَصَدِّعاً مِّنْ خَشْيَةِ}$$

$$\text{اللَّهِ وَتِلْكَ الْأَمْثَالُ نَضْرِبُهَا لِلنَّاسِ لَعَلَّهُمْ يَتَفَكَّرُون}$$

This phenomenon at the same time was accompanied by an unshakable conviction that the message was from God, and the Qur'an describes itself as the transcript of a heavenly "Mother Book" written on a "Preserved Tablet". The conviction was of such an intensity that the Qur'an categorically denies that it is from any earthly source, for in that case it would be liable to "manifold doubts and oscillations."[38]

Fazlur Rahman will maintain the Islamic peripatetic conception that the prophet considered that a prophet is distinguished from the rest of humanity by his overall conduct, however, particular to his conception is that the prophet is impatient with history and firmly desires to recreate it. The prophetic insight is so strong that it generates new values and is creative of knowledge. Hence, the prophet's overall behavior is deemed the *Sunnah* (the trodden path) or the 'perfect model'.

Doctrine of Miracles (*mu'jiza*)

Traditional *kalām* considered the doctrine of miracles (*mu'jiza*) to be foundational for the establishment of prophethood. Nur al-Din al-Sabuni (d.580 A.H./1203 C.E.) states: "that whence God decrees an individual to be the recipient of His divine revelation then he does so through sound inspiration or clear revelation and he informs others with God's commandments and establishes for him an authoritative symbol (*imarat*) that verifies the truthfulness of his claim and that is nothing other than miracles."[39] Al-Laqqani (d.1041 A.H./1664 C.E.) defines a *mu'jiza* as 'a supernatural event accompanied by a challenge without any opposition'. His definition contains seven elements: (1) An action performed or not performed by God; (2) Should not be in conformity with natural events, not that it was a habitual occurring act; (3) The occurrence should appear on the claimant of prophethood; (4) Should be in comparison to the claim in reality or authoritatively; (5) Should be inconsonance with the claim; (6) Should not be proven false; and (7) The claim should not be opposed except from another prophet like himself.[40]

Al-Taftazani (d.791 A.H) in his commentary on the *Creed of al-Nasafi* states that someone that claims prophethood amongst the people that have no book or wisdom, and clearly expressed before them the book and wisdom, and taught them the commandments and ordainments, and presented the best of conduct, and assisted in taking many people to the highest stations of actions and thought, and enlightened the world with belief and good works, and God made his religion above all other religions, as He had promised. Thus, there is no other definition of prophethood (*nubuwwat*) or messengership (*risalat*) other than this.[41]

The doctrine views that the person claiming to be a prophet puts forth a challenge to those that deny his claim to be a prophet. If his opponents fail in fulfilling the challenge then the truthfulness of the prophet is established and his claims to prophethood are accepted. Fazlur Rahman affirms that the Qur'an is the only miracle professed by the Prophet (ṣ) and only by its veracity the Prophet is proven to be a prophet. However, Fazlur Rahman rejects the copious accounts of miracles attributed to the Prophet (ṣ) in the Hadīth literature and deems them to be an accretion due to Christian and Jewish influences.[42] However, it is important to point out that Ibn Sīna does not reject prophetic miracles as being instrumental in establishing the veracity of the prophet himself.[43]

Doctrine of the Moral *élan* of the Qur'an

The second essential component in Fazlur Rahman's concept of prophethood is the doctrine of the moral *élan* of the Qur'an, throughout his writings he reiterates this doctrine as the guiding factor and criterion by which Islamic thought has to comply with. This characteristic elucidates the influence of Herbert Spencer upon Fazlur Rahman to elaborate Islam in a systematic manner.[44] Fazlur Rahman comments that Ibn Sīna consistently mentions his chief doctrines repeatedly and this is a sign of a systematic thinker. The moral *élan* of the Qur'an is that purpose of Islam is to establish a socio-moral order and the prophet is the individual who has been divinely selected to complete this task. Further, the method that the prophet adopts in achieving this objective serves as a model for the rest of humanity. This model is referred to the *uswa hasana* and this is the *Sunnah* or well-trodden path taken by the Prophet (ṣ).[45] Now since the prophet is guided by divine revelation in order to achieve the goal of establishing a socio-moral order the nature of prophetic intellection or prophecy and divine revelation is critical. Further there is an intimate connection between the two and in the following section we will address Fazlur Rahman's doctrine of prophecy.

Fazlur Rahman asserts that Avicenna's whole philosophical system has been constructed with the conscious purpose, if not philosophically interpreting Islam, at least of adapting the entire range of philosophy so far as it impinges upon religious questions to Islamic beliefs. Fazlur Rahman argues that the real point of contact between the Islamic tradition and the philosophic system built on Greek bases is the doctrine of prophethood.[46] Ibn Sīna objective is to rationally understand and explain the prophetic revelation that he develops the doctrine of his symbolic character of imagination and its relationship to the prophetic intellect.

Doctrine of Prophecy (Prophetic Intellection) and Divine Revelation

Fazlur Rahman dedicated two independent studies to the doctrine of prophecy in Islam. In his doctoral thesis on *Avicenna's Psychology*, he examines the Aristotelian construction of the mind. According to Fazlur Rahman, Ibn Sīna's main ideas "are no doubt taken from his predecessors, [but] it would be incorrect to suppose that there is nothing new in his work."[47] What was new for Fazlur Rahman was Ibn Sīna's theory of prophecy, namely, that the rational soul acquires knowledge on a variety of levels, the highest level being achieved by one who "can acquire knowledge from within himself," which Rahman referred to as "intuition."[48]

Intuition occurs when the soul immediately perceives knowledge without prior instruction. Although Ibn Sīna argues that the level of knowledge varies with the individual, a man can either intuitively know the "truth within him"[49] or the truth concerning "all or most problems." [50] Thus, according to Rahman, Ibn Sīna argues that:

> "there might be a man whose soul has such an intense purity and is so firmly linked to the rational principles that he blazes with intuition, i.e., with the receptivity of inspiration coming from the active intelligence concerning everything. So, the forms of all things contained in the active intelligence are imprinted on his soul either all at once or nearly so, not that he accepts them merely on authority but on account of their logical order which encompasses all [things] … for beliefs accepted on authority concerning those things which are known only through their causes possess no rational certainty. This is a kind of prophetic inspiration, indeed its highest form and the one most fitted to be called Divine power; and it is the highest human faculty."[51]

Therefore, according to Ibn Sīna, intuition is the basis of prophetic inspiration. God's active intelligence possesses all knowledge and reaches out to those who are pure of heart and mind. The purity of an individual, according to Ibn Sīna, increases his or her rational abilities and makes one more receptive to contact with God. When contact occurs, the individual intuits the knowledge that God's active intellect dispenses, and this knowledge becomes part of the individual's being. The sudden realization of new knowledge is accepted not because one realizes that it originated with God, but because of the inherent logic of the information.

In his commentary on the above passage, Fazlur Rahman maintains that Ibn Sīna is probably correct in his assessment of the role that intuitive intelligence plays in prophecy. He proposes, however, that knowledge does not have to be dispensed all at once, for this assumes that the intellect starts with no knowledge and then suddenly attains complete knowledge. To the contrary, Rahman argues that the intuitive intellect receives instantaneous divine knowledge only "where there is no prior proposition, or in other words, only in those situations where the native intuition is not enough to handle the problems which confront the individual at any particular moment." [52] Thus, prophetic knowledge occurs when the intuitive intellect of the prophet reaches out to the active intellect of God when the prophet is faced with crises that his native intellect is unable to resolve.

Much of Fazlur Rahman's theory on the nature of prophecy is laid out in his book *Prophecy in Islam*. In this book, written during his days at McGill University, Rahman builds on the ideas developed in his doctoral dissertation to demonstrate various theories of prophecy. Rahman provides a survey of both the philosophic and orthodox (Sunni) views of prophecy and suggests that although there are many aspects of Greek thought that the orthodox theologians disputed, the core elements of philosophical positions were incorporated into Sunni *kalām* (speculative theology).[53] In *Prophecy in Islam*, Rahman begins by examining the theories of al-Fārābi (d. 950) to support his own emerging ideas on the function of prophecy. Like Ibn Sīna, al-Fārābi maintains that the intuitive intellect is the highest level of knowledge that a person can achieve.[54] When the intuitive intellect of a person has reached its highest capacity, it makes contact with the active intellect of God, which, according to Muslim philosophical traditions, is the lowest of ten levels of intelligence issuing from God.[55] At the highest end of these intelligences exists "the transcendent intelligence," and at the lowest exists the "holy ghost."[56] It is only the lowest level of intelligence with which a human can potentially have contact.

Fazlur Rahman demonstrates that, according to classical philosophic thought, there are two kinds of prophetic activities: the intellectual revelation and the imaginative revelation.[57] The intellectual revelation, according to Ibn Sīna, occurs "when a man has actually attained all knowledge and gnosis (by himself) and he is not in need of anyone to direct him in any matter. This happens only when his soul attains contact with the active intelligence" of God.[58] Rahman goes on to show that contact between the rational soul of man and the active intelligence of God occurs through the agency of an intermediary. He quotes Ibn Sīna, who argued that "revelation is [the] … emanation (from the active intellect into the prophet's soul) and the angel is this (extra) faculty or power received (by the prophet as a part of his nature)."[59] Thus, for Ibn Sīna, the angel is not a creature in the real sense, but a power that connects God to the prophet. The final aspect of the intellectual revelation concerns how much knowledge is gained and when. Rahman paraphrases Ibn Sīna when he says that:

> "the ordinary consciousness is, for the most part, receptive, not creative and receives piecemeal what the active intellect creates as a totality. The ordinary mind has only reflections in the mirror, not real, veritable knowledge which can be possessed only when a man's phenomenal self-unites itself

with the ideal personality, the angelic intellect. Hence the [intellectual] prophet is described as a divine being, deserving of honors and almost to be worshipped.[60]

Thus, Rahman argues that the intellectual prophet, because of his total instantaneous knowledge of all things past, present, and future, is raised almost to the level of God. On the other hand, imaginative or technical revelation represents a "strong imaginative faculty" on the part of the prophet.[61] This prophet, due to this increased imaginative faculty, is able to receive sensations or realizations from the active intellect of God while awake, whereas ordinary people only receive it while asleep.[62] The distinction is important. Since the imagination is so strong in this type of intellect, that which is perceived spiritually is deemed by the perceiver to exist in reality. Such a person "becomes a prophet giving news of the divine realm, thanks to the intelligibles' he has received. This is the highest degree of perfection a person can reach with his imaginative powers."[63] As with the intellectual revelation, "the appearance of an angel and the hearing of the angel's voice [are] ... purely mental phenomena."[64]

Technical revelation goes hand in hand with imaginative revelation. Technical revelation occurs when the masses are unable to understand the spiritual – symbolic – truth that originates in the imagination of the prophet. Rahman argues that this form of revelation is political "in the wider sense of the word."[65] He states that "since the masses cannot grasp the purely spiritual truth, the prophets communicate this truth to them in materialistic symbols and metaphors."[66]

This of course raises the issue of how to interpret these symbolic truths. Rahman held that, within "orthodox" Sunni Islam, the prophetic message is taken as literal. The philosophers held, however, that "if a person speaks the bare truth to the public, his message must be considered to be devoid of divine origin."[67] But this position fails to take into account the "religio-moral" experience of the prophet. Rahman parted with the philosophers in that, for the philosophers,

> a moral principle is, in its cognitive aspects, exactly like a mathematical proposition. They do not realize that religio-moral experience, although it certainly has a cognitive element, radically differs from other forms of cognition in the sense that it is full of authority, meaning and imperiousness for the subject whereas [the] ordinary form of cognition is simply information.[68]

Thus, for the masses, revelatory symbols must be interpreted and placed in context in light of the moral experience of the prophet. Rahman argued that, in this regard, the prophet is inherently different from the philosopher. The classical school of Islamic philosophy held that the philosophers and the prophets were essentially the same thing. Both were seen to employ the same intuitive mechanisms in the formation of knowledge, and both religious and philosophical knowledge were thought to be composed of the same truths. Religious truths for the masses were, however, to be couched in simple terms, on a level acceptable for the mass intellect.[69]

In *The Philosophy of Mulla Sadra*, Rahman continued his quest to develop a theory concerning the philosophical roots of prophecy. According to him, Mulla Sadra (Sadr al-Din al-Shirazi, d. 1640) kept alive the philosophic traditions thought to have died with al-Ghazālī (d. 1111).[70] Mulla Sadra, a Shi'i scholar and lawyer, stood outside the "philosophy of illumination" traditions of his day and the peripatetic traditions of Ibn Sīna.[71] The philosophy of illumination (*hikmat al-ishraq*) was a non-

Aristotelian philosophy developed by the Shi'i philosopher al-Suhrawardī (d. 1191). The details of his philosophical ideas are beyond the scope of this paper, but Mulla Sadra stands out in 17th century Muslim philosophical thought because he was one of the few scholars to continue to employ aspects of Neoplatonist and Aristotelian philosophy that cut against the dominate ideas of al-Suhrawardī.

According to Rahman, Mulla Sadra argued that the mechanism of prophetic knowledge is God's command to "be."[72] Rahman argued that "although other levels of existence also come into existence by this command to "be," the difference is that whereas at this level the command to "be" is an end in itself the realm of the intellect is identified by Sadra with the realm of *qada'* or God's eternal Decree."[73] Secondarily, Mulla Sadra argued that the active intelligence that Ibn Sīna described did not exist solely within humans but was in some kind of union with the active intelligence of God. When this union reaches its highest level of development, "a complete identification takes place and they are able to create all knowledge from within themselves without external instruction. These are the prophets."[74] Mulla Sadra, therefore, proposes that God created the capacity of prophetic knowledge as an instantaneous act of creation – of the command "be." In doing so, the creative act allows humans to enter into direct union with God's spirit. The knowledge imparted through this union, the divine decree, is what the Qur'an portrays by terms like "the pen," "the preserved tablet," "the root of all books," that is, the fundamental knowledge of God.[75] Mulla Sadra also contends that divine decree is constituted of higher angels, intelligences, or God's attributes, in other words, that God's essence and decree are united and inseparable.[76] Finally, Mulla Sadra argues that all those things outside God's absolute essence are *qadar* (God's power or ability). *Qada'* and *qadar*, taken together, mean that while God's divine decree is a part of his essence and is, thus, eternal and unchanging, its manifestation outside his essence (*qadar*) occurs in time, is changing, and is malleable. The extension of God's *qadar*, according to Mulla Sadra, is also referred to in the Qur'an as a "book" whose text is constantly changing. As with *qada'*, angels also act as intelligences that transmit knowledge.[77] These two realms of prophetic knowledge and their transmission are central to Fazlur Rahman's own theories of revelation. Prophets, according to Fazlur Rahman, intuit God's knowledge through a process of intellectual realization that is, in turn, passed on to others through symbolic language that is meant to convey the meaning of the experience. It is therefore necessary to have a clearer understanding of the context of the revelation because the prophet's understanding of these symbols is influenced by his religio-moral experience of the world. Thus, to understand the Qur'an, it is necessary to come to an unbiased understanding of Muḥammad's (ṣ) experience of the world.

Doctrine of Prophetic Infallibility (*'isma*)

Etymologically, *'isma* is from the root word *'i-s-m*. Al-Jawhari states *'isma* means 'to restrain or hold something'.[78] Ibn Manzur states that *'ismatullah* means that 'God's divine grace prevents someone from doing evil (*ma'siyya*)'. Ibn Taymīya defines *'isma* means 'God protection of someone responsible for carrying out certain tasks from sin with impossibility of falling into sin itself'. He goes onto state that *'isma* means that Allah protects and prevents His prophets' and messengers from physical sins such as – adultery, drinking alcohol, theft and lying; also from inner sins such as – jealousy, arrogance and hypocrisy.[79]

Al-Bajuri (d.1223) states that the objective of God to render someone infallible is "to provide a psychological ability (*malaka nafsaniya*)" that prevents someone from sin.[80] Muhammad Tabatabai' (d.1982) contends that "'*isma* is God's protect of His prophets' and messengers from wrong and sin and it is the reason that allows them to do voluntary acts correctly and out of obedience, and it is a form of firm knowledge (*'ilm rasikh*) and an ability (*malakat*)."[81] On the other hand, orthodoxy (*Ahl ul Sunnah wa'l Jama'ah*) claim that '*isma* is rationally obligatory because if the prophets were not infallible from wrong doing or sin, their claim to performing miraculous acts would be contradictory.[82] Al-Iji writes that there is consensus (*Ijmā'*) between Muslims upon the infallibility of the prophets with the permissibility of forgetfulness (*al-Sahw wal' Nisyan*).[83] He further clarifies sins (*dhunub*) include deeds which are: disbelief (*kufr*) and wrong doings (*ma'si*). As for the former the Ash'arites are unanimous that it is impossible for prophets to commit before or after attaining prophethood. With regard to wrong doings (*ma'si*) he classifies them into four categories:

1. Major (*kaba'ir*) sins committed intentionally (*'amadan*)

2. Major (*sagha'ir*) sins committed inattentively (*sahw*)

3. Minor (*kaba'ir*) sins committed intentionally (*'amadan*)

4. Minor (*sagha'ir*) sins committed inattentively (*sahw*)

5. The Ash'rītes and Qadī 'Abdul Jabbār claim that the prophets committing major sins intentionally before attaining prophethood is not plausible rationally particularly if there is a question of a miracle being put forth. As for them committing major sins inattentively

after attaining prophethood is plausible. Minor sins committed intentionally are considered possible by the majority of the sects (*jumhur*).

Razī in his *'asmat ul-Anbiya* provides fifteen dialectical proofs (*hujaj*)[84] for the proof of the infallibility of the prophets and has categorized them into two categories: (1) concept of connection (*itisal*) between the prophet and God: God has paired every human being with a devil, and Allah has assisted every prophet over their devils and they submitted to Islam and so they (devils) do not command except that which is good. (2) The promulgation of the message (*tabligh al-Risalat*) from the prophet to the masses, thus if the prophets commit an evil deed then they are: (i) most deserved of receiving punishment in earnest over the severest evildoers of this community (*ummah*); (ii) their testament (*shahada*) does not merit any credibility; (iii) deserve ridicule and humiliation for commanding good and forbidding evil; (iv) if Muhammad (ṣ) commits an evil deed then we would be commanded to do it and that is not plausible and if we are not commanded to do it despite the prophet (ṣ) committing it then implausible.[85]

Muhammad Tabatabai' categorizes prophetic infallibility (*'isma*) into three categories:

1. Protection (*'isma*) from error (*khata'*) in receiving revelation.

2. Infallibility (*'isma*) from error (*khata'*) in the promulgation of the message.

3. Protection from error in actions.

Ahmad Amin (d.1954) considers that the orthodoxy failed in properly presenting the correct concept of prophetic infallibility (*'asmat ul-Anbiya*) according to Islamic teachings and also against human nature. Amin takes the opinion of the Islamic philosophers (*falasifa*) *viz.*, that human nature is comprised of carnal desires (*shahwāt*) and propensities towards good (*khayr*) and evil (*shar*). The two are blended together and this forms different tendencies. The virtue of an elevated human being is not that he is infallible (*ma'sūm*), rather that he is capable of doing both good and evil and he is attracted to both of them and he is most of the time attracted to good and repulsed by evil on the basis of a moral imperative that is established by divine law (*shari'ah*). This is the 'virtuous balance' (*miqyas al-Fadila*) in leaders and great people and is referred to spiritual wealth and is linked to his moral worldly actions and its implementation is the real obligation which the divine law mandates. Whereas, the infallible nature that the scholars of Islam claim the prophets have is referred in the Qur'an to only belong to the angels:

يَا أَيُّهَا الَّذِينَ آمَنُوا قُوا أَنفُسَكُمْ وَأَهْلِيكُمْ نَارًا وَقُودُهَا النَّاسُ وَالْحِجَارَةُ عَلَيْهَا مَلَائِكَةٌ غِلَاظٌ شِدَادٌ لَّا يَعْصُونَ اللَّهَ مَا أَمَرَهُمْ وَيَفْعَلُونَ مَا يُؤْمَرُونَ (التحريم)

"...Angels who disobey not God in what He commands them and do what they are commanded." (al-Taḥrīm: 6)

He contends that if the prophets' carnal desires are removed from him he fails to remain a human being and losses his identity as one. Further, he is deprived from choosing being amongst the lowest of the low (*safilin*) or the venerable (*'aliyyin*). Thus, according to Amin a prophet is a normal human being whose moral standards are more virtuous and noble than all of mankind and that distinction elevates him as a prophet.

It seems that Amin's opinion is a literal understanding of the concept of *'isma* as the prophets psychologically and morally altered by God himself. The orthodoxy, as indicated above, considered that the prophets were given an additional psychological ability that prevented them from performing evil deeds. Further, before the reception of revelation all prophets' were considered truthful (*sadiq*) and reliable (*amin*) and sound of character. Thus, the behavior and character of the prophets' before and after receipt of revelation is in the prophet's choice but unlike the rest of humanity who do not receive divine guidance (*hidāyah*) directly, he is guided directly by God himself. Amin fails to take into consideration God's divine providence (*al-'Anayat ul-Illahiyah*) upon the Prophet (ṣ). It is this divine providence which Muhammad Tabatabai' term as sound knowledge and ability revealed to the Prophet (ṣ) to enable him to make decisions correctly and obediently.

Fazlur Rahman's agrees with the orthodoxy's doctrine of prophetic infallibility (*'isma*) however, he does so while being deeply rooted in his Avicennan concept of prophethood. He writes in *Islam*:

> "Now a prophet is a person whose average, overall character, the sum total of his actual conduct, is far superior to those of humanity in general. He is a man who is ab initio impatient with men and even with most of their ideals, and wishes to recreate history. Muslim orthodoxy, therefore, drew the logically correct conclusion that prophets must be regarded as immune from serious errors (*the doctrine of 'isma*). Muḥammad (ṣ) was such a person, in fact the only such person really known to history. That is why his overall

behavior is regarded by the Muslims as *Sunnah* or the 'perfect model'.[86]

Fazlur Rahman's concept of prophethood on the one hand is based upon the philosophical thought of Ibn Sīna. Ibn Sīna concept of prophecy provided Fazlur Rahman with a systematic, scientific and philosophical explanation for interaction between the prophetic intellect and divine revelation. Further, Fazlur Rahman relied upon Shah Walī Ullah Dehlawi and Muhammad Iqbal to describe the verbal character of the Qur'an. The doctrine of infallibility essentially ties in with two of the anchor points in Fazlur Rahman's thought *viz.*, prophecy and moral *élan* of the Qur'an. Fazlur Rahman considers the prophets moral perception which he identifies as 'moral intuition' increased to the extent that it came into direct contact with the moral law itself the divine word was given to him with the inspiration. Lastly, the divine word had an intimate connection with the prophet's inmost personality and hence the performance and behavior of the Prophet (ṣ) was declared to be the perfect model '*uswa hasana*'. Therefore, the actions, behavior and statements of the Prophet (ṣ) cannot be deemed fallible they have to be considered infallible and this is the *sunnah* of the Prophet (ṣ).

As we have alluded to in section on epistemology, that Fazlur Rahman's concept of *Sunnah* is based upon Ibn Sīna's *Kitab al-Najat fi-l Illahiyat wa-l Mantiq* where he dedicates a chapter *Fasl fi Ithbat al-Nabuwwah wa kaifiyat da'watul Nabi lla Allah wa'l Mi'ad* – that it is necessary that human beings are dependent upon one another and are unable to function without one another, thus, there exists a civil and social contract (*'aqd al-mudn wal Ijtima'at*) between members of a society. Further, every human being is responsible in fulfilling a particular function in the fabric of society; similarly, a prophet is responsible for fulfilling a particular function in society. It is necessary, therefore, that for the survival of the society and mankind in general that cooperation (*musharaka*) and interaction (*mu'amala*) exists between members of society. In this interaction there must be two essential elements (1) *Sunnah* (2) *'Adl*. The prophet must 'establish his path' (*sunnah*) and a legislator (*mu'addl*). The prophet should be able to communicate and commit to his *Sunnah*. He should not allow people to leave his *sunnah* or to disagree with his authority – his subjects should be aware of what is acceptable and unacceptable before him. It is of paramount importance to point out that his role permits the survival and existence of a good (*salih*) human being. This requires that the prophet establish a good order (*nizam ul-khayr*). Hence, the need and function of a prophet is fundamental (*wajib*) and his 'trodden path' (*sunnah*) must be *considered* as Law because it is imperative for the socio-political needs of his society. Thus, Fazlur Rahman considers that the doctrine of prophetic infallibility reforms it into the modern concept principle that the power of the legislator must not be challenged as falling prey to weakness, wrongdoing, sin, error, desire or passion. Rather the prophet's decisions and actions must be considered *infallible* for the socio-economic and political benefit (*maslaha*) of the community (*ummah*).

On the other hand the orthodoxy considered there to be a logical connection between prophetic miracles and prophetic infallibility in the sense that the prophet would challenge disbelievers in their ability to fulfill that challenge. If they failed then the doctrine of miracles would necessitate that if the prophet fulfilled that challenge then he was truthful and the disbelievers incapable of fulfilling the challenge put forth. Fazlur

Rahman rejects the doctrine of miracles and considers the only miracle to be the Qur'an itself.

Doctrine of Intercession (*Shifa'at al-Nabi*)

Fazlur Rahman's rejects the orthodox doctrine of intercession and considers it to be: (1) entirely against the Qur'anic *élan* and (2) an innovation accrued in the second and third century. He claims that the Muslim theologians rejected the idea of redemption even though at a later stage in the development of Muslim theology, in the later second and third century the doctrine of intercession was introduced. In this section we will attempt to discuss how different Muslim theologians treated the orthodox doctrine of intercession to determine the validity of Fazlur Rahman's judgment. Firstly we will present his argumentation in opposition to the doctrine of intercession and attempt to discover the underlying basis for his rejection.

In *Status of an Individual in Islam* (1966) Fazlur Rahman argued that the doctrine of intercession was in contradiction with his purported 'doctrine of responsibility'. Here it is important to point out that historically there is no mention of a 'doctrine of responsibility' and it is his personal addition to Islamic Theology (*kalām*). It seems that the basis of the doctrine is to establish theologically 'hard work and accountability' which many reformers in the Muslim world deemed the antithesis *viz.*, 'laziness and moral deprecation' to be reason for the Muslim world's backwardness.

Fazlur Rahman based his doctrine upon verses from the Qur'an (al-An'ām: 94, 165), (al-Isrā': 15), (Maryam: 80), (Fāṭir: 18), (al-Zumar: 7) and (al-Najm: 38).

"Now there is no doubt that the primary locus of responsibility in Islam is the individual". The Qur'an says:

$$وَلَقَدْ جِئْتُمُونَا فُرَادَىٰ كَمَا خَلَقْنَاكُمْ أَوَّلَ مَرَّةٍ وَتَرَكْتُم مَّا خَوَّلْنَاكُمْ وَرَاءَ ظُهُورِكُمْ وَمَا نَرَىٰ مَعَكُمْ شُفَعَاءَكُمُ ٱلَّذِينَ زَعَمْتُمْ أَنَّهُمْ فِيكُمْ شُرَكَاءُ لَقَد تَّقَطَّعَ بَيْنَكُمْ وَضَلَّ عَنكُم مَّا كُنتُمْ$$

(al-An'ām: 94)

"Today (on the Day of Judgment) you have come to us as individuals (*furada*), just as We created you in the first place..."

Again, the Qur'an tells us:

$$وَٱتَّقُواْ يَوْماً لاَّ تَجْزِي نَفْسٌ عَن نَّفْسٍ شَيْئاً وَلاَ يُقْبَلُ مِنْهَا عَدْلٌ وَلاَ تَنفَعُهَا شَفَاعَةٌ وَلاَ هُمْ يُنصَرُونَ$$

(al-Baqarah: 48)

"Every soul earns but for itself, and no soul shall bear the burden of another, and even thus shall you return to your Lord".[87]

He goes on to trace the historical emergence and development of this doctrine as originating in Murjite circles, used to counter the Khariji tendency of considering that the perpetrator of major sins to be destined to hell, eternally and with no chance of redemption. Subsequently, the reaction of the orthodoxy in line with their policy to promote social cohesion and unity forged hadiths that advocated the doctrine of intercession most likely in favor of God's divine mercy and the prophet's position as law giver. Later the Mu'tazila also rejected the doctrine of intercession on the basis of its conflict with their doctrine of the promise and the threat. Here Fazlur Rahman is incorrect in stating that the Mu'tazila rejected the doctrine of intercession on the same basis of Khawarij:

> "and the Mu'tazilites rejected the doctrine of intercession in the next life based upon the same reasons as the Khawarij."[88]

Fazlur Rahman goes on to state in categorical terms: "it is on these grounds that Muslim theologians reject the possibility of redemption."[89] As we stated above, Fazlur Rahman's opposition to the doctrine of intercession was two fold: (1) the theological groups such as the Khawarij and Mu'tazila denying the existence of it and considering it an innovation accrued by later generations. (2) doctrine of responsibility which Fazlur Rahman purported in light of Gibb's thesis: "Islam is essentially a social movement pressed into religious channels."[90] Fazlur Rahman criticized Gibb's thesis and advocated that Islam stresses the role of the individual as a member of society and that on the day of judgment accountability will be taken individually. Fazlur Rahman's doctrine of responsibility is based upon various Qur'anic verses that point to the accountability of the individual in the afterlife which is connected to the doctrine of divine trust placed by God with man which necessitates that man fulfill the responsibilities of his sacred trust: "primary locus of responsibility in Islam is the individual"[91].

Here it is suggested that the doctrine of responsibility serves as an example of Fazlur Rahman's modern *mutakallim* activities *viz.*, that Fazlur Rahman accepting, rejecting, and refuting doctrines of both Western orientalists and Muslim traditionalists. As we have stated in the introduction that modern *kalām* can be described as continuation of traditional *kalām* controversies upon issues related to God's names and attributes and others, in addition to *kalām* issues discussions between different Muslim groups *viz.*, traditional, puritan, fundamentalist, neo-fundamentalist and modernist, and between non-Muslim Western orientalist. Fazlur Rahman records in his *Islam and Modernity* that Sir Syed Ahmad Khan advocated a new *kalām*, one that did justice to the Qur'an and to the modern world. It seems that Fazlur Rahman fulfilled Ahmad Khan's vision for a new *kalām*.

Khawārij on the Doctrine of Intercession

Here we would like to investigate and determine whether the Khawarij and orthodoxy (*Ahl ul Sunnah wa'l Jama'ah*) purported such arguments in rejection of the doctrine of intercession. Further, this will elucidate Fazlur Rahman's criticism towards *kalām* and demonstrate that it is a fixed point in his thought. The Khawarij chief principle that distinguished them from the remainder of the community was the 'doctrine of the perpetrator of a major sin'. They believed that the one who perpetrates a major sin invalidates his belief in God and hence he will be sent to hell eternally. Fazlur Rahman believes that had the doctrine of intercession been an integral part of faith then the Khawarij who were known to be extremely learned and pious would have not rejected it. However, since they had rejected it, it must be attributed to a later time. Fazlur Rahman estimates it to be after the second century and when it became documented as a hadīth that was in the third century. This projection of Hadith back into the mouth of the prophet is a practice of the community (*Ahl ul Hadith*) through the two sources of Islamic methodology, namely *Ijmā'* and *Ijtihād*.

Further, Fazlur Rahman considers this doctrine to be a product of the *I'rjā* that the orthodoxy (*Ahl ul Sunnah wal Ijmā'*) became so wont to do *viz.*, acquiring elements from different groups and fashioning them into hadīth by consensus.[92]

Mu'tāzilites on the Doctrine of Intercession

The Mu'tazilī theologian and Shafi'i jurist Qadī 'Abdul Jabbār (d. 415/1025) states the Mu'tazila rejected the doctrine of intercession because it was contradicted by Mu'tazilī the doctrine of the promise and the threat, is that this is one of the doubts (*shubh*) of the Murjia. They arrive at this conclusion criticizing the perpetual punishment of the evildoers (*al-fusāq*), and the crux of the issue in this doctrine is that there is no disagreement in the community of Muslims (*ummah*) that the intercession of the prophet (ṣ) is established (*thābit*) by the community of Muslims, but for whom is the intercession to be for? The Mu'tazila argue that the intercession of the prophet is for the repenters from the believers, and for the Murjia it is for the evildoers from the people of Salah (*Ahl ul-Salah*).

Shafā in its technical sense refers to when the issue of somebody else benefiting from someone else or protecting that person from harm and its paramount that there be an intercessor (*shaf'a*) and an intercession for him (*mashf'u lahū*) and subject matter in which intercession is made (*mashf'u fīhī*) and the intercessee (*mashf'u īlāhī*). The root of the matter is that the messenger (ṣ) is himself being asked to intercede on the request of the intercessee, will the intercessor agree and concede to intercede on the behalf of the intercessee? According to the Mu'tazila because the intercessee would not ask the intercessor to intercede had the intercessee thought that the intercessor would not intercede! Otherwise, how else could that intercession benefit him or protect him from harm had the intercessor (the Prophet (ṣ)) not answered.

Qadī 'Abdul Jabbār response is that from the punishment deserves to be permanent, otherwise how could the evildoer (*fasiq*) be taken out of from the hell fire by the intercession of the Prophet (ṣ) and the following prove otherwise:

وَٱتَّقُواْ يَوْماً لاَّ تَجْزِي نَفْسٌ عَن نَّفْسٍ شَيْئاً وَلاَ يُقْبَلُ مِنْهَا شَفَٰعَةٌ
وَلاَ يُؤْخَذُ مِنْهَا عَدْلٌ وَلاَ هُمْ يُنصَرُونَ

(al-Baqarah: 48)

"And fear a Day when no soul will suffice for another soul at all, nor will intercession be accepted from it, nor will compensation be taken from it, nor will they be aided"

وَأَنذِرْهُمْ يَوْمَ ٱلأَزِفَةِ إِذِ ٱلْقُلُوبُ لَدَى ٱلْحَنَاجِرِ كَاظِمِينَ مَا
لِلظَّالِمِينَ مِنْ حَمِيمٍ وَلاَ شَفِيعٍ يُطَاعُ

(Ghāfir: 18)

"And warn them, [O Muḥammad], of the Approaching Day, when hearts are at the throats, filled [with distress]. For the wrongdoers there will be no devoted friend and no intercessor [who is] obeyed"

أَفَمَنْ حَقَّ عَلَيْهِ كَلِمَةُ ٱلْعَذَابِ أَفَأَنتَ تُنقِذُ مَن فِي ٱلنَّارِ

(al-Zumar: 19)

"Then, is one who has deserved the decree of punishment [to be guided]? Then, can you save one who is in the Fire?"

$$\text{يَعْلَمُ مَا بَيْنَ أَيْدِيهِمْ وَمَا خَلْفَهُمْ وَلاَ يَشْفَعُونَ إِلاَّ لِمَنِ ٱرْتَضَىٰ}$$

$$\text{وَهُم مِّنْ خَشْيَتِهِ مُشْفِقُونَ}$$

(al-Anbiyā: 28)

"And they cannot <u>intercede</u> except on behalf of one whom He approves."

Thus our summary on that matter the benefit (*fā'idah*) of intercession is elevating the level of the intercessor and the import (*dalālah*) is the elevated status of the intercessor over the intercessee. With regards to the subject (*mawd'u*), there is disagreement amongst the people, with regards to our (Mu'tazila) standpoint the subject or content of intercession is so that the intercessee can receive what he needs (*hajatihi*) and his needs are either the obtainment of benefit or the removal of harm. But the Murjia disagree, and consider the subject – the quintessential need for intercession in the first place – is to receive protection from harm and not for the obtainment of benefit, our critique of the Murjia, is that the unsoundness is apparent because if the purpose of intercession is the prevention of harm then that this is a benefit which in itself. Thus the position of the Murjia is actually the same as ours which is the purpose of intercession (*shaf'a*) is to obtain benefit therefore we find the position of the Murjia to be unsound. And from the proofs from Hadiths we find that they are not sufficient since they are single chained *ahaad* and the Hadiths which are cited are nullified by other Hadiths which state to the affect that those that perpetrate certain evil actions will not enter paradise, hence it is understood irrespective of intercession or not.

The important points to be noted here from Qadī 'Abdul Jabbār are the following:

1. The doctrine of intercession is accepted by the community.

2. The Murjia disagree in the 'perpetual punishment of the evildoer'. He finds that it is due to their doubt on the logical connection between the doctrine of Shif'ā and the doctrine of the threat.

3. The Mu'tazila consider intercession to be for the people of heaven whereas the Murjia consider it to be for the believers in the hellfire.

4. The Mu'tazila argue that the benefit of intercession of the dwellers of heaven is that it elevates the Prophet (ṣ). Whereas the Murjia consider the benefit of intercession for the dwellers of hell to save them from a perpetual dwelling in hell.

5. The Mu'tazila adducing the same result from the verses of the Qur'an that Allah has categorically denied intercession for anyone on the Day of Judgment but have developed an argument that allows for the Hadiths of intercession to be accepted on the basis that it is for the honor of the Prophet (ṣ) that the people of heaven will be allowed to intercede with him and then the interceder may have his request fulfilled.

6. Qadī 'Abdul Jabbār being a Shafi'i jurist denied the strength of the Hadith transmissions deeming them to be singular reports (*ahaad*) and unreliable.

Fazlur Rahman is incorrect in categorically stating that the Mu'tazila rejected the doctrine of intercession which Qadī 'Abdul Jabbār states it is accepted by the community but it seems his argument is contradictory because the evidence that supports the community, he considers them to be unreliable. Fazlur Rahman position rejects the Mu'tazila opinion entirely and focuses his criticism on the very existence of the doctrine in the community in the first place. If the Hadiths are unreliable then what is the basis for the existence of the doctrine. Thus Fazlur Rahman, concludes the doctrine is an innovation (*bid'ā*). Next we will consider the defensive reaction of the Ash'arī.

Ash'arītes on the Doctrine of Intercession

The Ash'arītes unanimously agreed upon the affirmation of the 'doctrine of prophetic intercession' such as Abī Muzaffar Al-Isfara'īnī (d. 471 AH) in his *Al-Tabsīr*[93] on the intercession of the prophet Muhammad (ṣ): "The created shall be gathered and made accountable for their deeds, then those of the paradise will forever reside in paradise in perpetual bliss, additionally, they will see their lord because of their nobility and in completion of His grace upon them. And the disbelievers and the apostates shall forever reside in the punishment of the hellfire and they shall not have escape from it even for a brief moment. The first group from amongst the dwellers of hellfire shall be the evildoers be punished in it then removed from it by the intercession of the Prophet (ṣ), scholars, ascetics, pious worshipers and the children of the believers. The second group the one who does not manage to be worthy of receiving their intercession then on the condition of their previous belief they will be taken out of hell by the mercy of Allah Exalted is He. The third group evildoers from amongst the believers they shall be forgiven before they enter the hellfire either by the intercession of the Prophet (ṣ) or by the mercy of the Compeller. And no one shall remain in the fire that has an atom's weight of belief. And know that the believer does not become a disbeliever by committing a sin and he does leave the bounds of belief because his sin exists in a place amongst the places in his heart but his belief does not become nullified in his heart by it. Based upon what the Allah has said: "Indeed, those who have believed and done righteous deeds indeed, We will not allow to be lost the reward of any who did well in deeds"[94] and on the authority of 'Abdullah b. Mas'ud that the messenger of Allah observed: None shall enter the fire (of hell) who has in his heart the weight of a mustard seed of belief and none shall enter paradise who has in his heart the weight of a mustard seed of pride.[95] Pride here means disbelief (*kufr*) and 'an atoms weight of belief' means belief sincerely and absolutely free from polytheism (*shirk*), blasphemy (*i'fk*), doubts in the articles of faith (*shak*) or confusion in the articles of faith (*shubh*) cannot be considered. And any remote similarity to a similitude with disbelief and innovation does not warrant the name of belief as al-Shafi'i has stated: "Polytheism can tolerate associating another partner with God but with Islam it cannot tolerate being associated with polytheism" and his statement "An oath on one of His attributes is similar to an oath on His Being". God has cautiously informed about this meaning that Al Shafi'i has taken in: "And most of them believe not in Allah except while they associate others with Him".[96] Thus it has been decided by God that the articles of faith are imminently conditional in the description of belief, and it does not accept any innovation or atheistic properties because it is absolutely not belief in reality. And it has been mentioned about the meaning of intercession and it is: "And from [part of] the night, pray with it as additional [worship] for you; it is expected that your lord will resurrect you to a praised station".[97] The praised station is the station of intercession that no other prophet or messenger may have but Muḥammad (ṣ).[98]

Al-Isfarāi'nī states that there are three groups of people in hell: two of the three groups will attain the intercession of the prophet: (1) dwellers of hellfire shall the evildoers be punished in it then removed from it by the intercession of the Prophet (ṣ), scholars, ascetics, pious worshipers and the children of the believers (2) evildoers from amongst the believers they shall be forgiven before they enter the hellfire either by the intercession of the Prophet (ṣ) or by the Mercy of the Compeller. Here the addition of scholars, ascetics, pious worshipers and the children of the believers are considered as interceding possibilities. According to Fazlur Rahman's criteria as established by verse al-Baqarah: 254, that unequivocally states that God will not allow any intercession whatsoever in the afterlife. Further, Fazlur Rahman's categorical rejection of all Hadīths' relating to intercession despite some being narrated on the authority of Abdullah Ibn Mas'ud, for whose erudition Fazlur Rahman takes notice throughout his writings. Thus, Fazlur Rahman considers that the doctrine of intercession is the product of a reaction of the orthodoxy to foreign Christian influences. Lastly, we present the Maturidites whom Fazlur Rahman considers to be closer and sounder the early community's theological understanding.

Maturidites on the Doctrine of Intercession

Al-Farhārī states that the characteristic feature of this work is that it displays the latter day employment of logic and dialectics in refuting the arguments and doubts of the Mu'tazila. Al-Farhārī states:

> "Intercession in the Arabic language is referred to as *Shaf'a*. The root word from which *Shaf'a* originates from is *sh- fa- 'a* which literally means 'to single out'. *Shaf'a* is technical defined as: "A 'single' individual condemned to hell (*mujrim*) and he

was paired to someone who interceded on his behalf to remove him from Hell". In the Qur'an the word *Shaf'a* has been mentioned a total of twenty eight times and the word *shaf'a* has been used eleven times. The right of intercession will be given to the prophets, messengers, angels, scholars and martyrs.[99] The prophet's intercession is dedicated to those that have brought faith *la i'laha i'lla Allah* but they have not performed any good deeds. Further, this ability to seek intercession from God is based on the verse in:

$$ \text{وَمِنَ ٱلَّيْلِ فَتَهَجَّدْ بِهِ نَافِلَةً لَّكَ عَسَىٰ أَن يَبْعَثَكَ رَبُّكَ مَقَامًا مَّحْمُودًا} $$

(al-Isrā': 79)

And as for the night, keep vigil a part of it, as a work of supererogation for thee; it may be that thy Lord will raise thee up to a laudable station."[100]

He interprets 'laudable station' in light of the Hadith mentioned in Bukharī and Tirmidhī that God will grant intercession to the Prophet (ṣ) on the Day of Judgment.[101] He also records on the basis of another hadith that the *maqām al-mahmūd* 'laudable station' refers to the Prophet (ṣ) being granted permission by God to sit on His throne.[102] According to Fazlur Rahman, the former hadīth would be rejected on the basis of anthropomorphism (although Fazlur Rahman has in no place articulated his position on the issue of anthropomorphism which leads to a lack of conviction in his reliance upon on Ibn Taymīya on the history of *kalām*). With regards to the latter hadīth Fazlur Rahman rejects it because it contradicts the clear verse of al-Baqarah: 254.

Intercession in the Qur'an

In the Qur'an the 'doctrine of intercession' has been rejected and affirmed in different verses. The Qur'an rejected the Makkans' claims to having intercessors that could intercede for them on their behalf and it is precisely these verses that Fazlur Rahman bases his rejection of the orthodox doctrine of intercession. However, he fails to take into consideration verses that deal with the Qur'anic affirmation of prophetic intercession as in surah ;

لاَّ يَمْلِكُونَ ٱلشَّفَاعَةَ إِلاَّ مَنِ ٱتَّخَذَ عِندَ ٱلرَّحْمَـٰنِ عَهْداً

(Maryam: 87)

"having no power of intercession, save those who have taken with the All-merciful covenant."

يَوْمَئِذٍ لاَّ تَنفَعُ ٱلشَّفَاعَةُ إِلاَّ مَنْ أَذِنَ لَهُ ٱلرَّحْمَـٰنُ وَرَضِيَ لَهُ قَوْلاً

(Ṭā Hā: 109)

"Upon that day the intercession will not profit, save for him to whom the All-merciful gives leave, and whose speech He approves."

Yahya Farghal states, the Qur'an rejects the popular belief in unqualified "intercession" by living or dead saints or prophets. The Qur'an speaks about the people that do not possess intercession with God except those that have taken a covenant (*'ahd*) with God. Thus, God will grant to His prophets on Judgment Day the permission to "intercede," symbolically, for such of the sinners as will have already achieved His redemptive acceptance (*ridā'*) by virtue of their repentance or basic goodness. In other words, the right of "intercession" thus granted to the prophets will be but an expression of God's approval of the latter. Furthermore, the above denial of the possibility of unqualified intercession stresses, indirectly, not only God's omniscience – which requires no "mediator" – but also the immutability of His will: and thus it connects with the preceding mention of His almightiness.[103]

Notes

[1] Fazlur Rahman "Divine Revelation and Prophethood", *Hamdard Islamicus 1* (2), (1978), p.67.

[2] Thomas Nelson, *Eastons Bible Dictionary: A Dictionary of Bible Terms*, 3rd ed., 1897, p.961.

[3] See n-b-a', Ibn Manzur, *Lisan al-'Arb*, Dar ul Ihya' al-Turath al-'Arabi, 3rd ed., (Beirut, 1999).

[4] See n-b-a', Al-Jawhari, *Al-Sahah*.

[5] See n-b-a', Al-Fayumi, *Al-Misbah Al-Munir*.

[6] See n-b-a', Shams ul-Din b. Mahmud al-Isfahani, *Sharh Matali' ul-Anzar 'ala Tawali' ul-Anwar*, 1st ed., Egypt, 1978.

[7] 'Abdul Karim 'Uthman, *Sharh al-Usul ul-Khamsa li Qadī 'Abdul Jabbār*, Maktaba al-Wahba, (Cairo, 1996), pp.563-564.

[8] Al-Ghazālī, *al-Iqtisad fi 'l-I'tiqad*, 'Insaf Ramadan, Dar Qutayba, (Beirut, 2003), p.100.

[9] Al-Maturidi, *Kitab al Tawhid*, edited by Bekir Topaloğlu & Muhammad Aruçi, Dar al-Sader, (Beirut, 2001), p.249.

[10] See entry *lutf* in *Encyclopedia of Islam*, Brill, Leiden, pp.833-834.

[11] Fakhr ul-Din al-Razi, *al-Mahsil*, pp.156-158.

[12] Al-Maturidi, *Kitab al Tawhid*, edited by Bekir Topaloğlu & Muhammad Aruçi, Dar al-Sader, (Beirut, 2001), pp.248-256.

[13] Ibrahim Madkur, *fi falsafat ul-Islamiyyat: Manhaj wa Tatbiq*, Dar ul

Ma'arif, Alexandria, 2003, p.8.

[14] *Ibid.*

[15] *Ibid*, pp.83-85.

[16] Fazlur Rahman, *Prophecy in Islam*, p.29.

[17] *Ibid*, p.671.

[18] Ibn Sīna, *A History of Muslim Philosophy*, p.499.

[19] Harry Austyn Wolfson, *Avicenna and Orthodox Islam: An Interpretative Note on the Composition of His System*, vol II, Jerusalem 1965, p.671.

[20] Fazlur Rahman, *Prophecy in Islam*, p.29. Also, Ibrahim Madkur, *fi falsafat ul-Islamiyyat: Manhaj wa Tatbiq*, Dar ul Ma'arif, Alexandria, 2003, p.86.

[21] Fazlur Rahman, *Prophecy in Islam*, p.39.

[22] Ali Mabruk, *al-Nabuwwat: min 'ilm al-nabuwwat i'la falsafat ul-tarikh muhawalat fi I'adat bina' al-'Aqa'id*, 1st ed., Dar al-Tanwir litiba't al-Nashr wa-l tauwz'i: (Beirut, 1993), p.151.

[23] *Ibid*, p.673.

[24] *Ibid*, p.675.

[25] Al-Kindī goes on to explain that whereas God is a "true" agent, since He is a cause of being and acts without being acted upon, all other agents are only "metaphorically" agents, because they both act and are acted upon. The force of the term "metaphorical" here is the same as it was in *On First Philosophy*: just as created things are both many and one, and thus not "truly" one, so they are both passive and active, and thus not "truly" agents. This short text raises two interesting questions about how al-Kindī conceived of divine action. First, what does he have in mind when he describes God's agency as being mediated by the action of "metaphorical agents" (God "is the proximate cause for the first effect, and a cause through an intermediary for His effects that are

after the first effect")? Second, what is involved in "bringing being to be from non-being"? Regarding the first question, one might suppose that al-Kindī is following Neoplatonic texts, and that he has in mind a mediated emanation of effects from the first principle. If this is right, then the "first effect" will be the "world of the intellect" mentioned in other Kindian texts (e.g. the *Discourse on the Soul*, repeating this phrase from the *Theology of Aristotle*). This is supported by a non-committal remark in *On First Philosophy* that "one might think the intellect is the first multiple" (Rashed and Jolivet, 1998). But it seems at least as likely that the "first effect" mentioned here is the world of the heavens: by creating the heavens and setting them in motion, God indirectly brings about things in the sublunary world. This would be a more Aristotelian version of the idea that divine causation is mediated.

Adamson, Peter, "Al-Kindī", *The Stanford Encyclopedia of Philosophy (Summer 2012 Edition)*, Edward N. Zalta(ed.).

[26] Fazlur Rahman, *Islamic Philosophy, Encyclopedia of Philosophy*, edited by Paul Edwards, Vol. 4, 1967, p.220.

[27] *Ibid*, p.220.

[28] Harry Austyn Wolfson, *Avicenna and Orthodox Islam: An Interpretative Note on the Composition of his System*, vol II, Jerusalem 1965, p.673.

[29] Ibn Sīna, *al-Nijat fi-l 'Mantiq wa Illahiyyat*, ed., Abdul Rahman 'Airat, Dar ul Jil, (Beirut, 1st ed., 1992), pp.172-174.

[30] Fazlur Rahman "Divine Revelation and Prophethood", *Hamdard Islamicus 1* (2), (1978), pp. 66-72.

[31] Fazlur Rahman, *Major Themes of the Qur'an*, p.56.

[32] (al-Nisā': 164) وَكَلَّمَ اللّهُ مُوسَى تَكْلِيماً (And Allah spoke to Moses [with] direct speech). Here in 4:164 the Qur'an speaks about God speaking directly to Moses without any medium. Rahman's concept of prophethood considers the agency of Gabriel to be fundamental in his

concept of prophecy, acting as an agency that *assists* in divine intuitionalism.

[33] Ibn Sīna, *A History of Muslim Philosophy*, p.481.

[34] Fazlur Rahman, *Avicenna's Psychology*, p.39.

[35] Fazlur Rahman challenged the notion of accident and essence that was prevalent at the time and reached the following definition of accident: Whenever two concepts are clearly distinguishable from each other, they must refer to two different ontological entities. Whenever these two concepts come together in a thing, Ibn Sīna describes their mutual relationship as being accidental, i.e., they happen to come together, although each must be found to exist separately. See his entry of Ibn Sīna, *A History of Muslim Philosophy*, p.485.

[36] Fazlur Rahman, *Islam*, pp.30-31.

[37] "If we were to send this Qur'an down on a mountain, you would see it split asunder out of fear of God."(al-Ḥashr: 21).

[38] Fazlur Rahman, *Islam, Encyclopedia of Britannica*, 15th edition, p.7.

[39] Nur al-Din al-Sabuni, *Kitab al-Bidayat min al-Kifayat fi al-Hidaya*, ed., Fathullah Khalif, Dar ul-Ma'arif, Egypt, 1969, p.86.

[40] Ahmad b. Muhammad al-Maliki, *Kitab Sharh al-Sawi 'ala Jauharat ul-Tauhid*, ed., Abdul Fattah al-Bazm, 2nd ed., Dar Ibn ul-Kathir, (Damascus: Syria), 1999, pp.298-300.

[41] Sa'd al-Din al-Taftazani, *Sharh al-Aqa'id al-Nisafiyyah*, ed., Ahmad Hijazi al-Saqa, Maktaba Kulliyat al-Azhar, (Cairo), Egypt, 1988, pp.87-88.

[42] Fazlur Rahman, *Islam*, p.3.

[43] Ibn Sīna, *al-Nijat fi-l 'Mantiq wa 'Illahiyyat*, ed., Abdul Rahman 'Airat, Dar ul Jil, (Beirut, 1st ed., 1992), p.175.

[44] Herbert Spencer, *First Principles*, London: Watts & Co., 6th ed., 1946, p.312.

[45] Fazlur Rahman, *Islam*, p.21.

[46] *Ibid*, p.670.

[47] Fazlur Rahman, *Avicenna's Psychology: An English Translation of Kitab al-Najat*, p.19.

[48] *Ibid*, 21.

[49] *Ibid*, 36.

[50] *Ibid*, 36.

[51] *Ibid*, pp.37-38.

[52] *Ibid*, p.95.

[53] Fazlur Rahman, *Preface to Prophecy in Islam: Philosophy and Orthodoxy*, (University of Chicago Press, Chicago, 1958).

[54] Although al-Fārābi uses the term "cognitive intellect," Rahman argues that they are talking about the same phenomena (*Prophecy in Islam*, p.11).

[55] *Ibid*, pp.11-12.

[56] *Ibid*, p.14.

[57] *Ibid*, pp.30-36.

[58] *Ibid*, p.30.

[59] *Ibid*, p.34.

[60] *Ibid*, p.35.

[61] *Ibid*, p.36.

[62] *Ibid*, p.37.

[63] *Ibid*, p.38.

[64] *Ibid*.

[65] *Ibid*, p.40.

⁶⁶ *Ibid.*

⁶⁷ *Ibid*, p.42.

⁶⁸ Fazlur Rahman, "The Post-Formative Developments in Islam-II", *Islamic Studies*, 2 (1963), p.301. Also, Frederick Denny, "Fazlur Rahman: Muslim Intellectual," *The Muslim World* 79 (1989), 1:93.

⁶⁹ Denny, *Fazlur Rahman: Muslim Intellectual*, pp. 92-93.

⁷⁰ Fazlur Rahman, *The Philosophy of Mulla Sadra*, (State University of New York Press, Albany, 1975), p.vii.

⁷¹ *Ibid*, pp.1-2.

⁷² *Ibid*, p.184.

⁷³ *Ibid*, pp.184-185.

⁷⁴ *Ibid*, p.241.

⁷⁵ *Ibid*, p.181.

⁷⁶ *Ibid.*

⁷⁷ *Ibid.*

⁷⁸ Al-Jawhari, *al-Sihah*, see *'i-s-m*.

⁷⁹ Jamal Muhammad Sa'id Abdul Ghani, *Ara' Ibn Taymīya fi 'ihmat ul-Anbiya'*, Maktaba zahra' al-Sharq, 1998, p.33.

⁸⁰ Al-Bajun, *Tuhfat al-Murid 'ala Jawharat ul-Tawhid*, Muhammad Ali Subayh and Sons Publishers, (Cairo, 1964), p. 274.

⁸¹ Muhammad Tabatabai', *al-Mizan fi al-Tafsir*, Dar Ihya' Al Turath, (Beirut, 2006), v.2, pp.134-139.

⁸² 'Abdul Qadir al-Natadji al-Kurdistani, *Taqrib al-Muram fi sharh tahzib al-Kalām*, al-Matb'a al-A'miriyat ul-Kubra, 1901, p.234.

⁸³ 'Adud ul-Din al-Iji, *al-Mawaqif*, p.356.

⁸⁴ Here we will only provide the rational (*'aql*) dialectical proofs and

not those that are provided by revelation (*naql*).

[85] 'Adud ul-Din al-Iji, *al-Mawaqif*, pp.359-361; Sa'd al-Taftazani, p.193-195, Fakhr al-Din al-Razi,*'Asmat ul-Anbiya*, ed., Muhammad Hijazi, Maktaba al-Thaqafa al-Diniya, 1st ed., 1986, pp.41-47.

[86] Fazlur Rahman, *Islam*, pp.32-33.

[87] Fazlur Rahman, "The Status of the Individual in Islam", *Islamic Studies vol. v (4)*, December 1966, p. 322.

[88] Fazlur Rahman, *Revival and Reform in Islam*, p.52.

[89] Fazlur Rahman, "The Status of the Individual in Islam", *Islamic Studies vol. v (4)*, December 1966, p. 327.

[90] *Ibid.*

[91] *Ibid.*

[92] See Fazlur Rahman, *Islamic Methodology and History*, pp.27-84; *Revival and Reform in Islam*, p. 55.

[93] *Al Tabsīr fil Dīn wa tamyīz Al Firkat Ul Najīyat 'an Al Firaq Al Halīkīn, Al Īsfarāīnī, Abī Muzaffar*, Kamāl Yūsuf Al Ḥuwṭ, 'Aālm Al Kutub, (Beirut, 1983), pp.170-175.

[94] al-Kahf: 30.

[95] Muslim, *Sahih Muslim*, Book of Belief, Chap. 40: Forbiddance of Pride, Book no.1, Hadith no.165.

[96] Yūsuf: 106.

[97] al-Isrā': 79.

[98] Bukharī, *Sahīh Bukharī*, vol. 8, Book 76, Number 570.

[99] Al Farhārī, *Nibras sharh Al Aqaid*, Maktaba Haqqanīya, Multan: Pakistan 1237 AH, p.238-241.

[100] Fuad Abdul Baqī, *Al Mu'jam Al Mufahras li-Alfaz Al Qur'an*, Dar ul Kutub, Egypt, 1945, p.384.

[101] *Tafsir al-Baghawī*, Dar Tibah, Riyadh, Saudi Arabia, n.d., Vol. 5, p. 115,

[102] *Ibid,* p.116.

[103] Yahya Farghal, *al-Usus al-Manhajiyat li-bina' al-'Aqidat ul-Islamiyah*, Dar al-Fikr al-'Arabi, Matba'a Dar al-Qur'an, (Cairo), 1971, pp.134-135; Also, see Muhammad Asad, *The Message of the Qur'an*, Dar al-Andalus, Cordoba, 1980.

Bibliography

Abdul Baqi, Muhammad Fuad, *Al Mu'jam Al Mufahras li-Alfaz Al Qur'an*, Egypt: Dar ul Kutub, 1945.

Abu Bakr, Ibrahim, "Islamic Modernism in Malaya as Reflected in Hadi' Thought", MA Thesis, Montreal: McGill University, 1992.

Abu Laylah, Muhammad, *In Pursuit of Virtue: The Moral Theology & Psychology of Ibn Hazm*, London: Ta-Ha Publishers Ltd., 1990.

Ahmad, Aziz, "Jamal al-din al-Afghani and Muslim India", *Studia Islamica No. 13*, 1960.

Ahsan, Abdullah, "Late 19th Century Muslim response to the Western Criticism of Islam: An Analysis of Amir 'Ali's Life and Works", MA Thesis, Montreal: McGill University, 1981.

Al- Shaf'i, Hasan, *Madkhal ila 'ilm ul-kalām*, Karachi: Idarat ul-Qur'an wa'l Islamiyah, n.d.

Al-Baghawi, *Tafsir al-Baghawi*, Saudi Arabia: Dar Tibah, Riyadh, 1997.

Al-Bajuri, *Tuhfat al-Murid 'ala Jawharat ul-Tawhid*, Cairo:

Muhammad Ali Subayh and Sons Publishers, 1964.

Al-Baqillani, Abu Bakr Muhammad, *Kitab al-Tamhid*, R.J. McCarthy (ed.), Beirut: 1957.

Al-Bukharī, Muhammad, *Sahīh Bukharī*, Riyadh: Maktaba al-Salafiyah, 1379 AH (2000 CE).

Al-Farhārī, *Al Nibras Sharh Al Aqaid*, Pakistan: Maktaba Haqqaniya, Multan: 1237 AH (1858).

Al-Fayumi, Ahmed Ali al-Muqri, *Al-Misbah Al-Munir*, Cairo: Maktaba al-Salafiya, n.d.

Al-Ghazālī, Abu Hamid Muhd., *Deliverance from Error: Five Key Texts Including His Spiritual Autobiography*, R.J. McCarthy (tr.), Kentucky: Fons Vitae, 1980.

Al-Hajjaj, Muslim, *Sahih Muslim*, Riyadh: Maktaba al-Salafiyah, 1379 AH (2000 CE).

Ali Mabruk, *al-Nabuwwat: min 'ilm al-nabuwwat i'la falsafat ul-tarikh muhawalat fi I'adat bina' al-'Aqa'id* (1st ed.),, Beirut: Dar al-Tanwir litiba't al-Nashr wal tauwz'I, 1993.

Al-Iji, Adud ul-Din, *al-Mawaqif*, Beirut: Dar al-Kutub al-Ilmiyah, 1998, pp.359-361.

Al-Isfaraini, Abi Muzaffar, *Al-Tabsīr fil Din wa tamyiiz Al Firkat Ul Najiyat 'an Al Firaq Al Halikin*, Cairo: Matba'at al-Anwar, 1940.

Al-Jawhari, *Al-Sihah*, Cairo: Maktaba al-Salafiya, n.d.

Al-Maliki, Ahmad Muhammad, *Kitab Sharh al-Sawi 'ala Jauharat ul-Tauhid*, Abdul Fattah al-Bazm (ed.), 2nd ed., Damascus: Dar Ibn ul-Kathir, 1999.

Al-Maturidi, *Kitab al Tawhid,* Bekir Topaloğlu & Muhammad Aruçi (eds.), Beirut: Dar al-Sader, 2001.

Al-Natadji, Abdul Qadir, *Taqrib al-Muram fi sharh tahzib al-Kalām,* al-Matb'a al-A'miriyat ul-Kubra, 1901.

Aloysuis Adiseputra,"The Doctrine of the Impeccability of the Prophet as Elucidated by Fakhr al Din Razi", MA Thesis, Montreal: McGill University, 1981.

Al-Razī, Fakhr ad-Din, *'Asmat ul-Anbiya,* Muhammad Hijazi (ed.), Cairo: Maktaba al-Thaqafa al-Diniya (1st ed.), 1986.

______, *Mahsil afkar al-Mutaqadimin wa al-Muta'khirin min al-Ulama' wa al-Hukama' wa al-Mutakalimin.*

Al-Taftazani, Sa'd al-Din, *Sharh al-Aqa'id al-Nisafiyyah,* Ahmad Hijazi al-Saqa (ed.), Cairo: Maktaba Kulliyat al-Azhar, 1988.

Anwar, Etin, "Ibn Sīna & Mysticism: A Reconsideration", M.A. Thesis, Montreal: McGill University, 1998.

Arberry, A.J., *Avicenna on Theology,* Conneticut: Hyperion Press Inc., 1951.

______, *Reason and Revelation in Islam,* London: George Allen and Unwin Ltd., 1957.

Asad, Muhammad, *The Message of the Qur'an,* Cordoba: Dar al-Andalus, 1980.

Easton, M.G., *Illustrated Bible Dictionary* (3rd ed.), Tennessee: Thomas Nelson, 1897.

Eliade, Mircea (Editor in Chief), *The Encyclopedia of Religion,* 16 vols., New York & London, 1987.

Encyclopedia Britannica, 24 vols., Chicago, London & Toronto, 1953.

Encyclopedia of Islam (new edition), Leiden & London, 1954 (in progress).

Encyclopedia of Islam, The, 4 vols., Leiden & London, 1913-1934; Supplement (in 5 parts), 1934-1938.

Encyclopedia of Philosophy, The, 4 vols., New York, 1984.

Encyclopedia of Philosophy, The, 8 vols. New York & London, 1967.

Encyclopedia of Religion and Ethics, 13 vols., Edinburgh & New York, 1908-1927.

Encyclopedia of Religion, an, ed. by Vergilius Ferm, New York, 1945.

Encyclopedia of the Social Sciences, 14 vols., New York, 1950.

Erickson, Millard J., *Christian Theology*, Michigan: Baker Book House, 1994.

______, *Introducing Christian Doctrine* (2nd ed.), Michigan: Baker Book House, 2001.

Ess, Josef Van, "The Beginnings of Islamic Theology", in *The Cultural Context of Medieval Learning*, John E. Murdoch and Edith Dudley Sylla (eds.), Boston: Reidel (1975), pp.87-111.

Fakhry, Majid, *A History of Islamic Philosophy*, New York: Colombia University Press, 1970.

______, *Islamic Occasionalism and Its Critique by Averroes and Aquinas*, London: George Allen and Unwin Ltd., 1958.

________, *Ethical Theories in Islam*, Leiden: E.J. Brill, 1991.

Farghal, Yahya, *al-Usus al-Manhajiyat li-bina' al-'Aqidat ul-Islamiyah*, Cairo: Dar al-Fikr al-'Arabi, 1971.

Frank, Richard M., *Beings and their Attributes: The Teachings of the Basrian School of the Mu'tazila in the Classical Period*, Albany: SUNY Press, 1978.

Gibb, H.A.R., *Mohammedanism: An Historical Survey* (2nd ed.), New York: Oxford University Press, 1962.

Hasan, Ahmad, *The Doctrine of Ijmā' in Islam*, Islamabad: Islamic Research Institute, 1976.

Ibn Manzur, *Lisan al-'Arb*, (3rd ed.), Beirut: Dar ul Ihya' al-Turath al-'Arabi, 1999.

Ibn Sīna, *al-Nijat fi-l 'Mantiq wa 'Illahiyyat* (1st ed.), Abdul Rahman 'Airat (ed.), Beirut: Dar ul Jil, 1992.

Imamat, Adnan Muhammad , *Al-Tajdid fi al'Fikr al-Islami* (1st ed.), Dar Ibn ul-Jawzi, 1424 AH (2003).

Iqbal, Muhammad,, *The Reconstruction of Religious Thought in Islam*, M. Saeed Sheikh (ed.), Lahore: Institute of Islamic Culture, 1986.

Jamal Muhammad, Sa'id Abdul Ghani, *Ara' Ibn Taymīya fi 'ismat ul-Anbiya'*, Maktaba zahra' al-Sharq, 1998.

Jordan, Jeff, "Pragmatic Arguments and Belief in God", *The Stanford Encyclopedia of Philosophy (Spring 2011 Edition)*, Edward N. Zalta (ed.), California: Stanford University, 2011.

Khan, Sayyid Ahmad, *Al-Tahrir fi usul al-Tafsir*, Agra, 1892.

Liadain, Sherrard, *Seal of the Saints: Prophethood and Sainthood in the Doctrine of Ibn 'Arabī*, Michael Chodkeiwicz (tr.), Lahore: Suhail Academy, 1993.

Madkur, Ibrahim, *fi falsafat ul-Islamiyyat: Manhaj wa Tatbiq*, Alexandria: Dar ul Ma'arif, 2003.

Mahmud al-Isfahani, Shams ul-Din, *Sharh Matali' ul-Anzar 'ala Tawali' ul-Anwar* (1st ed.), Egypt, 1978.

Makari, Victor E., *Ibn Taymiyyah's Ethics: The Social Factor*, California: Scholars Press, 1983.

Makdisi, George, "Ash'arī and al-Ash'arītes in Islamic Religious History II", *Studia Islamica no.18*, (1963).

Margoliouth, David Samuel, *Mohammed and the Rise of Islam*, New York: G.P. Putnam's Sons, 1905.

______, *The Early Development of Mohammedanism*, London: Williams and Norgate, 1914.

Rahman, Fazlur, "A Survey of Modernization of Muslim Family Law", *International Journal of Middle East Studies 2*, (1980): pp. 451-465.

______, "Approaches to Islam in Religious Studies: Review Essay", in *Approaches to Islam in Religious Studies*, Richard C. Martin (ed.), Arizona: The University of Arizona Press (1985): pp. 189-202.

______, "Avicenna and Orthodox Islam: An Interpretative Note on the Composition of his System", Harry Austryn Wolfson Jubilee Volume on the Occasion of his Seventy Fifth Birthday, Vol.2, Jerusalem: *The American Academy for Jewish Research*, (1965): pp. 667-676.

________, "Currents of Religious Thought in Pakistan", *Islamic Studies 1*, (1968): pp. 1-7.

________, "Divine Revelation and the Prophet", *Hamdard Islamicus 1 (2)*, (1978): pp.66-72.

________, "Dream, Imagination and Alam al-Mithal", *Islamic Studies 4 (2)*, (1964): pp.167-80.

________, "Economic Principles of Islam", *Islamic Studies 8 (1)*, (1969): pp.1-8.

________, "Essence and Existence in Avicenna", *Mediaeval and Renaissance Studies 4*, (1958): pp.1-16.

________, "Essence and Existence in Ibn Sīna: The Myth and Reality", *Hamdard Islamicus 4 (1)*, (1981): pp.3-14.

________, "Essence and Existence in Ibn Sīna", A lecture delivered at McGill Institute of Islamic Studies, April 29, 1970.

________, "Fazlur Rahman" in *The Courage of Conviction: Prominent Contemporaries Discuss Their Beliefs and How They Put Them into Action*, Phillip L. Berman (ed.), Santa Barbara, California: Dodd, Mead & Co., (1985): pp.153-159.

________, "Functional Interdependence of Law and Theology", in *Theology and Law in Islam*, G.E. von Grunebaum (ed.), Wiesbaden: Otto Harrassowitz, (1971): pp.89-97.

________, "Ibn Sīna's Theory of the God-World Relationship", in *God and Creation: An Ecumenical Symposium*, D. B. Burrell and B. McGinn (eds.), Indiana: University of Notre Dame Press, (1990): pp.38-52.

________, "Implementation of the Islamic Concept of State in the

Pakistani Milieu", *Islamic Studies 6 (3)*, (1967): pp.205-224.

________, "Internal Religious Developments in the Present Century of Islam", *Journal of World History 2 (4)*, 1955), pp.862-879.

________, "Interpreting the Qur'an", *Inquiry 3 (5)*, (May 1986): pp.45-49.

________, "Islam and Health: Some Theological, Historical and Sociological Perspectives", *Hamdard Islamicus 5 (4)*, (1982): pp.75-88.

________, "Islam and the Constitutional Problem of Pakistan", *Studia Islamica 32*, (1970): pp.275-287.

________, "Islam and the Problem of Economic Justice", *The Pakistan Economist 24*, (1974): pp.14-39.

________, "Islam in Pakistan", *Journal of South Asian and Middle Eastern Studies 8 (4)*, (1985): pp.34-61.

________, "Islam: Challenges and Opportunities", in *Islam: Past Influence and Present Challenge*, A.T. Welch and P. Cachia (eds.), Edinburgh: Edinburgh University Press, (1979): pp.315-330.

________, "Islam: Legacy and Contemporary Challenge", *Islamic Studies 19 (4)*, (1980): pp.235-246.

________, "Islam", in *The Encyclopedia of Religion*, M. Eliade (ed.), New York: Macmillan Publishing Co., 7 (1987): pp.303-322.

________, "Islamic Modernism: Its Scope, Method and Alternatives", *International Journal of Middle East*

Studies 1, (1970): pp.317-333.

__________, "Islamic Philosophy", *Encyclopedia of Philosophy*, Paul Edwards (ed.), New York: Macmillan, 4 (1967): pp.219-224.

__________, "Islamic Studies and the Future of Islam", in *Islamic Studies: A Tradition and its Problems*, Malcolm H. Kerr (ed.), Malibu: Undena Publications, (1980): pp.125-133.

__________, "Islamization of Knowledge: A Response", *The American Journal of Islamic Social Sciences 5 (1)*, (1988): pp.3-11.

__________, "Law and Ethics in Islam", in *Ethics in Islam: Ninth Giorgio Levi Della Vida Biennial Conference*, Richard G. Hovannisian (ed.), Malibu: Undena Publications, (1985): pp.3-15.

__________, "Mulla Sadra's Theory of Knowledge", *Philosophical Forum 4*, (1972): pp.141-152.

__________, "Mulla Sadra", in *The Encyclopedia of Religion*, M. Eliade (ed.), New York: Macmillan Publishing Co., 10 (1987): pp.149-153.

__________, "Muslim Modernism in the Indo-Pakistan Sub Continent", *Bulletin of the School of Oriental and African Studies 21 (1)*, (1958): pp.82-99.

__________, "On Schact's Origins of Muhammadan Jurisprudence" by M.M. Azami, *Journal of Near Eastern Studies, Vol. 47 (3)*, (1988), pp.228-229.

__________, "Perception of the Desirable Societies in Different Religions: The Case of Islam", Unpublished article presented at United Nations University, Bangkok: March 12-15, 1984.

______, "Pre-Foundation of the Muslim Community in Makkah", *Studia Islamica 43*, (1976): pp.5-24.

______, "Revival and Reform in Islam", *Cambridge History of Islam*, P. M. Rolt, Ann K.S. Lambton, et al. (eds.), Vol.2B, Cambridge: Cambridge University Press, (1970): pp.632-656.

______, "Riba and Interest", *Journal of Islamic Studies 31*, (Karachi), March 1964: pp.1-43.

______, "Roots of Islamic Neo-Fundamentalism", in *Change and the Muslim World*, P.H. Stoddard, D.C. Cuthell, et al. (eds.), Syracuse: Syracuse University Press, (1981): pp.23-35.

______, "Shari'ah", in *Islam*, New York: Anchor Book, (1968): pp.117-137.

______, "Some Islamic Issues in the Ayub Khan Era", in *Essays on Islamic Civilization*, D. P. Little (ed.), Lieden: E.J. Brill, (1976): pp.299-302.

______, "Some Key Ethical Concepts of the Qur'an", *Journal of Religious Ethics 1 (1)*, (1983): pp.170-185.

______, "Some Recent Books on the Qur'an by Western Authors", *The Journal of Religion 64 (l)*, (1984): pp.73-95.

______, "Some Reflections on the Reconstruction of Muslim Society in Pakistan", *Islamic Studies 2*, (1967): pp.103-120.

————, "Status of Women in the Qur'an", in *Women and Revolution in Iran*, G. Nashat, Boulder (ed.), Colorado: Westview Press, (1983): pp.37-54.

————, "The Concept of *Hadd* in Islamic Law", *Islamic Studies 4 (3)*, (1965): pp.237-251.

————, "The Controversy Over the Muslim Family Law", in *South Asian Politics and Religion*, D.E. Smith (ed.), New Jersey: Princeton University Press, (1966): pp.414-427.

————, "The Eternity of the World and the Heavenly Bodies in Post-Avicennan Philosophy", in *Essays on Islamic Philosophy and Science*, G.F. Hourani (ed.), Albany: SUNY Press, (1975): pp.222-237.

————, "The God-World Relationship in Mulla Sadra", in *Essays on Islamic Philosophy and Science*, G.F. Hourani (ed.), Albany: SUNY Press, (1975): pp.238-253.

————, "The Ideological Experience of Pakistan", *Islam and the Modern Age 2 (4)*, (1971): pp.1-20.

————, "The Impact of Modernity on Islam", *Islamic Studies 5 (2)*, (1966): pp.113-128.

————, "The Message and the Messenger", in *Islam: The Religious and Political Life of a World Community*, M. Kelly (ed.), New York: Praeger Publications, (1984): pp.29-54.

————, "The Principle of Shura and the Role of Ummah in Islam", in *State, Politics and Islam*, Mumtaz Ahmad (ed.), Indianapolis: American Trust Publications, (1986): pp.1-13.

________, "The Qur'anic Concept of God: the Universe and Man", *Islamic Studies 6 (1)*, (1967): pp.1-19.

________, "The Qur'anic Solution of Pakistan's Educational Problem", *Islamic Studies 6 (4)*, (1967): pp.315-326.

________, "The Religious Situation of Makkah from the Eve of Islam up to Hijra", *Islamic Studies 16 (1)*, (1977): pp.289-301.

________, "The Sources and Meaning of Islamic Socialism", in *Religion and Political Modernization*, D. E. Smith (ed.), New Haven and London: Yale University Press, (1974): pp.243-258.

________, "The Status of the Individual in Islam", *Islamic Studies 5 (4)*, (1966): pp.319-330.

________, "The Status of Women in Islam: A Modernist Interpretation", in *Separate Worlds: Studies of Purdah in South Asia*, P.H. Papanek and G. Minault (eds.), Columbia: South Asia Books, (1982): pp.285-310.

________, "The Thinker of Crisis: Shah Waliy-Ullah", *Pakistan Quarterly 6 (2)*, (1956): pp.448.

________, "Translating the Qur'an", *Religion and Literature 20 (1)*, (1988): pp.23-30.

________, *Health and Medicine in the Islamic Tradition*, New York: Crossroad Pub. Co., 1987.

________, Ibn Sīna, *A History of Muslim Philosophy*, M.M. Sharif (ed.), Vol.1, Wiesbaden: Otto Harrassowitz, (1966): pp.480-506.

__________, *Islam and Modernity: Transformation of an Intellectual Tradition*, Chicago: University of Chicago Press, 1982.

__________, *Islam* (2nd ed.), Chicago: University of Chicago Press, 1979.

__________, *Islamic Methodology in History*, Karachi: Central Institute of Islamic Research, 1965.

__________, *Major Themes of the Qur'an*, Chicago: University of Chicago Press, 2009.

__________, *Prophecy in Islam: Philosophy and Orthodoxy*, London: George Allen and Unwin Ltd., 1958.

__________, *Revival and Reform in Islam*, Ebrahim Moosa (ed.), London: Oneworld Publications, 1999.

Renard, John, *All the King's Falcons: Rumi on Prophets and Revelation*, Lahore: Suhail Academy, 2012.

Sabuni, Nur al-Din, *Kitab al-Bidayat min al-Kifayat fi al-Hidaya*, Fathullah Khalif (ed.), Egypt: Dar ul-Ma'arif, 1969.

Saleem, Abdul Qadeer, "A Critical Study of Mujaddid-e-Alf Thani's Philosophy", Phd. Thesis, Karachi: University of Karachi, n.d.

Smith, Wilfred Cantwell, *Modern Islam in India*, Lahore: Ripon Printing Press, 1947.

Tabatabai', Muhammad, *al-Mizan fi al-Tafsir*, Beirut: Dar Ihya' Al-Turath, 2006.

'Uthman, Abdul Karim, *Sharh al-Usul ul-Khamsa li Qadī 'Abdul Jabbār*, Cairo: Maktaba al-Wahba, 1996.

Walzer, R., "Al Farabi's Theory of Prophecy and Divination", in *The Journal of Hellenic Studies* 77 (1), (1957): pp.142-148.

Index